A *Primer of Psychophysiology*

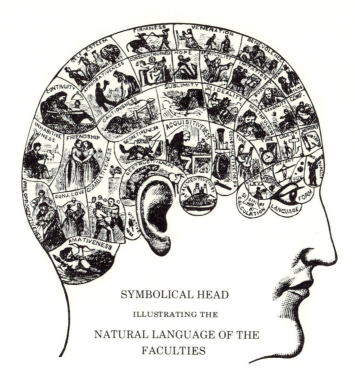

SYMBOLICAL HEAD

ILLUSTRATING THE

NATURAL LANGUAGE OF THE
FACULTIES

A nineteenth-century attempt to depict localization of personality traits in the brain. Current theories about brain function may seem equally naïve in the year 2050. (Reprinted from Wells, 1868.)

A Primer of Psychophysiology

James Hassett
Boston University

with a Foreword by Gary E. Schwartz
Yale University

W. H. Freeman and Company
San Francisco

Library of Congress Cataloging in Publication Data

Hassett, James.
    A primer of psychophysiology.

    (A Series of books in psychology)
    Bibliography: p.
    Includes index.
    1. Psychology, Physiological.   I.   Title.
[DNLM: 1.   Psychophysiology.   WL102 H355p]
QP360.H35   612'.8   77-20913
ISBN 0-7167-0038-7
ISBN 0-7167-0037-9 pbk.

Printed in the United States of America

1   2   3   4   5   6   7   8   9

Contents

Foreword

Psychophysiology: A Perspective on Human Nature

by *Gary E. Schwartz*
Yale University

More than ever before, people are coming to recognize that they are psychophysiological beings. This recognition is no longer restricted to academicians and clinicians studying the relationship between mind and brain, behavior and body. Research results linking biology with psychology are becoming common knowledge to the general public. We read and hear everywhere that mind and brain are intimately associated and that the relationship between mental and neurophysiological processes is one of the great mysteries yet to be unraveled by science. Many adults and children are learning first-hand how various drugs affect their consciousness and emotions. Even the foods we eat are now being seen as complex chemicals that ultimately become part of our brain and body and thereby influence our consciousness and behavior.

Articles and books from the lay press are rapidly spreading the word about man's fundamental psychophysiological nature, both in health and in disease. Although much of this material is inherently interesting, it is often sensationalized and not infrequently misstated. Public accounts of biofeedback, the physiology of meditation, and the extended use of the "lie detector" are common examples of this twentieth-century problem. The beginning student is forced either to read the highly interesting but often inaccurate accounts available in the lay press or must attempt to decipher the more accurate, but typically complex and dry, writings of high-level academic books and journal articles.

A *Primer of Psychophysiology*, by Jim Hassett, is an attempt by one psychophysiologist to bridge the gap between interesting writing and content and the realities of theory and research in this field. Committed to the needs of the introductory student interested in the measurement of physiological processes in human beings in relation to environmental and behavioral processes, Hassett has taken the position that good writing must be coupled with content that emphasizes a comprehensive *perspective* about psychophysiology. This perspective is a theme that reoccurs throughout the book and touches all aspects of the field today.

As Hassett points out, there are numerous practical issues involved in the procedures by which physiological responses are currently monitored. Clearly, to understand psychophysiology, the student must understand biomedical technology and appreciate its potentials and limitations. It follows that to understand this technology, the student must also understand the basic biological properties of the tissues that are being monitored. This would include understanding the intimate relationships between their structure, on the one hand, and their function, on the other.

The perspective of psychophysiology I wish to underscore, however, goes beyond the technology of today or the potential technology of tomorrow. Even if every neural, humoral, and physiological process in the body could be accurately and unobtrusively measured in people, we would still have the *conceptual* problem of putting all this information back together to produce a psychophysiological being that can read, experience emotions, and think. That is exactly the challenge facing us.

All human activities involve the complex regulation of multiple psychophysiological processes. Although this is often taken for granted, it is truly miraculous how the brain manages to coordinate all the complex processes involved in such seemingly simple tasks as regulating our limbs and eyes to hold this book and read these words. For example, the brain must coordinate multiple physiological processes just to keep our body alive and healthy while we are engaged in this task. (Consider what would happen, for example, if our brain "forgot" to regulate our respiratory system while we were reading these words.) In addition, the brain must process all the neural information coming from the eyes into the visual system and convert this information into conscious gestalts that can have "meaning" to us.

Hassett suggests that we conceive of the human organism engaged in such tasks as being a symphony of biological organs that are orchestrated and conducted by the brain. This is a good analogy and one with which I concur. Each organ, like each instrument, plays a unique role in producing what we describe as behavior. Each organ, like each instrument, has a unique set of potentials and limitations. The conductor, like the brain itself, must coordinate all the various instruments to produce the unique patterns comprising the particular symphony. The conductor, in turn, communicates the written score in his own way.

In a real sense, the human brain is comprised of multiple scores that are selected and played according to environmental demands. These neural scores are continually updated and modified by the brain's experience in a cultural setting. In this way, the human brain is one that continually monitors the feedback generated by the organs so as to coordinate the entire bodily system. The brain, in turn, brings its own unique qualities to bear on the dynamically changing pattern of organ activity that we see overtly as behavior and experience as consciousness. Whereas a musically unsophisticated person hears a symphony as a complex pattern of sounds, the well-rounded musician learns to attend to the multiple *component* melodies making up the symphony and, furthermore, tries to understand the *structure* that brings together the melodies played by various instruments to produce the complex pattern of the orchestrated work. We can see the challenge facing the well-rounded psychophysiologist in the same light. His goal is to examine complex behavior, like a symphony, as though it were composed of multiple organs *structured* in a unique fashion. He must first isolate and measure each of the separate organs and understand their *interrelationships*, so as to infer higher-level neural structures that coordinate their activity.

Hearing and understanding a symphony is no easy task. Trying to do the same thing for human psychophysiology is even more difficult. However, we shouldn't be frightened by this complexity, even if it turns out that the psychophysiologist of tomorrow never fully comprehends Hassett's perspective on the person in the same way that Tchaikovsky understood a symphony. I was trained in music and at one time wanted to become performer, composer, and conductor. Although I never learned to play the guitar like Segovia or to compose and conduct like Tchaikovsky, I developed a deeper and broader understanding of what a good performer is and what a symphony is all about. My *perspective* on music expanded as a result of being a student of music, and my appreciation for music has grown accordingly.

The same should be possible for students who wish to develop a psychophysiological perspective on human nature. Research is currently at the stage where investigators are struggling to monitor the individual organs and trying to learn something about how they are regulated. Unfortunately, the technological problems sometimes prevent researchers and students from realizing that each organ is but one component of the total bodily *system* comprising a person. However, if we can adopt a perspective of psychophysiology that takes the multiple components comprising a person and brings them back together as a *functional psychophysiological* system, we will have learned an important lesson about the nature of human activity. For the student who never goes beyond A *Primer of Psychophysiology*, this may be more important than remembering any one fact about the measurement and characteristics of any one response. For the student who goes further in this field, the present volume should provide a useful foundation for developing expertise in measuring and studying the biological components, and describing the challenge of putting them back together in the form of a living, psychophysiological person.

Preface

This short volume was planned as a concise and readable introduction to the measurement of human physiological response. It is aimed at the serious student, whether a Ph.D. in clinical psychology or a curious undergraduate with little natural science background.

Students and colleagues deluge me with requests for a basic reference to help them understand physiological studies within their own specialties. The recent spurt of interest in biofeedback and meditation- research has intensified their demands. My stock reply has always been: "There is no such text, *yet*." This book was written to meet that demand.

Since the specific needs of its readers are expected to vary so widely, the book was organized to be used in several different ways. The main body of the text presents a narrative overview of the field. This is not meant as an exhaustive survey of the field but rather as an historical introduction. Some current research areas are developed in detail (for example, biofeedback, cerebral asymmetry); others are not (for example, classical conditioning, habituation). The book was written to whet the appetite, not satisfy it. Material less likely to be of interest to *every* reader is segregated in a series of Appendices at the end of the volume. Some of these sections summarize very basic material (for example, an introduction to electricity); others present material that is much more advanced (for example, filtering the EEG).

The emphasis throughout is on providing a text that is in fact a primer—a source of basic information for the interested novice. Besides being a beginning textbook for courses in psychophysiology, the volume should serve as an ancillary source for courses in experimental, social, and clinical psychology with a biological orientation. It also might serve as one of several required texts in such divergent courses as physiological psychology, human psychobiology, biofeedback, and altered states of consciousness. In Chapters 1 through 3, psychophysiology is introduced and placed in historical perspective. Key concepts in physiology, anatomy, and electronics are also included here. The main body of the book (Chapters 4 through 9) focuses on each of the major psychophysiological measures in turn—its history, physiological basis, and psychological significance. The measures are organized from the most peripheral (the skin) to the most central (the brain), reflecting a natural, historical, and anatomical progression.

This book grew out of my work, first as a laboratory instructor and later as a lecturer, in Harvard's Introductory Psychophysiology course. When this course was begun in 1965 by David Shapiro, it was the only one of its kind. My involvement came several years later, when the course was taught by Gary Schwartz.

Psychophysiologists reading this book will recognize Gary's influence throughout. The emphasis on the patterning of physiological responses, the centrality of focus on the brain, and an overwhelming enthusiasm even for the ambiguities of the field—all these are lessons I learned from Gary. His active role in shaping this book cannot be stressed too much. We argued every step of the way, as teacher and student so often do, but in the end he was usually right. Without his continuing support as my editor and friend, this book would never have been completed.

There are, of course, countless others who contributed to this work. I would especially like to thank Theodore Zahn and William Lawlor, for introducing me to both psychophysiology and good science; Annelise Katz, for supervising the kind of library that makes scholarly research a joy; the Permanent Members' Committee of Harvard's Department of Psychology and Social Relations, for helping to shape my present commitment to the field; Terry Bergman, Richie Davidson, and Larry Young, who provided much of the inspiration, many of the references, and sometimes even the words; Gail Bloom, Rhonda Redd, Judy Holman, and Paul Guay for typing; W. Hayward Rogers, of W. H. Freeman, for believing that this book should be written and that I should write it; Patricia Salt, Laurie Fogelson, Abby Stewart, Richard Thompson, Joseph Campos, and David Shapiro for their feedback on earlier versions of the manuscript; Joseph Musacchia, Alan Sieber, Patricia Salt, and Larry Young for helping me to generate some of the polygraph records reproduced here; Mom and Dad for being Mom and Dad; and, finally, the countless legions whose hearts, heads, and sweat glands made this research possible.

October 1977   *James Hassett*

A *Primer of Psychophysiology*

1

What Is Psychophysiology?

Psychophysiological observation is as old as the first young man who noted a woman's blush. In this ancient and honorable event lay the seeds of several modern scientific conceptions. A mental state was inferred from a well-defined physiological change (increasing blood flow to the face). Further, the physiological change was believed to be more valid than words could ever tell. The more vigorously the young lady denied her embarrassment, the more emphatically her partner believed in it.

Pragmatic applications of the knowledge achieved through physiological observations were soon to appear. Several cultures developed crude lie-detection techniques. The Chinese, for example, had a man accused of a crime chew a mouthful of dried rice; if he could spit it out, he was judged innocent. The Anglo-Saxons employed a similar ritual: If the accused could easily chew and swallow a piece of dry bread, he was freed. Both of these tests of innocence are crudely based on the physiological fact that the sympathetic nervous system is activated by stress. One of its responses to stress is to slow down salivation. In retrospect, the theory underlying these techniques is that the guilty party would be anxious, his mouth would be dry, and thus he would find it difficult to swallow or spit. Unfortunately, it ignores the fact that an innocent man might also very well be scared spitless.

The ancient Roman scientist Galen was among the first to make more systematic observations of bodily changes to detect emotional state (Mesulam and Perry, 1972). An emotionally distraught woman came to the famous physician, complaining of a variety of physical ills. At one point during her examination, a bystander mentioned that he had recently seen a young man named Pylades dancing at the theatre. Galen noted that when his patient overheard this remark, "her pulse was irregular—suddenly violently agitated, which points to a troubled mind." He proceeded during subsequent examinations to drop the names of several young male dancers; the woman's pulse changed only when she heard Pylades' name. Galen finally diagnosed his patient as suffering from lovesickness, a malady that remains incurable to the present day.

Man, science tells us, is an animal. But once we go beyond examples like feeling our hearts pound in fear or exultation, we rarely think of ourselves as the biological beings that we are. You may be keenly aware of your body in moments of acute physical or emotional excitement, but under more commonplace circumstances all of our bodily processes go on outside of awareness.

Even the act of sitting quietly and reading this book demands a complex symphony of bodily functions. Virtually all of these are regulated by the brain without any conscious awareness on your part. Imagine how difficult it would be to make any sense out of the written word if you constantly had to will your eyes from one key word to the next: "All right, eyes. What word should I read now? Let's try the next phrase to the right." Instead, all bodily systems continue to function almost by themselves as the eyes systematically scan the text for bits of information and the integrated meaning. And the eyes are only the most obvious starting point for our analysis. Every turn of the page involves the synchronous action of hundreds of muscle fibers in the hand, arm, and shoulder. Blood must be redistributed throughout the body to allow this simple act. Meanwhile, your brow may knit in concentration, your lips may tense or contort, and you may even shift position to get more comfortable without thinking about it. All this is regulated by the brain, even as it concentrates on the meaning of these words or drifts off into a fantasy about the person sitting at the other end of the library.

Psychophysiology is the scientific study of the role of these many bodily processes in behavior and conscious experience. The word itself invokes a convenient combination of the root *psyche*, referring to mental events, and *physiology*, implying an emphasis on related bodily changes. It is an attempt to observe the workings of all our hidden machinery—from the second-by-second regulation of blood flow by the heart to the patterns of neural firing in the cortex that represents our noblest ideals.

We now live in a time when advances in medical engineering are making it ever easier to peer into inner space. As Chester Darrow put it in the first issue of the journal *Psychophysiology* (1964a), "Even as electronic engineers have extended our view into outer space, they have also offered an almost unlimited insight into what were once the inaccessible recesses of the living organism." We are at the beginning of a long journey into the human body, tracing its complex adjustments to an ever-changing world. This short volume is meant to serve as an introduction to this search; it reviews what we have learned so far and what remains to be done. We know far more about rocks on the moon than we do about how an astronaut could bend down to pick them up. The profound mysteries of the biological processes underlying human consciousness and behavior are just beginning to be unraveled.

In its essence, psychophysiology emphasizes the role of bodily processes in human experience. As a distinct discipline, it is a relatively young science.

In the first half of this century, many researchers used the term *psycho-physiology* loosely, to refer to many different kinds of physiological research. We shall attempt to define the word with somewhat more precision here. Our goal is not to sketch in the boundaries of still another academic discipline, single-mindedly pursuing its own esoteric problems. Psychophysiology is a child of psychobiology, which in turn is an offspring of the marriage between the physical and the social sciences. However, it is still useful to distinguish the field from its siblings.

Physiological psychology is the academic discipline most closely related to psychophysiology. Most often, the physiological psychologist manipulates physiology while he observes behavior (Stern, 1964). To understand the function of the occipital lobe of an animal's brain, he may destroy the occipital lobe and note that his subject now has visual problems. Or, to understand body chemistry, he may inject an animal with a drug that is known to affect synaptic transmission in a certain way and see how the animal responds.

Given its intrusive ways, most research in physiological psychology has been limited to lower animals. We can do all sorts of things to rats, pigeons, and monkeys that we would hesitate to do to another human being. We can make them hungry and thirsty while we shut them up in a box with nothing to do but press a lever for hours or days on end. We can stick electrodes deep in their brains and their bodies.

Since Darwin's theory of evolution swept the scientific world, there has been a theoretical justification for the long-standing medical practice of experimenting on lower species. Darwin's doctrine of species continuity implies that the monkey is our cousin, while the rat might be a second uncle twice removed. Thus, since all animals are from the same stock, there are bound to be important similarities in the structure and function of the nervous system of all animals. And indeed much of our understanding of human physiology and its relation to behavior is based on just this sort of experimentation.

While the psychophysiologist frequently refers to this body of data, his focus is on complex human behavior under more ordinary circumstances. His independent variable is more frequently behavioral, while his dependent measure is physiological. Thus he might deprive a person of sleep or make him happy or sad, while observing how the body reacts to these changes. (This distinction between physiological psychology and psychophysiology on the basis of whether the independent variable is behavioral or physiological should not be seen as an unbreakable "rule." Such rules too often pigeonhole experiments or experimenters and serve no very useful purpose.)

Where the physiological psychologist often sacrifices the relevance afforded by working with humans, the psychophysiologist sacrifices simplicity. It is much easier to specify the actual brain area destroyed in a rat than to say with any precision just how happy an experimental subject became. The vagaries of the human condition are a constant source of frustration to the psychophysiologist, who must attempt both to control the environment and to keep it from becoming too artificial. Just as the physicist has an advantage in precision over the chemist, so physiological psychology is a "harder" science than psychophysiology. But when the time comes to discuss human experience, the physiological psychologist may have to extrapolate his findings in a way that the psychophysiologist does not.

While we have now distinguished psychophysiology from its nearest relative, we have not yet defined it. In pragmatic terms, the field is often "defined" by a certain set of methods: It involves the measurement of human physiology under varying psychological conditions. Most frequently, this measurement begins with the polygraph, an electronic device for recording minute electrical changes (see Chapter 3). The actual responses from the surface of the body that have been monitored most commonly in the past are those stressed throughout this book: sweat gland activity, heart rate, blood pressure, and the electrical activity of muscles (EMG) and the brain (EEG). As we trace the history of this field, these traditional measures will often seem the most important, if only by the sheer volume of data now available. But we must not allow ourselves to fall into the trap of defining an endeavor solely by its past. As biomedical technology advances, many other measures are being added to our basic list. For example, new methods of thermography (temperature measurement—in this case an index of blood distribution near the skin's surface) are now being developed (see Chapter 5) and will probably play an increasing role in the psychophysiology of the future. Defining psychophysiology in terms of its methods (see Sternbach, 1966) has the advantage of bringing the field as it now exists into sharp focus. But with that goes the risk of blinding ourselves to new directions for growth.

Another set of definitions of psychophysiology revolves around certain basic *problems.* Thus a scientist who studies the structure of the sweat gland and its relation to the electrical activity of the skin would be called a psychophysiologist. This is similar to the methods definition, but it is not precisely the same. In the example of our sweat-gland researcher, for example, there is no requirement that he use a polygraph, work with humans, or even manipulate psychological variables.

Defining psychophysiology in terms of its methods or its problems is an empty pursuit. The psychophysiologist should answer any question he is clever enough to ask with any method his ingenuity can propose. For, most of all, psychophysiology is developed here as a *perspective,* a strategy for studying human behavior and experience. Its subject matter is the subject matter of all psychology. The psychophysiologist hopes to bring new insights into old problems by seeing man as a biological being.

Consider the case of a young man who hopes to become a pilot but is afraid to fly. Different schools of psychology would attempt to understand this problem in quite different ways. A psychoanalyst might seek the roots of this disabling fear by studying his client's dreams and memories of childhood. A behaviorally oriented clinician would focus on specific manifestations of the phobia (Does the man avoid airports all together?) and view the problem as a function of learning. The psychophysiologist would focus on the physiological basis and characteristics of the fear response. He might suggest a treatment procedure that emphasizes physiological responses and freely borrows from other psychological theories. For example, the client might use biofeedback to learn how to relax as he imagined flying from Toledo to Akron.

Note that here psychophysiology provides a different perspective on a quite ordinary problem. It is not simply a matter of using a polygraph; it involves conceptualizing every person as the biological being that he is. Thus, the subject matter of psychophysiology is the subject matter of psychology itself. Its problems are as old as the first person who wondered, "What is he thinking?" or "Why is he doing that?"

2

Mind and Body

In 1926, a physician, who had long been a close friend of mine, lost his left arm as a result of . . . infection. . . . In spite of my close acquaintance with this man, I was not given a clear-cut impression of his sufferings until a few years after the amputation, because he was reluctant to confide to anyone the sensory experiences he was undergoing. He had the impression, that is so commonly shared by layman and physician alike, that because the arm was gone, any sensations ascribed to it must be imaginary. Most of his complaints were ascribed to his absent hand. It seemed to be in a tight posture with the fingers pressed closely over the thumb and the wrist sharply flexed. By no effort of will could he move any part of the hand. . . . The sense of tenseness in the hand was unbearable at times, especially when the stump was exposed to cold or had been bumped. Not infrequently he had a sensation as if a sharp scalpel was being driven repeatedly, deep into . . . the site of his original puncture wound. Sometimes he had a boring sensation in the bones of the index finger. This sensation seemed to start at the tip of the finger and ascend the extremity to the shoulder, at which time the stump would begin a sudden series of clonic contractions. He was frequently nauseated when the pain was at its height. As the pain gradually faded, the sense of tenseness in the hand eased somewhat, but never in a sufficient degree to permit it to be moved. In the intervals between the sharper attacks of pain, he experienced a persistent burning in the hand. This sensation was not unbearable and at times he could be diverted so as to forget it for short intervals. When it became annoying, a hot towel thrown over his shoulder or a drink of whiskey gave him partial relief.

I once asked him why the sense of tenseness in the hand was so frequently emphasized among his complaints. He asked me to clench my fingers over my thumb, flex my wrist, and raise the arm into a hammerlock position and hold it there. He kept me in this position as long I could stand it. At the end of five minutes I was perspiring freely, my hand and arm felt unbearably cramped, and I quit. But you can take your hand down, he said.

From Livingston, 1943 (quoted in Melzack, 1973).

Every thought, every action, every sensation begins with some electrochemical event in the brain. In the case of a person with a phantom limb, pain may persist in an extremity even after it has been amputated. This dramatically underlines the fact that a feeling of tenseness in your hand corresponds to the electrical activity of certain brain cells. Even after the hand is lost, this same pattern of electrical activity can still be perceived as tenseness in that nonexistent hand.

And so, if we wish to understand human behavior and consciousness, we must first understand the nervous system. In a very real sense, all of psychology is the study of brain processes.

The central role of the brain in our mental lives has not always been understood. Ancient philosophers, seeing all natural phenomena as mysteries, put the problem thus: How does the "spirit" or "soul" interact with the body? Not sure *what* the soul was, early thinkers wanted to discover *where* it was in the body. Approximately 700 years before Christ's birth, Herophilus of Alexandria argued that the fourth ventricle of the brain was the seat of the soul (the ventricles of the brain are simply cavities filled with cerebrospinal fluid). Herophilus' claim began a still-unresolved controversy, which extended beyond the Middle Ages, as to whether the soul resided in the brain or the heart.

Galen was responsible for many advances in concepts of cerebral organization. Among other things, he stressed the functional importance of the *rete mirabile* ("marvellous net")—a network of fine vessels at the base of the brain (Clarke and Dewhurst, 1972). This area was believed to be critical in the production of "animal spirits" that mediated sensation and movement. This idea remained popular until it was discovered in the nineteenth century that the human brain lacks a *rete mirabile*; Galen's observations had been based on dissections of oxen and pigs. The long acceptance of this erroneous belief may serve as a gentle warning to those who would extrapolate too quickly from studies of lower animals to humans.

Over the centuries, it was the gradual accumulation of evidence from the unfortunate victims of brain damage that proved the brain's central importance. The Greek physician Hippocrates was the first to note that injuries to the head often yielded disturbances of thought, memory, and behavior. In the twenty-five centuries since his observations, many attempts have been made to explain how this mass of soggy gray tissue could create the Theory of Relativity, the Mona Lisa, and the Los Angeles Freeway. But the mind remains a mystery to itself.

How is it that you decide to read this book, focus your eyes on a critical illustration, or wonder what the author meant by that? Scientists are still struggling with what Gary Schwartz has called the "brain self-regulation paradox"—how does the brain tell itself what to do? The mind-body problem has hardly been resolved. But psychophysiology promises many clues.

Some psychologists remain content to view the human organism as a "black box," a complicated machine that can best be understood by simply studying what goes in (environment) and what comes out (behavior). The psychophysiologist is interested in all the complicated steps in between. He would like to open the black box to discover the processes that underlie and, indeed, define human behavior and conscious experience. Sometimes this involves direct recording of the electrical activity of the brain in the electroencephalogram, or EEG. A less direct attack concentrates on more "peripheral" measures—heart rate, sweat-gland activity, muscle contraction, and so on. (Note that these, too, ultimately reflect regulation by the brain.)

Organization of the Nervous System

The nervous system consists of billions of separate cells (neurons) that communicate with each other via electrical and chemical messengers. The point at which two neurons meet is called a synapse; a single neuron may synapse with hundreds of other neurons. The result is infinitely more complicated than any machine ever created by man.

To make some sense out of the nervous system's overwhelming complexity, we must turn to various classification schemes. The body did not evolve to meet the specifications of these "systems," and we should not expect too much of them. Each of the following subdivisions of the nervous system reflects an attempt to simplify, to separately examine the parts of what is really an integrated whole.

Some schemes for subdividing the nervous system emphasize structure (how the body is built; anatomy) while others concentrate on function (what the body does). Throughout this text, we shall stress the intimate relation between structure and function. These are really two sides of the same coin; after all, the structure of the body evolved to serve certain functions.

As a first approximation, we might want to distinguish between the central nervous system (CNS) and the peripheral nervous system on the basis of structures. (PNS sometimes appears as an abbreviation for the peripheral nervous system. Since the parasympathetic nervous system is more commonly referred

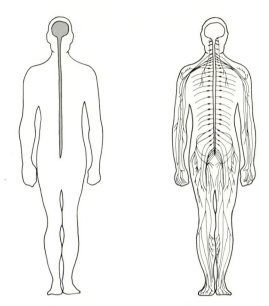

Figure 2.1 *The Central Nervous System vs. the Peripheral Nervous System.* The central nervous system *(left)* consists of the brain, brain stem, and spinal cord; the peripheral nervous system *(right)* includes all nerve fibers to and from the rest of the body.

to as PNS, we will save the abbreviation for it to avoid confusion.) The CNS includes the brain, brain stem, and spinal cord; the peripheral nervous system includes all other nervous system fibers (see Figure 2.1). The CNS always acts on the world via the peripheral nervous system; a brain without a mouth cannot speak. Similarly, the CNS learns about the world through the peripheral nervous system; a brain without eyes can see nothing.

The peripheral nervous system is usually further broken down into the somatic nervous system (here again we shall avoid the abbreviation SNS, since this may be confused with the sympathetic nervous system discussed below) and the autonomic nervous system (ANS). Once more, this distinction is a simplification; the ANS, for example, is usually defined on functional grounds and may include CNS connections. The somatic nervous system consists of nerves to and from sensory and motor organs. The ANS is also referred to as the visceral nervous system since it controls the internal organs, or viscera, of the body. The somatic nervous system activates voluntary muscles (also called striate muscles, because of their striped appearance). The ANS innervates the so-called involuntary (or smooth) musculature.

The motor branches of the somatic system are often of considerable interest to us. The behavioral domain (to which many psychologists limit themselves) very simply reflects complicated series of muscular movements. A rat pressing a bar and a philosopher discussing the mind-body problem each interacts with the world by means of the muscular system. The psychophysiologist records the electrical activity of the musculature directly in the electromyogram (EMG). The summated electrical activity of large muscle groups can be recorded from the surface of the body to provide an index of very subtle changes that ordinarily precede observable behavioral events.

As we proceed to parcel up the body into neat little packages, it may be useful to remind ourselves that every thought and every action involves a complicated pattern of nervous system activity that does not necessarily respect the lines we are drawing. These categories help us to understand, but they must not be allowed to limit our understanding.

For example, the distinction between the somatic nervous system and the autonomic (visceral) nervous system is just a convenient shorthand for their overall functions. CNS connections of our two systems are by no means independent; there is considerable anatomical overlap between somatosensory pathways and the functional centers of ANS integration in the CNS. Thus, when we discuss measurement of any ANS response system, we should not think of the response as occurring in a vacuum. The body always acts as an integrated whole. Somatic and autonomic responses often occur in tandem. For example, when body temperature drops, the ANS reacts via SNS constriction of peripheral blood vessels to prevent the loss of heat from the body surface. At the same time, the somatic nervous system reacts by generating heat through the contraction of voluntary muscles—as seen in the extreme case of slapping your hands together and stamping your feet while you wait for the bus on a cold morning. We will see many examples of this interaction between bodily responses as our study of psychophysiology proceeds.

With this warning in mind, let us proceed to orient ourselves to CNS and ANS structure and function.

The Central Nervous System

The CNS consists of the brain, brain stem, and spinal cord. The spinal cord is a column of nerve fibers running through the middle of the body and protected by a bony structure. It serves as a link between the brain and the peripheral nervous system; its fibers transmit information between brain and body. A few very simple reflexes can be mediated strictly by the spinal cord (for example, the knee-jerk reflex), but under ordinary circumstances the brain oversees everything.

For simplicity's sake, one might think of the brain as organized in a series of layers. The innermost kernel of the brain consists of the phylogenetically oldest life-support systems. As the spinal cord enters the skull, it widens to form the brain stem, which includes structures overseeing basic bodily processes: breath-

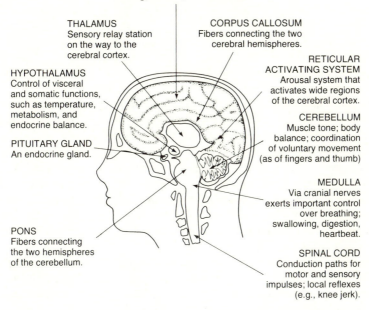

CEREBRUM
(Surface: cerebral cortex)
Sense perception; voluntary
movements; learning, remembering,
thinking; emotion; consciousness.

THALAMUS
Sensory relay station
on the way to the
cerebral cortex.

CORPUS CALLOSUM
Fibers connecting the two
cerebral hemispheres.

HYPOTHALAMUS
Control of visceral
and somatic functions,
such as temperature,
metabolism, and
endocrine balance.

RETICULAR
ACTIVATING SYSTEM
Arousal system that
activates wide regions
of the cerebral cortex.

PITUITARY GLAND
An endocrine gland.

CEREBELLUM
Muscle tone; body
balance; coordination
of voluntary movement
(as of fingers and thumb)

MEDULLA
Via cranial nerves
exerts important control
over breathing;
swallowing, digestion,
heartbeat.

PONS
Fibers connecting
the two hemispheres
of the cerebellum.

SPINAL CORD
Conduction paths for
motor and sensory
impulses; local reflexes
(e.g., knee jerk).

Figure 2.2 *Cross Section of the Brain.* Major structures of the brain and their functions. (From *Introduction to Psychology*, Sixth Edition, by Ernest R. Hilgard, Richard C. Atkinson, and Rita L. Atkinson, copyright © 1975 by Harcourt Brace Jovanovich, Inc. and reproduced with their permission.)

ing, heartbeat, digestion, and so on. Also included in this central core is the reticular activating system, a network of fibers that govern sleep and wakefulness. The limbic system surrounds the central core and is intimately related to our emotional lives. Finally, the cerebral cortex surrounds all other structures. In the cerebrum are our highest mental powers, the faculties that distinguish man from beast. Figure 2.2 represents a cross section of the brain, summarizing major anatomical subdivisions and their functions.

Psychophysiologists' interest in brain function spans many different kinds of questions. When we discuss peripheral measures like heart rate and blood pressure, we will return to an analysis of specific brain structures that regulate these variables. A topic of considerable current interest involves the extent to which the hemispheres (symmetrical sides) of the brain are involved in different kinds of mental events (see Chapters 7, 9). Another controversial area involves the localization of mental processes in the cortex (see Chapter 9).

Clearly, we cannot begin to describe all the fascinating details of what we do and do not know about brain function in a few pages (see Rose, 1976). What we can do here is begin to emphasize the critical regulatory role of the brain. All of psychology is, in the end, the study of the brain. For psychophysiology, this is especially true.

The Autonomic Nervous System

Historically, psychophysiologists' greatest interest has been in the autonomic (visceral) branch of the nervous system (although this is changing as improved techniques for direct recording of the CNS are developed). The ANS can be divided into the sympathetic nervous system (SNS) and the parasympathetic nervous system (PNS). These antagonistic branches work to maintain stable conditions inside the body in the face of an ever-changing world. Such physiological measures as sweat secretion, heart rate, blood pressure, and pupil dilation (all regulated by the ANS) have been the stock-in-trade of the psychophysiologist. Let us consider in some detail, then, the structure and function of the SNS and PNS.

The autonomic nervous system regulates the state of the heart, the glands, and the involuntary (smooth) muscles without our awareness or active involvement. Indeed, for many years it was believed that autonomic functions were beyond normal self-control. Recent experiments in biofeedback and studies of Eastern mystics who have a long religious tradition of bodily training suggest that, under special conditions, the so-called involuntary musculature can become voluntary. The clinical and theoretical implications of this recent evidence will be discussed in some detail later in this volume (see Chapter 10). But this new perspective does not change the fact that we ordinarily do not exert conscious control over the internal milieu. Nature has wisely built the body so that it is not necessary for us to tell our hearts to beat, 70 times each minute, for every moment of our lives. If, in fact, these internal systems were under our everyday control, we would have precious little time for anything but the complicated business of keeping ourselves alive.

The basic function of the SNS is mobilization of the body to meet an emergency. Technically, this is referred to as catabolism. It involves a series of complicated responses ranging from the breakdown of glycogen in the liver (to supply additional energy in the form of sugar) to changes in the circulation of the blood. In evolutionary terms, each of the SNS changes can easily be understood as an adaptation to an emergency situation. The increased access to the stored energy of the body provides the organism with its maximum physical resources to meet the emergency. Decreased blood flow near the surface of the skin reduces the likelihood of excessive bleeding after injury, while the rechannelling of blood to the internal muscles allows vigorous physical activity. Cannon (1927) christened this entire complex bodily pattern the "fight or flight reaction," and his theorizing about its importance has had a major impact on the historical development of psychophysiology, as we shall see below when we discuss it in its modern form of "arousal theory."

The action of the SNS tends to be diffuse (that is, involving the entire body) and to be maintained for a relatively long period of time. The anabolic action of the PNS to conserve and maintain bodily resources, on the other hand, is localized and of relatively short duration. Sternbach (1966) uses the analogy of the rifleman for the PNS, as opposed to the shotgun approach of the SNS.

The PNS counteracts SNS action. While the SNS acts to speed the heart, the PNS slows it down. Blood flow is increased to the gastrointestinal tract and blood sugar is stored as glycogen in the liver by the PNS. Most, but not all, internal bodily systems receive input from both the SNS and the PNS. Because they work so closely together, it is difficult to determine whether a given bodily change should be attributed to SNS or PNS activity. A dilation of the pupil, for example, may reflect increases in SNS activity or decreases in PNS activity, or both. Similarly, a decrease in heart rate may indicate increases in PNS activity or decreases in SNS activation. (However, as we shall see in Chapter 5, recent evidence suggests that, except under stressful conditions, increases *and* decreases in heart rate are mediated by appropriate action in the PNS.)

Table 2.1 summarizes the major structural and functional differences between the SNS and the PNS. The major difference is, of course, that the SNS mobilizes the body for action (catabolism) while the PNS restores the body's energy (anabolism). Next in importance is the fact that the SNS tends to act quickly and all of a piece, while the PNS has a shorter, more discrete pattern of activation.

This latter functional difference between the SNS and PNS is based on their differing structural organizations. For the somatic nervous system, each *neuron* (cell body) in the CNS is connected by a long *axon* (a nerve fiber that delivers the electrochemical impulses), which finally makes its way to the target organ. In the case of voluntary muscles, there is a *synapse* at the motor end plate of the muscle. Thus, the somatic nervous system is said to have "one neuron linkage." The ANS, on the other hand, has two neuron linkages; there is an additional cell body between the last neuron in the CNS and the target organ. The linkage between these two neurons takes place at a *ganglion*. Differences between SNS and PNS ganglia account for some of the differences between the diffuse SNS and localized PNS activity.

As you can see in Figure 2.3, axons from the SNS emerge from the middle regions of the spinal cord. Technically, these areas are called the thorax and lumbar regions. Thus, the SNS is sometimes referred to as the thoracolumbar system. These axons soon meet in a set of sympathetic ganglia located just to the side of the spinal cord. There is a great opportunity for electrical "cross-talk" in these tightly linked ganglia. Thus, an electrical impulse from any portion of the SNS will tend to activate the entire SNS system. On the other hand, as Figure 2.3 suggests, PNS fibers synapse close to their target organs. They emerge from

Table 2.1 Comparison Between the Sympathetic
and the Parasympathetic Nervous Systems

	SNS	PNS
Function	Catabolism	Anabolism
Activity	Diffuse, long-lasting	Discrete, short-acting
Anatomy		
Emerges from spinal cord	Thoracolumbar	Craniosacral
Location of ganglia	Near spinal cord	Near target organs
Postganglionic neuro-transmitter	Noradrenaline*	Acetylcholine
Specific Actions		
Pupil of eye	Dilates	Constricts
Lacrimal gland	—	Stimulates secretion
Salivary glands	Scanty, thick secretion	Profuse, watery secretion
Heart rate	Increase	Decrease
Contractility of heart (force of ventricular contraction)	Increase	—
Blood vessels	Generally constricts*	Slight effect
Bronchial tubes of lungs	Dilates lumen	Constricts lumen
Sweat glands	Stimulated*	—
Adrenal medulla	Secretes adrenaline and noradrenaline*	—
Genitals	Ejaculation	Erection
Motility and tone of gastrointestinal tract	Inhibits	Stimulates
Sphincters	Stimulates	Inhibits (relax)

* The postganglionic SNS neurotransmitter is acetylcholine for most sweat glands and some blood vessels in skeletal muscles. The adrenal medulla is innervated by preganglionic cholinergic sympathetic neurons.

Source: Based on Noback and Demarest, 1972.

the spinal cord above and below SNS fibers from the cranial and sacral regions. Hence, the PNS is sometimes referred to as the craniosacral system. The ganglia for the PNS are located far from each other, and thus PNS impulses tend to be considerably more specific (limited to a single organ) than their SNS counterparts.

The anatomical differences between the systems do not end here. You will notice in Figure 2.3 that one connection from the SNS goes to the adrenal

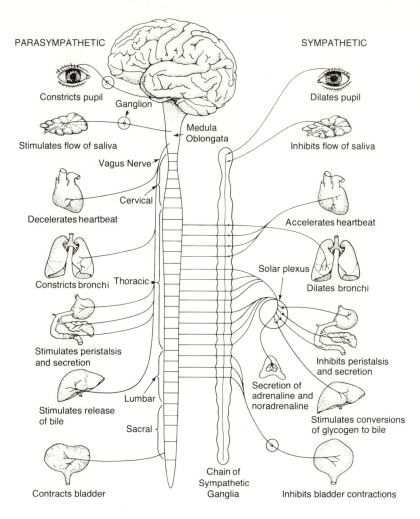

PARASYMPATHETIC

Constricts pupil

Ganglion

Stimulates flow of saliva

Medula
Oblongata

Vagus Nerve

Decelerates heartbeat

Cervical

Constricts bronchi Thoracic

Stimulates peristalsis
and secretion

Stimulates release
of bile

Lumbar

Sacral

Contracts bladder

Chain of
Sympathetic
Ganglia

SYMPATHETIC

Dilates pupil

Inhibits flow of saliva

Accelerates heartbeat

Solar plexus

Dilates bronchi

Inhibits peristalsis
and secretion

Secretion of
adrenaline and
noradrenaline

Stimulates conversions
of glycogen to bile

Inhibits bladder contractions

Figure 2.3 *The Autonomic Nervous System.* (From *Introduction to Psychology*, Sixth Edition, by Ernest R. Hilgard, Richard C. Atkinson, and Rita L. Atkinson, copyright © 1975 by Harcourt Brace Jovanovich, Inc. and reproduced with their permission.)

medulla, an endocrine gland that sends chemical messages through the bloodstream in the form of hormones. There are no corresponding connections from the PNS. (Note here, and in Table 2.1, that the antagonistic actions of SNS and PNS do not extend to every organ.) If a mugger came up behind you in a dark alley, your SNS would send impulses to all of its target organs telling your body to get ready for the worst. The adrenal medulla, when it got its electrochemical message, would then respond by secreting the hormones adrenaline and noradrenaline into the bloodstream. And then the story would get a little more complicated. For noradrenaline is the neural transmitter (the chemical substance released by electrical impulses at the synapse) of the SNS. The hormonal noradrenaline would find its way to SNS synapses and increase their effect still further. Some neurotransmitters are quickly destroyed at the synapse after they have caused increased electrical firing rates. Some take a longer time to be destroyed. Noradrenaline falls into this latter category. These facts provide still more anatomical reasons to explain why SNS activity is relatively diffuse and takes some time to subside. (You would probably still feel "wired" for some period of time after the mugger had departed with your money.) And all of which gives us still another name for the "fight or flight" thoracolumbar SNS: *the adrenergic system* (from the word *adrenaline*).

Needless to say, the PNS has a different neurotransmitter: acetylcholine. Thus the anabolic, craniosacral PNS is also referred to as cholinergic. Acetylcholine is promptly deactivated at PNS synapses by the enzyme cholinesterase. Thus, in addition to having a very localized action, the PNS tends to act quickly and decisively.

Like any "rule" for the structure of the nervous system, this simple equation of SNS activity with noradrenaline and PNS activity with acetylcholine (ACh) has its little exceptions. Preganglionic fibers for the entire ANS have ACh as the neurotransmitter. That is, we have been discussing electrical transmission only in the postganglionic second link of the two-neuron chain. More importantly for our purposes, not all SNS postganglionic transmission is adrenergic. The most notable exception is the sympathetically innervated fibers to the sweat glands, which are activated by ACh. Since the sweat glands are atypical in this sense, electrodermal activity (EDA, the electrical measurement of the sweat glands) must be considered an atypical SNS response.

Thus we have seen a distinction drawn between the catabolic action of the SNS and the anabolic action of the PNS, and we have seen how differences in the *function* of these interdependent systems are grounded in their anatomical *structure*.

Emotion and Arousal

Many of the concepts presented in this discussion of the ANS were proposed by Walter B. Cannon and his students in their attempts to understand physiological processes associated with emotion. The distinctions he drew between SNS and PNS function have contributed to arousal theory and to the understanding of arousal and emotion. Let us review the notion of arousal, then, in the light of the anatomical information presented above and of some recent evidence that suggests a more sophisticated alternative.

Emotion is the spice of life and the source of all its drama. For love did Othello kill Desdemona and Romeo and Juliet destroy themselves. For love did Shah Jehan build the Taj Mahal. If psychology is ever to understand the lustful, spiteful, idealistic world of humans, it must explain *how* it is that we feel the things we do.

This has proven to be such a difficult subject to study that many scientists have found themselves becoming quite emotional as they tried to win colleagues to their own points of view. A few have gone so far as to vehemently deny that human emotion is even a useful scientific construct.

According to Webster, emotion is "a physiological departure from homeostasis that is subectively experienced in strong feelings (as of love, hate, desire, or fear) and manifests itself in neuromuscular, respiratory, cardiovascular, hormonal, and other bodily changes preparatory to overt acts which may or may not be performed."

This definition emphasizes the critical role of internal bodily changes in any emotion. In emotional situations of all sorts we clearly see the interaction of mind and body. The two oldest psychological theories of emotion, the James-Lange and the Cannon-Bard, recognize this interaction but differ over whether mind or body comes first.

Near the end of the nineteenth century, the great Harvard psychologist William James and a Scandinavian named Carl Lange independently proposed a theory of emotion which at first glance seems contrary to common sense. According to the mythical man in the street, we laugh because we are happy, cry because we are sad, and tremble because we are afraid. What came to be known as the James-Lange theory turns this relation around: Some event in the environment automatically sets off a pattern of bodily changes. The brain then recognizes this pattern as belonging to a specific emotion and proceeds to label it. Thus the sight of a stranger in a dark alley may elicit pounding of the heart and sweaty hands. The brain browses through this complex of signals from the viscera until it realizes, in a flash, "My body is reacting this way, I must be afraid!" Thus, according to James, we feel happy *because* we laugh, sad *because* we cry, and afraid *because* we tremble.

Walter Cannon rejected this view. He wished instead to emphasize the evolutionary role of strong emotions in preparing the organism for vigorous activity during an emergency—the "fight or flight" response of the SNS. (At least an implicit acceptance of this view can be seen in the above dictionary definition of *emotion.*) He also wanted to stress the importance of the brain (particularly the hypothalamus) as initiator and an integral part of an emotional experience. In the Cannon-Bard theory of emotion, the brain is far more than a passive sensory receiver checking to see which internal organs are "on" and which "off."

In a classic paper, Cannon (1927) marshaled several bodies of experimental evidence to argue against the James-Lange peripheralist view. He noted that, even when input from the viscera is cut off from the brain surgically, an experimental animal still behaves "emotionally." More importantly for the history of psychophysiology, he argued that the same visceral changes occur in many different emotional states. Implicit in the James-Lange theory is the idea that each emotion is physiologically distinct. If the brain is to know when the body is angry and when afraid, two different patterns of physiological activity must be associated with these key emotions. In a slightly different form, this question of the patterning of physiological activity continues to be a vital one for contemporary psychophysiology.

Neither the Cannon-Bard nor the James-Lange theory stands today as an adequate framework in which to view our complex emotional lives. Even Cannon's ideas about the evolutionary value of SNS "fight or flight" activation have been questioned: The release of adrenaline, for example, breaks down muscular glycogen and thus might hinder activity. (See Grossman, 1967, for an excellent review of contemporary evidence on theories of emotion.) But each theory helped to provide the germinal ideas for today's psychophysiology.

Intellectual descendants of Cannon include Duffy's (1934) concept of "energy mobilization" and Lindsley's (1951) influential "activation theory of emotion." Lindsley incorporated findings from the early 1950s on the critical role of the reticular formation of the brain in maintaining alertness. He went on to argue that emotion can be seen as a simple continuum ranging from coma (or, for the purists, death) to the extreme emotions like rage, which could be detected in the complex rhythms of the EEG. Although this hope of finding clear-cut EEG correlates of the various emotions was never realized, the time was ripe in psychophysiology for a convenient unifying theory like the arousal approach.

The notion of a continuum of arousal or activation underlying behavior slipped into the mainstream of psychology, where it remains to the present day. "Arousal" came to be applied not only to a simple emotional state but also to a more general mental alertness. Many studies attempted to manipulate arousal in a behavioral sense. Experimental subjects who were instructed to pay special attention to their tasks, for example, might be said to be aroused. What started out as a physiological theory was watered down, then, into a behavioral construct of assumed value.

In 1958, John Lacey wrote a classic paper challenging the validity of the arousal concept. Among Lacey's arguments were the following: (1) EEG and behavioral arousal are clearly dissociated by certain drugs; (2) there is no compelling evidence that common psychophysiological measures vary together; (3) there is some evidence that cardiovascular *increases* are associated with *decreases* in cortical activation. This last point, the Lacey baroreceptor hypothesis, will be discussed in some detail in Chapter 5. For our purposes here, the second point is the most critical.

The notion of one underlying continuum of arousal was taken by many researchers to mean that any psychophysiological variable was interchangeable with any other. Thus, for example, if one were interested in studying the relation of arousal to visual thresholds, he might choose to measure sweat gland activity (Lykken et al, 1966), the electrical activity of the brain (Venables and Warwick-Evans, 1967), or heart rate (Boissonneault et al., 1970), depending on the available facilities. All were thought to reflect, however imperfectly, the same underlying state. Lacey argued quite correctly that, if this were so, then experimenters who measured two or more of these variables simultaneously should find them to be highly correlated. A person whose palms were sweating should also give evidence of an activated EEG and a relatively high heart rate. In point of fact, all the evidence available did *not* support this point of view; correlations between psychophysiological measures in any study tended to be rather low.

Defenders of the arousal theory viewpoint were quick to point out that an easy interchangeability of measures is not a necessary implication of arousal theory. Even its staunchest advocates would agree, as Duffy (1972) put it, that "The organism does not react as a massive undifferentiated whole." Woodworth and Schlosberg (1954) used the analogy of economic prosperity as a general descriptive variable. Although any single economic variable (like the median income of all families or total assets of the banks in a community) may be only slightly related to the presumed underlying variable, nevertheless it is valid to talk about one community's being more prosperous than another. "Similarly," they argued, "we do not have much trouble in deciding whether an individual is highly activated or half asleep, without meaning that all his (physiological) functions are activated."

The notion that there is some continuum of arousal underlying the intensity of behavior is a seductive one that has figured prominently in many psychological theories. Certain types of schizophrenics, for example, have been characterized by many theorists as suffering from a physiological deficit that leaves them under- or over-aroused (see Maher, 1966). But any attempt to order all the many human behavioral and mental states along a single continuum is doomed to failure. The "arousal" of playing tennis is quite different from sexual "arousal" or the "arousal" of preparing for a difficult exam.

Arousal theory led many researchers to conceptualize a variable like the sweat-gland response as a simple key to a single internal state rather than one integral component in a total pattern of bodily response. The point of view emphasized throughout this book is that the sweat glands were biologically built in a different way from the heart and the brain and that each of these systems provides yet another clue to the puzzle of humanity.

3

Recording Human Physiological Response

When Galen took the pulse of his lovesick patient, his fingers sensed the distention of the radial artery of the wrist with each beat of the woman's heart while he mentally noted when the pulse was "faster" or "slower." Important as Galen's conclusions were, his procedure was a crude one, far from adequate for building a science. The history of science is intimately bound up with advnaces in scientific engineering. The human senses are poorly designed to peer into the organism's inner world, to see how the human biological machine is put together. Scientific instruments extend man's limited vision: The telescope brought the stars within an arm's reach, while the microscope magnified the tiniest particle. Similarly, the stethoscope placed over the chest replaced the simple feel of the pulse and provided new information about the periodic beating of the heart.

An understanding of modern psychophysiology, then, demands an understanding of the methods now at our disposal for observing changes inside the body. Indeed, psychophysiological researchers sometimes find themselves devoting as much time to keeping an arsenal of complicated electronic gadgets in good repair as they do to actually using them. It is easy to become mesmerized by a roomful of flashing lights, noisy relays, and hastily scribbling pens.

We shall now trace the evolution of relevant medical technology and provide the information necessary for understanding current recording techniques.

Early Approaches to Physiological Recording

Direct observation is, of course, the simplest procedure. Recent research on hemispheric asymmetry indicates that a person using the left side of his brain tends to move his eyes to the right, and vice versa (see Chapter 7). In many recent studies of this relationship, the experimenter simply sits directly in front of his subject and notes the direction in which his eyes move when he answers questions that emphasize right- or left-hemisphere thinking. Such a procedure is quite appropriate and, of course, very convenient for this research question. But if the researcher were interested in the more subtle eye movements that occur during reading, for example, this method would not be entirely adequate. And so early students in this area devised various telescope-like devices that focused on the reader's eyes and allowed the experimenter to note the very minor changes in eye position that are so characteristic of this task. Similarly, when Darrow (1932) wanted to directly observe the formation of sweat droplets in emotional situations, he had people press their fingertips against a glass plate, which he then observed through a microscope. Like many of his contemporaries, Darrow supplemented his direct observation by taking a moving picture of his experiment. The human observer is notoriously unreliable, and this photographic record of his observations was thus available for later, more leisurely analysis. This idea of a permanent record of physiological changes through photography is still used in contemporary studies of eye movements.

Not all physiological changes are visible, even with the aid of high-power magnification; for this reason many methods of indirect observation were gradually developed.

Many of the early studies that indirectly measured physiological change depended on entirely mechanical recording systems. For example, to study the knee-jerk reflex, Wendt (1930) developed an elaborate series of rods, levers, and pulleys that attached the quadriceps muscle of the knee directly to a writing device. A pen was jerked across a piece of paper whenever this muscle thickened, signaling the jerking of the knee.

Clearly, this sort of mechanical arrangement demanded a mechanical writing system. Physiologists at first adapted the kymograph of behavioral researchers. Basically, this consisted of a slowly revolving cylinder that was covered with a sheet of paper. A pen, or stylus, came in contact with the paper and moved across its surface as the drum rotated. In this case, as long as the quadriceps muscle remained stationary, a straight line would appear across the paper. A sudden jerking of the pen as it was mechanically moved by thickening of the muscle permanently recorded the occurrence of the knee jerk.

Many different writing systems were used in early research. For the "smoked drum kymograph," a piece of special paper was passed through a smokey flame until it was covered with soot. This was then placed on the drum and a sharp stylus merely traced away the carbon deposit as it moved across the cylindrical surface. Once a record was completed, the paper was shellacked so that it could be kept indefinitely. This was preferred to using an ink-bearing pen because the stylus was physically lighter and thus could respond more quickly to mechanical changes in the system. Various other writing systems for registering changes on the kymograph were also available. These were the precursors of what is today the major research apparatus of the psychophysiology laboratory: the polygraph. The term *polygraph* simply means "many pens" and implies the simultaneous recording of several channels of information. Although technically the pens could be recording anything (for example, polygraphs may be used in a weather station to simultaneously record temperature, humidity, and barometric pressure), the term gradually came to refer primarily to psychophysiological recording. Indeed, professional lie-detection experts (who typically measure sweat-gland, respiratory, and blood-pressure changes—see Chapter 10) refer to themselves with the more neutral term "polygraphers."

Simple mechanical linkages of the type described above were, of course, used to measure more than the knee jerk. Early studies of eye-blinking, for example, frequently involved attaching a simple rod to the eyelid. Any blink would move the rod and ultimately the recording stylus. Finger tremor and other physiological changes were also studied with ingenious devices of this sort.

A similar but more complicated system came with the development of pneumatic recording devices. These converted a change in pressure to a mechanical change that would cause the stylus to move. The plethysmograph, for example, is a simple volume recorder. When blood flows to most parts of the body, the influx of liquid makes the body part swell; that is, it increases its volume. Figure 3.1 illustrates one simple device for studying blood flow to the hand. The hand is immersed in a liquid-filled container that is tightly sealed

Figure 3.1 *Francke's Hand and Wrist Plethysmograph.* A is a heavy glass jar filled with water up to the level of the expanded glass tube at E. Changes in the water level are then transfered to a pneumatic system for recording. A rubber membrane, D, covers the top of the jar and fits around the arm. The hand clasps a wooden grip, B, in the water. (After C. A. Ruckmick, *The Psychology of Feeling and Emotion.* Copyright 1936. By permission of McGraw-Hill Book Company.)

with a diaphragm (called a tambour) of stretchable rubber or metal. As blood flows into the hand, its volume is increased; this lightly displaces some of the liquid, which then stretches the diaphragm. When this moves, it activates a lever connected to a stylus and the movement is recorded on a kymograph. Thus, a permanent and continuous (although admittedly crude) measure of blood flow to the hand is obtained.

Probably the most popular pneumatic recording device is used for the study of respiration. As you breathe in and out, abdominal and chest muscles expand and contract.

For the pneumograph, an airtight, thin rubber tube that stretches like an accordion is placed around the chest. As the subject breathes in, the hose stretches and its volume is increased, sucking in a tambour that is sealed at the end of the tube. A series of rods communicates this movement to the polygraph stylus. The entire operation of this device is illustrated in Figure 3.2. This type of apparatus is still used in professional lie detection, although more modern systems are preferred by the psychophysiologist. A more complicated system for measuring blood pressure that relies on similar principles will be discussed in Chapter 5.

This brief review of direct observation and the mechanical measurement of physiological change gives us our first clues to the crucial role of instrumentation in psychophysiology. The techniques outlined thus far are often rather uncomfortable for the subject and may have obvious effects on the responses under study. It is a questionable assumption that a person's eye-blink rate will

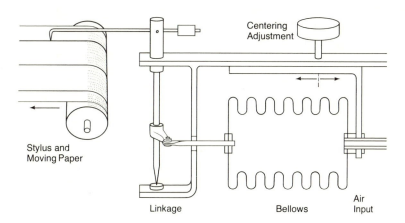

Figure 3.2 *A Pneumatic System for Recording Respiration.* A respiration recorder operates by dead-air displacement. An accordionlike tube fitted to the subject's chest is connected to the thin-walled metal bellows. As the subject inhales or exhales, air is withdrawn from or returned to the bellows, rotating the vertical shaft that carries the pen. (After B. M. Smith, "The Polygraph." Copyright © 1966 by Scientific American, Inc. All rights reserved.)

be representative of normal conditions when he is forced to sit quietly with a thread taped to his eye. Advances in our understanding of human physiology, then, often depend on the development of instruments that allow us to observe many different kinds of physiological responses without disturbing the subject. Most contemporary psychophysiological methods depend on the recording of electrical changes associated with bodily processes.

Electricity and the Body

Luigi Galvani was the first to suggest that electricity was a critical force in energizing biological tissue. On September 26, 1786, Galvani was performing dissections in his cramped laboratory while a colleague was simultaneously experimenting with a static electricity generator a few feet away. When one of his assistants happened to touch a scalpel to a nerve in a dead frog's leg, the leg twitched dramatically. The incident inspired Galvani to perform a series of experiments that gradually convinced him that it was the fortuitous electrical charge that had caused the muscle to contract.

Galvani believed that he had discovered the essential life force, which he named "animal electricity." He became embroiled in a scientific feud with a colleague, Alessandro Volta. Volta argued that Galvani had unwittingly produced primitive batteries in many of his experiments and that there was in fact only one kind of electricity.

After Galvani was forced to retire (upon refusing to swear allegiance to Napoleon), his nephew Aldini upheld the family's honor by touring Europe, arguing for the unique nature of "animal electricity." Many of Galvani's contemporaries believed that it would soon be possible to bring the dead back to life merely by restoring their "animal electricity." Aldini fed this belief with dramatic demonstrations of his uncle's discovery. Legend has it that he would show an audience the severed head of a dead chicken and make its eyes blink and its beak open and close. On special occasions, he even secured the bodies of recently executed criminals and would move their limbs in a macabre demonstration of his viewpoint.

Despite such imaginative public relations, Galvani's theory was finally rejected; there is only one kind of electricity. Our understanding of the fundamental nature of this one kind, however, still leaves much to be desired. (See Appendix A.)

Psychophysiological Recording

We can think of contemporary recording of psychophysiological processes as involving three related stages, schematically represented in Figure 3.3. In the first stage, some physiological process is detected as an electrical signal or somehow converted into an electrical impulse. Then, in the next stage, this signal is electronically processed by a series of amplification circuits so that it is presented in a meaningful way to the final stage, a device to display the electrical changes. Let us consider each of these stages in turn.

Stage 1: Detecting the Signal

As we suggested above, the human body is in a very real sense a complicated electrochemical machine. It is often possible to directly monitor the electrical events of the body by simply placing electrodes (in the simplest case, any good conductor) on the body's surface.

If we place two electrodes anywhere on the surface of the body, there will be a measurable potential difference between them. (Note that there must always be two electrodes, so that there will be a complete electrical circuit. Electrons must flow from one place to another.) These biopotentials reflect the normal electrical functioning of the body. If the two electrodes are placed over the skull, we will be recording primarily the electrical activity of the brain, the electroencephalogram, or EEG. If we place one electrode on the left arm and a second on the right, we can record the electrocardiogram (EKG), which reflects electrical events associated with the contraction of heart muscles. If we place two electrodes close to one another on the back of the arm, we obtain a record of the muscular activity at this site, or electromyogram (EMG). Two electrodes placed on either side of the eyes will be sensitive to changes in the orientation of the eyes. The electrical record of these changes is called the electrooculogram, or EOG. Note that these procedures provide a rather crude measure of electrical activity. Each neuron acts on the basis of electrical impulses. It is possible to record the electrical activity of a single neuron, but it is usually necessary to insert microelectrodes deep into the body to isolate each cell. Single-cell recording is generally the province of the physiological psychologist or physiologist, and is ordinarily limited to studies of lower animals. The psychophysiologist, recording from the surface of a normal person's body, studies the complex interactions of large masses of neuromuscular tissue and their relation to behavior and conscious experience.

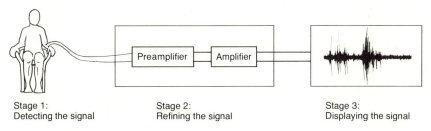

Stage 1:
Detecting the signal

Stage 2:
Refining the signal

Stage 3:
Displaying the signal

Figure 3.3 *Stages in Psychophysiological Recording.* (See text for details.)

Needless to say, the body is not neatly organized into mutually exclusive electrical circuits. We cannot be sure that two electrodes placed on the top of the head will record nothing but brain activity. If our subject tenses the muscles of the scalp, there may be contamination by unwanted EMG signals. Frontal scalp areas are affected by the potential associated with the eyes. We may even detect the powerful EKG signals from our leads. These unwanted electrical signals are termed artifacts; they superimpose electrical "noise" on the signal that we are interested in. This is one reason that we need electronic filters in Stage 2 to emphasize the electrical waves that are of primary interest in a given experiment.

All of the recordings discussed above were bipolar—that is, both electrodes were located at or near the tissue under study. Each of these electrode positions is termed an "active" site. In other cases, a researcher may prefer monopolar recording, in which one of the two electrode sites chosen serves as a relatively inactive site, a reference point electrically. Thus we may record monopolar EEG by placing one electrode on the surface of the scalp and the other on an earlobe. In some senses, this electrical recording is less ambiguous than the bipolar arrangement. It is giving us relatively pure information about electrical activity at a single body site rather than a complicated interaction of the activity at two different points. The electrogastrogram (EGG), a record of electrical activity associated with stomach contraction, is typically recorded with one electrode over the stomach and another on one leg. Skin potential (SP), a measure of electrical activity of the sweat glands on the palms or soles of the feet, is also best recorded with a monopolar configuration—one electrode on the palm and another on the back of the arm.

The actual reason for preferring monopolar or bipolar recording technique depends both on the specific physiological system in question and the experimenter's intent. These issues will be discussed as we consider each physiological measure in turn. The important point to remember is that two electrodes placed anywhere on the surface of the body will have a potential difference between them. Exactly where we place the electrodes and how we relate these electrical signals to underlying physiological activity is one of the key questions of psychophysiology, to which we will return throughout this book.

Thus far, we have been talking as though the electrodes themselves are almost irrelevant, and, if we were to strap two strips of aluminum foil to pieces of wire, they would be quite adequate. For some of the stronger physiological signals, like the EKG, this is almost true. Any good conductor of electricity held firmly to the surface of the body will do. But when we discuss electrical signals that are more difficult to detect (because of their smaller magnitude), the nature of the electrodes becomes increasingly important. For we want to be sure that the electrical signals we receive are coming from the body and are not another kind of artifact—unwanted electrical signals produced by the equipment itself. And, in some instances, the substances that come in contact with the skin (for example, in sweat-gland recording) may themselves affect the tissue. A conducting medium, a special chemical solution, is almost always placed between the skin and the electrodes. This, too, may affect the underlying tissue. A particularly troublesome problem for measurement of the very small voltages of psychophysiology is electrode polarization. Ionic polarization occurs with many substances, so that the electrodes begin to act as miniature batteries generating a potential of their own. Electrodes made of silver and coated with silver chloride are very stable; that is, they resist polarization. Silver/silver-chloride electrodes in a variety of sizes and shapes are now commercially available and routinely used in most psychophysiological research. A number of ingenious systems have also been devised for fastening them securely to the body.

Before we leave the topic of potentials, we should refer to one other frequently measured electrical characteristic of the skin, its resistance to a minute current. This is not a true biopotential since, although it is a measurable variation in the body's electrical characteristic, it is not a voltage generated by the body. Skin resistance (SR) and its reciprocal skin conductance (SC) are alternative measures of sweat-gland activity. This is the most common psychophysiological variable that requires imposing external electrical currents on the body. Of course, only very small currents (in the order of 10 μamps), well below the threshold of feeling, are ever applied to the body.

But the interest of the psychophysiologist does not end with physiological changes that are easily associated with electrical events at the body's surface. And so he often employs *transducers*, devices that translate pressure, heat, or light changes into electrical events.

We have already seen how the rhythmic contractions of the chest can be used to monitor breathing. In the modern psychophysiology laboratory, these contractions are not monitored with the mechanical pneumograph described above. Rather, a device called a strain gauge, for example, is strapped around the chest. A strain gauge consists of an electrical conductor that decreases its resistance when it is stretched. Thus the changes in the circumference of the chest are recorded as a variable change in electrical resistance. Similarly, a strain gauge taped horizontally across the eyelids can measure the distention of the lid as the eyes of the dreamer move back and forth in REM (rapid eye movement) sleep (see Chapter 7).

Other transducers are also available. If one is interested in measuring the temperature of the skin (an index of localized blood flow; see Chapter 5), one may use a thermocouple, which generates a variable electrical potential according to its temperature. Alternatively, one may use a thermistor, which changes its electrical resistance as a function of temperature.

Thus we have seen that, in the first stage of psychophysiological recording —detecting the signal—biopotentials (the natural electrical events of the body) may be recorded or various nonelectrical events may be recorded electronically with the aid of transducers.

Stage 2: Refining the Signal

The electrical signal detected at the surface of the body is, in its raw form, not a very useful one. Although there is a difference in electrical potential between any two sites on your head, it is not enough to turn on a flashlight or drive an electrical motor. Therefore, the signal must be amplified, or made larger, until it is electrically useful, that is, until it is powerful enough to drive the devices that in Stage 3 will physically record its progress. Further, some characteristics of the signal may be more directly linked to underlying physiological processes than others. We mentioned earlier that two electrodes on the head might pick up electrical changes associated with eye movement as well as the EEG record of brain activity. Therefore, the crude electronic signal

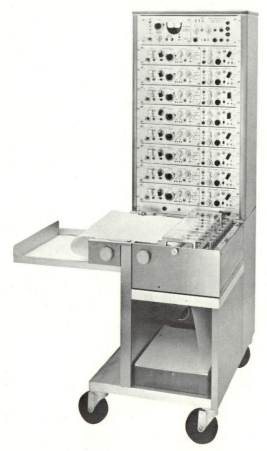

Figure 3.4 *A Grass Model 7 Polygraph.* (Courtesy of Grass Instrument Company, Quincy, Mass.)

frequently must be filtered to accentuate the changes that are of greatest interest to the researcher.

This second stage of refining the signal consists, then, of amplification and filtering. This is done electronically by a series of complicated circuits that are usually subdivided into a preamplifier and a power amplifier. As these names indicate, most of the major signal boosting occurs in the power amplifier while the preamplifier is more concerned with filtering the physiological signal.

Commercial polygraphs include amplifiers and preamplifiers with a great deal of built-in flexibility in amplification and filtering. This allows the experimenter to record many different physiological responses, with quite different electrical characteristics, on one set of equipment. It also permits him to experiment with the effects of various ranges of amplification and filtering on a given physiological signal. But with this flexibility comes complexity: The control panel of the polygraph may appear rather forbidding to the novice, and an impressive array of switches and dials must be set properly before recording can begin (see Figure 3.4). The discussion here will not teach you how to use the polygraph, but it will impart a few of the general principles of signal refinement that can be helpful in studying psychophysiological literature.

The principles of amplification are quite straightforward. The goal is to increase the electrical signals of the body to a magnitude that is large enough to drive the recording apparatus. In a research report, the actual amount of amplification is usually indicated as a scale at the bottom of a physiological recording. Thus, if in a recording of EEG, we see the following legend:

$$\mathsf{I}\;50\,\mu\mathrm{V}$$

we know that a line equal to that shown indicates an actual voltage of 50 microvolts.

The concepts of electrical filtering are not so simple, nor can they be so straightforwardly described. (See Appendix A.) But once the signal is increased in amplitude and its frequency characteristics are altered by filtering, all that is left is the final stage, in which the reshaped electronic signals are displayed for the eye to behold.

Stage 3: Displaying the Signal

The preferred method of making a permanent record of the physiological changes observed in the laboratory involves some variation on the kymograph paper record described earlier. Historically, one major problem in psychophysiological recording has been that of developing a writing apparatus sensitive enough to faithfully record the small-magnitude, high-frequency changes of the body.

In 1903, Einthoven developed the string galvanometer for recording the

EKG. In this system, a fine thread is suspended between the poles of a powerful electromagnet. As the current to be recorded passes through this string, other magnetic fields are generated and the string bends in proportion to the electrical voltage. In many early polygraphs, the string was connected to a mirror that deflected a light beam to a moving roll of photographic paper (see Figure 3.5). This system had the advantage of relatively little mechanical inertia; the force required to move a pen across a piece of paper was far greater.

Since that time, a variety of light pens and powerful galvanometers have been developed. The basic principle of current polygraph recording is simply to put a pen on the tip of a very sensitive electrical meter. A special motor moves a roll of paper under the tip of the pen at a constant speed. This speed can be preset by the experimenter, depending on the detail he is interested in. (This may be somewhat confusing to the beginner; see Appendix A.) However, even contemporary systems have their mechanical limitations; in many polygraphs, the pen simply cannot reverse direction more quickly than 75 times each second. Thus, physiological signals with high-frequency components greater than 75 Hz (like the EMG) cannot be adequately recorded on the polygraph.

The experimenter who is interested in very high-frequency responses may therefore use an oscilloscope. This elaborate device includes a small TV screen that can display electrical changes at a very fast rate. Of course, if he wants a permanent visual record of these changes, the experimenter must take a motion picture of the oscilloscope screen.

Even after a polygraph record or oscilloscope movie is made, the researcher's job has barely begun. Now that he has recorded physiological responses, he must somehow begin to make some sense out of them, to analyze his data. In the early days of psychophysiological research, and often today, that may mean taking out a ruler and manually measuring the size of various deflections.

Some of this burden has been lifted by high-speed computer facilities. In this

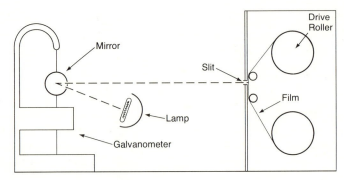

Figure 3.5 *A Mirror Galvanometer.* (See text for details.)

case, an electronic record of physiological changes is kept along with the reassuring visual record. This electronic record, on a special tape recorder, is then fed into the computer and more elaborate data analysis procedures become possible.

The polygraph, however, remains the bread and butter of the psychophysiology laboratory.

4

The Sweat Gland

The lowly sweat gland may seem like an unlikely place to begin our study of the body. We all know how important the brain is, or the heart, but few of us have ever stopped to think seriously about perspiration. Its functions seem comparatively mundane and perhaps even mildly embarrassing.

But modern psychophysiology was born when a French physician named Féré first noted that the electrical properties of the skin change in emotional situations. We now know that Féré was indirectly observing sweat-gland activity. And so it seems appropriate that we should begin our study here. For even at the biologically primitive level of the sweat gland, we will find a story of fascinating complexity. The psychophysiologist confronting this data often feels like a traveler in a strange land. He has the task of translating an unknown tongue, the long-forgotten cryptic language of the body.

History

In 1888, Dr. Féré published the case history of an hysterical anorectic (tastefully referred to as Mme. X) who came to him complaining of electrical tingling in her hands and feet. Féré noticed that these sensations increased when his patient sniffed an odor, looked at a colored piece of glass, or listened to a

32

tuning fork. We do not know whether Mme. X's extremities ever stopped tingling, but in the course of this research Féré found that, when a weak electrical current was imposed on his patient's forearm, systematic changes in the resistance of the skin occurred. Just two years later, Tarchanoff independently reported that similar electrical changes could be observed without the imposition of an external current. Thus he discovered skin potential and further showed that it changed in response to mental activity as well as to sensory stimulation.

This electrical activity of the skin gradually became known as the "galvanic skin reflex" or GSR, a term that survives to the present day. Despite the relative difficulty of measuring these subtle changes with the primitive electrical apparatus available at the turn of the century, the predictability and the melodrama of the GSR attracted the attention of many researchers. If you have never seen an example of this simple phenomenon, it may be difficult to recapture the excitement of these early researchers, who saw no limits to its potential. Imagine, if you can, attaching your fingers with an elaborate set of wires to a huge machine in a musty lab at the turn of the century. And then you notice that every time you imagine a friend's face, the needle on the meter moves!

Among the first students of the GSR was Carl Jung, who saw the GSR as a physiological and objective window to the unconscious processes postulated by his mentor, Freud (Peterson and Jung, 1907). It was this study that first noted that the magnitude of the skin's electrical response seemed to reflect the magnitude of the emotional experience—the more deeply your image affected you, the more the needle moved.

In this atmosphere of pioneering enthusiasm, hundreds of scientists set about the task of using their bulky equipment to determine just what situations elicited GSRs. In one such study of fear, Nancy Bayley (1928) subjected fellow students to the following stimuli: listening to an article about cattle drowning at sea; holding a lighted match until it burned the fingers; firing a .38 revolver loaded with an extra loud blank cartridge about four feet from the subject; and even, for a few subjects, being handed the revolver with the request that they shoot themselves. She concluded, both from subjective reports and the physiological reactions, that there were two types of fear: startle and apprehension. In other studies from this period, Waller (1918) looked at the GSR to an imagined German air raid of London, and Linde (1928) found that the funniness of jokes had a lawful relation (to the delight of psychophysicists, a logarithmic Weber-Fechner curve) to GSR magnitude.

The electrical changes of the skin are so dramatic and so easy to measure that, while psychologists sought basic behavioral laws, others saw a more commercial potential. Advertising agencies at one time experimented with the possibility that GSRs to advertisements could predict their effects on sales. Indeed, in one preliminary test (Eckstrand and Gilliland, 1948), a group of housewives showed their largest GSR responses to a pancake flour ad that did yield higher sales than control advertisements. However, a similar test of baby-food ads with the same group was less successful. Such a result is not surprising. The assumption implicit in this study (and many other studies of advertising)—that an advertisement that caused people to respond emotionally would also boost sales—may or may not be true. In any case, the use of GSR in advertising proved to be just one more fad in a faddish industry.

Many electronics supply houses now sell inexpensive gadgets which emit tones of varying pitch or volume depending on the resistance in the circuit. One is invited to be the life of the party by attaching the machine to the hands of unsuspecting friends and asking them intensely personal questions, the machine presumably emitting a telltale whine if they lie. These are in fact harmless toys as long as they are not used to invade the privacy of innocent bystanders. We shall return to the question of whether observed electrical changes really reflect lying when we discuss the lie-detection industry (see Chapter 10).

More expensive versions of these gadgets have been sold in the names of both science and religion. As a rough rule of thumb, we might suggest that the less sophisticated the user, the more he is likely to pay to measure his sweat glands' responses.

What Does the Sweat Gland Respond To?

Running throughout these early experiments and commercial ventures was the belief that the GSR was an indicator of emotion, perhaps even better than the subject's own report of what he felt. Hans Syz (1926–1927), for example, found that a group of medical students showed GSRs to such terms as *prostitute*, *misspent youth*, and *unpaid bills*, although they claimed to feel no emotion to these words. He argued that social taboos kept these emotional responses from awareness but that they were emotions nonetheless. This is an appealing line of argument to the operationalist who wants to get away from the confusing and often conflicting reports that people typically give of their feelings. Still, it doesn't seem quite right to equate emotions with GSRs, since this is clearly not the commonsense meaning of the word. Alternatively, the medical students' GSRs could be classified as "orienting responses," the reflex responses to novel stimuli that will be discussed later in this chapter.

But such attempts at glib labeling are doomed to failure. The sweat gland did not evolve to conform to English words like *emotion*, and the task of the psychophysiologist is to try to transcend everyday language as he searches for the common features of those events which elicit sweat gland responses. Much of this chapter is an attempt to answer the question, "What does the sweat gland respond to?" and we shall see that the sweat gland has many different ways of responding that give us many kinds of information. But there are two major conclusions we can draw at this point:

1. *Sweat-gland activity is an index of events in the brain.* Sweat-gland re-

sponses and other measures of ANS function have sometimes been referred to as "peripheral," somehow apart from CNS function. This is quite misleading. Responding to a phrase like *unpaid bills* clearly involves complicated cognitive processes. Bernstein, Taylor and Weinstein (1975) developed elaborate experimental procedures in which physically identical stimuli are given quite different meanings. "Psychological significance," as complicated a construct as one is likely to find in social research, was the key element in predicting sweat-gland response. The behavioral scientist does not by-pass the complexity of human experience by studying the sweat gland; rather he confronts it directly.

2. *The amount of sweat-gland response is lawfully related to the intensity of conscious experience.* Consider the following list of words: *chair, desk, flower, fuck, ashtray, pencil.* In all probability, your largest sweat gland response was to the unexpected obscene word. The unanimity of studies on the topic of increased sweating to emotionally charged stimuli is quite compelling. McCurdy (1950) summarizes this evidence in a review forbiddingly titled "Consciousness and the Galvanometer." Every researcher who has measured the electrical activity of the skin is familiar with this phenomenon, although the difficulty in precisely stating the relationship (for example, finding a more specific label than "conscious intensity") has limited research on the field. The behaviorist bias of American psychology has also curtailed the study of consciousness, but one of the great promises of psychophysiology is the reintroduction of this taboo topic into the mainstream of social science. The fact that more intense experiences yield more intense sweat-gland responses is one good place to start.

Beyond these two major points, one can ask the more general question of sweat-gland function: Why did evolution build our sweat glands to respond to intense stimuli? The answer is buried in our ancestry, but there are several major theories to explain the biological significance of this emotional sweating. The traditional view is attributed to Darrow (1936): Increased sweating improves the grip. For example, a laborer may spit on his hands before gripping an ax. (In the Chinese and Japanese languages, the phrase *spitting on the hands* is an idiom for a situation involving general mental and physical stress.) Increased sweating on the hands also leads to greater tactile sensitivity. Further, the wetness of the palms and soles makes them very resistant to abrasion and cutting. All of these changes are helpful in threatening situations, at least for Man the Hunter. Thus, it is easy to see them in evolutionary terms. There are other, more complicated views of subtle physiological effects of this sweating (see Edelberg, 1972).

Overview of Electrodermal Measures

One common characteristic of many early studies was their cavalier disregard of whether an external current was imposed on the subject ("Féré method") or not ("Tarchanoff method"). It was widely held that both methods yielded the same results, and so the specific recording procedure used was a technicality. For many years, some of the more casual users of electrodermal activity failed to make their recording methodology clear.

In fact there are subtle differences between the two measures in the physiological basis and consequently in the results observed. For this reason, psychophysiologists are now trying to eliminate the old term GSR, even though they may find themselves using the term through force of habit. A more precise terminology substitutes the phrase skin resistance (SR) for the exosomatic method of imposing a current source and skin potential (SP) for the endosomatic procedure of measuring the voltage changes of the skin itself. Correct use of this nomenclature also includes a description of the events considered. *Level* means that relatively long periods of time are analyzed (tonic activity), and *response* refers to short duration changes (phasic activity, just a few seconds) that occur in response to a specific stimulus. Responses that are not readily attributable to some external stimulus are called *spontaneous*. Finally, the general term for referring to all of these events is *electrodermal activity* (EDA) rather than GSR. Table 4.1 summarizes the most common abbreviations for the various measures.

Figure 4.1 illustrates simultaneous recordings of SC and SP. Note the distinctive responses recorded during a casual conversation; during a period of rest, both SC and SP could be straight lines. The SCR is an upward deflection of the pen representing an increase in conductance (due to increased sweating), while the SPR is usually characterized by increased negativity relative to baseline. Tonic SCL and SPL could be computed by noting values at regular intervals (for example, every 15 seconds for 2 minutes) and averaging them. The responses seen on Figure 4.1 would be classified as spontaneous (see below) because they do not follow discrete stimuli.

Relatively few researchers now discuss *resistance*; the alternative, *conductance*, is generally preferred (Lykken and Venables, 1971). (Conductance units are mathematically equivalent to resistances and can be computed from them by the formula *ohms* = 1/*mhos.*) There are a number of lines of evidence

Table 4.1   Kinds of Electrodermal Activity (EDA)

SPL	=	Skin Potential Level
SPR	=	Skin Potential Response
SSPR	=	Spontaneous Skin Potential Response
SRL	=	Skin Resistance Level
SRR	=	Skin Resistance Response
SSRR	=	Spontaneous Skin Resistance Response
SCL	=	Skin Conductance Level
SCR	=	Skin Conductance Response
SSCR	=	Spontaneous Skin Conductance Response

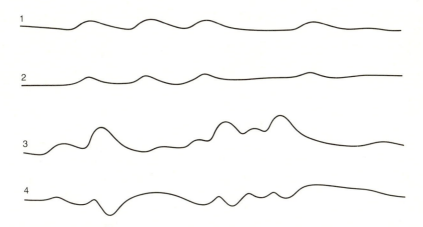

Figure 4.1 *Simultaneous SC and SP Recordings.* Simultaneous recordings of SP (channels 1 and 3, recorded from left palm and forearm) and SC (channels 2 and 4, recorded from right palm). Channels 1 and 2 were simultaneously recorded during a period of relaxed conversation; channels 3 and 4 are a continuation of this record after a lapse of several minutes. The precise correlation between SC and SP is not entirely understood. See Figure 4.3 for one suggested model. (Courtesy of Larry Young.)

suggesting the superiority of SC (skin conductance) units. The most compelling argument, based on biological grounds, is that sweat glands act like a number of resistors in parallel (Treager, 1966). Since the resistance of a group of resistors in parallel is the sum of their reciprocals, or conductances, an increasing conductance gives a directly proportional representation of the number of sweat glands coming into play. Darrow (1964b) independently showed that SC is linearly related to sweat secretion, while SR is not. SC is also preferred to SR on statistical grounds; SCs tend to be more normally distributed than SRs.

This may seem like a rather minor distinction, but it is not. Since conductance is a nonlinear transformation of resistance, use of the two sets of figures may lead one to very different conclusions. (See Appendix B for an example.) On electronic grounds, resistance is cheaper and easier to record directly, and so most researchers continue to use SR measuring circuitry, converting these values to SC later. The point to remember is that conclusions should be drawn from SC rather than SR.

Of course, there are many ways of measuring sweating that do not rely directly on EDA. For example, Strahan, Todd and Ingliss (1974) developed a "sweat bottle" technique that involves simply placing a small bottle of distilled water against the palm and later measuring electrical characteristics of the water. This has the advantage of being extremely portable and thus very useful in naturalistic research. For example, one study using this procedure (Strahan and Ho, 1976) was able to demonstrate increased sweating in patients about to undergo surgery. New techniques like this will, no doubt, play a large role in the psychophysiology of the future.

Physiological Basis

We have been talking up to this point as if it were intuitively obvious that EDA reflects sweat-gland activity. Early researchers suspected several other influences; some believed EDA reflected muscle activity, while others stressed possible contributions of the peripheral blood vessels. The muscle theory was discredited fairly early. The vascular theory was somewhat more robust, but a series of elegant experiments also ruled out this possibility. For example, in 1962 Lader and Montagu showed that if sweat gland responses are suppressed pharmacologically, the SCR disappears. A similar blocking of peripheral vasomotor activity left the SCR unaffected. It is still not clear whether there may be some vascular basis for SP. However, it is now widely agreed that sweat-gland activity is largely responsible for EDA.

Although the neural transmitter of the sweat glands is acetylcholine (normally the parasympathetic transmitter), sweat glands are under sympathetic control. Destruction of the SNS on one side of the body, for example, destroys EDA only on that side (Schwartz, 1934). Because of this sympathetic control and the widespread belief in the diffuseness of sympathetic reaction, EDA has been used in the past as a crude indicator of overall sympathetic arousal. A review of sweat-gland connections to the central nervous system, however, undercuts this simplistic view (Edelberg, 1972; Rickles, 1972).

Anatomically, there are at least two separate pathways from the brain to the sweat glands: one from the cortex and a second from structures deep inside the brain, including the hypothalamus and the reticular system. These findings give us our first indication that even the "simple" sweat gland is an organ of unexpected biological sophistication. We shall see as this review continues that different measures of EDA may be giving us very different information about underlying processes. The simple assumption that any EDA measure is a reliable and valid indicator of sympathetic arousal is no longer tenable.

Before concentrating on those sweat-gland changes that are responsible for EDA, let us briefly review some of the major features of human perspiration as a whole.

In 1614, Sanctorius Sanctorio began a series of experiments on human perspiration that lasted 30 years. With admirable dedication to his work, he spent hour after hour sitting on a very sensitive scale. He demonstrated that perspiration goes on constantly, even when sweat droplets do not appear on the skin, a phenomenon termed *insensible perspiration*. On a typical day, he lost about a pound of sweat, an estimate that modern scientists have verified (Kuno, 1956).

The average person has between two and three million sweat glands scattered over his body. Their concentration varies widely according to part of the body. Typically, there are about 2500 sweat glands per square inch on the palms and soles of the feet, about 1300 on the forehead, and about 400 on the back, for example (Champion, 1970). Although the actual numbers per square inch vary widely between people, the rank order of sites is very consistent (Kuno, 1956). That is, there will always be more sweat glands on the palms and soles than on the forehead, and still fewer on the back.

There are two different kinds of sweat glands. The less common *apocrine* glands develop from hair follicles and are found primarily in the armpits and genital areas. It is believed that these glands are exclusively responsible for body odor (Champion, 1970). They respond primarily to stressful stimuli and have little or no role in heat regulation, although heat-responsive glands are also present in these areas.

The apocrine glands become functional around the time of puberty. Their secretion is somewhat different from the salt-watery substance with which we identify sweat; in fact, they secrete their cytoplasm, that is, part of the cellular substance.

The biological significance of this apocrine sweating is poorly understood, although scientists have made some fascinating speculations. In general, these theories are based on the fact that, in lower animals, many odors serve as sexual signals to other members of the species. These odor-producing substances are called pheromones.

There are tantalizing bits of evidence that similar substances may be an important factor in human biology. A study by Vierling and Rock (1967), for example, demonstrated that certain odors can be detected only by ovulating women. One of these, exaltolide, is a musky-smelling substance found in male urine. Men cannot smell this substance, nor can women before the menarche or after menopause. Woman of child-bearing age can detect this odor best during the few days of each cycle when it is possible for them to get pregnant. Although apocrine sweat has not been tested for the presence of exaltolide, it is possible that this substance is a human pheromone or sexual signal of some sort. Another study by Martha McClintock (1971) implicates pheromones in the timing of menstrual cycles.

Thus, although relatively little scientific attention has been devoted to apocrine sweating, it is possible that it plays some primeval role in our sexual behavior (Thomas, 1974). Further evidence for this hypothesis comes from the fact that, in women at least, the amount of apocrine sweating decreases with rising estrogen levels (Rothman, 1954). It may be for future generations of scientists to find that our society's widespread use of deodorants has depressed more than body odor.

The second type of sweat gland is called *eccrine*. These glands cover the entire body and produce a NaCl solution. They are well developed only in man and the apes (Champion, 1970).

Their major function is thermoregulation, the maintenance of a constant body temperature. Heat is created both by muscular exertion and by metabolic processes. The body struggles to maintain a constant internal environment of 97° to 99° F by heating the air we breathe and the contents of our digestive tracts and by giving off heat through the skin. One method for this final heat loss is thermoregulatory sweating.

During a normal day, about one pint of liquid is lost as sweat. It was this "insensible" perspiration which Sanctorius Sanctorio was the first to demonstrate. At an air temperature of roughly 88° F, sweat begins to appear as small droplets on the body. Under conditions of extreme heat, as much as three quarts of sweat may be lost in an hour, up to a total of twelve quarts per day (Rothman, 1954). Heat is lost as this liquid is turned into a vapor. The amount of sweat that can be vaporized is also influenced by the humidity, or amount of moisture in the air. Thus, our sluggishness on muggy days may be an instinctive way of maintaining a constant body temperature.

All of this activity is governed by a reflex center in the hypothalamus that responds to the warmth of the blood. Reflex sweating occurs automatically, before the body has a chance to overheat.

Other eccrine glands are not particularly responsive to heat changes but respond instead to external stimuli and stress. These sweat glands are concentrated on the palms and the soles of the feet and, to a more limited extent, on the forehead and underarms. The different classifications are relative rather than absolute. Under conditions of extreme heat the "emotional" glands may respond; under conditions of extreme stress, the thermoregulatory glands may respond.

EDA is normally a measure of this "emotional" sweating. It is ordinarily recorded from the fingertips or the palm of the hand, although it can also be measured on the feet and possibly the forehead and underarms. Traditionally, many psychophysiologists have acted as though, beyond this, the actual recording site made little difference. This is probably true for the simple sorts of studies we have been considering thus far. Bull and Gale (1975) reported that, as people listened to a series of tones, responses from the two hands, while not identical, showed similar trends. However, some recent research, as well as biological common sense, suggests that this may not always be the case. For example, Varni (1975) demonstrated that, when one arm is shocked in a classical conditioning procedure, larger SSRs appear on that hand. In a more controversial study, Myslobodsky and Rattok (1975) recently reported larger left-hand responses to visual than verbal stimuli, a finding consistent with current notions of cerebral asymmetry (see Chapters 7 and 9).

Figure 4.2 outlines the basic anatomy of an eccrine sweat gland. The extreme outer layer of the skin, the stratum corneum, consists of a dead layer of cells that form a protective shield for the delicate internal organs, serving much the same function as the furry coat in certain lower animals. The next major

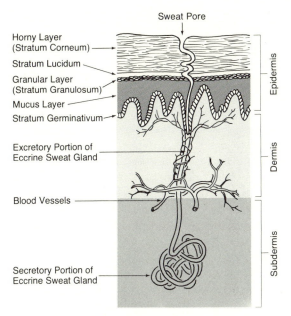

Sweat Pore

Horny Layer
(Stratum Corneum)

Stratum Lucidum

Granular Layer
(Stratum Granulosum)

Mucus Layer

Stratum Germinativum

Excretory Portion of
Eccrine Sweat Gland

Blood Vessels

Secretory Portion of
Eccrine Sweat Gland

Epidermis

Dermis

Subdermis

Figure 4.2 *An Eccrine Sweat Gland.*

layer of the epidermis (stratum Malphigii) consists of germinating cells that continually replace the dead surface cells. The entire epidermal layer is relatively unresponsive electrically, and so most changes appear to be occurring in the dermis and through the sweat ducts themselves.

Remember that much human sweating under normal conditions does not actually appear as sweat droplets on the skin. The route for insensible perspiration is ordinarily *not* via the sweat glands but rather by a more direct path through the skin.

As pointed out above, the sweat glands themselves are primarily responsible for EDA. The precise details of this mechanism remain in doubt, but we shall describe Robert Edelberg's (1972) sweat-circuit model—probably the most thorough of the current views.

The cavity of the sweat duct, Edelberg says, has a substantial negative potential with respect to surrounding tissue. This is the basic electromotive force of SP. The sweat ducts are ordinarily filled to the Malphigian layer. It is this standing amount of sweat which determines tonic level measures of EDA. If sweat is pushed up the duct (either by sympathetic increase of the secretion of the sweat gland or by contraction of the more hormonally controlled myoepithelial muscle fibers) SCR or SPR is seen.

The sweat does not just remain standing at this new level. It may gradually diffuse through the duct wall into the corneum or be more actively reabsorbed

by a change in the selective membranes of the duct. These two alternatives
work to shape the precise form of later components of the response.

To understand the implications of this difference, we must return for a closer
look at the response topography. Up to this point, we have discussed only the
simplest type of SPR, in which all change consists of a transient increase in
negativity. However, more complex SPR wave-forms are commonly observed.
Figure 4.3 illustrates the classical uniphasic and biphasic SPRs and their relation to the SCR recovery limb (return to prestimulus values).

Let's return now to our original response. If the sweat gradually diffuses
through the duct wall, the SCR will gradually return to prestimulus values—a
slow recovery that is typically associated with a uniphasic negative SPR. If
changes in the ducts' selective membranes yield active reabsorption of sweat
and thus a fast recovery limb, we are likely to see a biphasic SPR.

In the simplest terms, then, electrodermal level measures refer to the amount
of sweat standing in the duct. A slowly recovering SCR or uniphasic negative
SPR implies sudden movement up the duct, as a result of either increased
sweating or muscular contraction at the base of the gland. A biphasic SPR or a
fast recovery rate for the SRR informs us of the active reabsorption of sweat.
Note that, theoretically at least, all of these changes could occur below the
surface; EDA measures the underlying activity of many sweat glands rather
than just the amount of sweat produced. Note also that this model implies that
not only different measures of EDA, but different components of the same

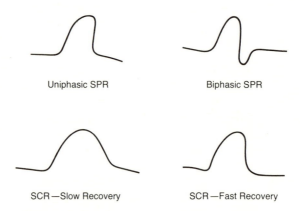

Uniphasic SPR   Biphasic SPR

SCR—Slow Recovery   SCR—Fast Recovery

Figure 4.3 *Idealized Relations Between SCR and
SPR. Left:* Uniphasic SPR (negative response relative to
baseline) tends to be accompanied by slow recovery
SCR (defensive reaction). *Right:* Biphasic SPR (both
negative and positive components) is associated with an
SCR that returns more quickly to prestimulus values
(goal-directed activity). Actual responses tend to be
somewhat more complicated. (See Edelberg, 1970.)

response, may be telling us about different biological processes. We shall discuss the possible implications of such differences for biological categories of behavior below.

Differences Between Electrodermal Measures

The first major distinction, critical for any psychophysiological response measure, is between tonic and phasic measures of activity. Tonic measures consider relatively long-term changes (like SCL) while phasic measures are concerned with more transient responses to stimuli (like SCR). One tonic measure that we have not considered in detail up to this point is the rate of spontaneous EDRs.

Frequently, experimenters observe relatively sudden changes in SC and SP in the apparent absence of external stimulation. That is, an experimental subject gives what appears to be an SCR, but no stimulus has been presented to him. In a case like this, we might suspect that the person in our experiment is generating internal stimuli of his own—an emotion-laden image suddenly popped into consciousness in the midst of his daydreaming. Or perhaps our subject has suddenly taken a deep breath or noticed something on the wall facing him.

From the point of view of the experimenter, such EDRs are classed as spontaneous (sometimes abbreviated SSCRs or SSPRs), since no identifiable stimulus has been imposed. The total number of such phasic responses for a given time period—the rate of spontaneous activity—is a tonic measure of EDA. If a person sitting quietly for two minutes shows five such sudden changes in SC, his rate of SSCRs is said to be 2.5/minute. (The exact magnitude that qualifies a response for this category is a matter of some dispute and may vary from one study to the next. See Appendix B.)

Ordinarily, SCRs are classified as elicited (or nonspontaneous) whenever external stimuli can be identified. But there are exceptions. For example, one may talk about the rate of SSCRs during meditation (Orme-Johnson, 1973), while taking an IQ test (Kilpatrick, 1972), or while watching a stressful movie (Goleman and Schwartz, 1976). In the latter cases at least, it is clear that the external environment contributes substantially to the number of SSCRs. However, since it is difficult to talk about exactly which scenes in the movie, for example, yielded responses, the total rate of responses for the film as a whole was computed.

A number of recent studies suggest that these two tonic measures of SC may represent different sorts of activity. Kilpatrick (1972), for example, found that during an IQ type of test, most subjects showed increases in SCL without corresponding changes in SSCRs. However, when the same test was billed as a measure of brain damage, both SCL and SSCRs increased. This finding was consistent with a growing body of evidence that spontaneous activity increases under emotional stress, while level changes reflect both emotional and cognitive problem-solving demands. This type of research is a sign of the coming of age of psychophysiological research—even at the level of the sweat glands, biologically based distinctions can be made that emphasize the importance of focusing attention on response-patterning.

At present, the exact psychobiological implications of differences between recording SC and SP are not as clearly understood. Edelberg (1973) believes that SP includes a nonsweat-gland epidermal component that SC does not. Therefore, we might expect that when precise relations between the two are mapped out, SP will be the more informative of the measures.

We have already emphasized the relation between the SPR's direction relative to baseline and the recovery rate of the SCR, uniphasic negative SPRs being associated with a slow recovery and biphasic SPRs accompanying a quicker return to baseline values. In behavioral terms, this distinction may also be a critical one for today's new psychophysiology of patterning. For example, in one experiment, when subjects heard a loud-tone, slow-recovery SCRs were observed. However, when the same tone served to warn the subject that he must press a button as quickly as possible, the SCR recovery rate was accelerated. Along with a number of other lines of evidence, this sort of finding led Edelberg (1970) to argue that the active process of reabsorption seen in fast recovery is a sign of goal-directed activity—reabsorption being a biologically adaptive process that keeps the skin from getting so moist that fine tactile manipulations become difficult. The slow-recovery SCR is taken as a defensive reaction in which sweat remains on or near the surface to minimize abrasion.

Whatever the final verdict on this particular explanation of the distinction, we are once more reminded of patterning within the electrodermal system.

Orientation and Habituation

If you are sitting quietly in your room reading this book and the window shade suddenly snaps up, you will automatically turn your head to look at it. Any organism presented with a new or unexpected stimulus automatically undergoes a series of physiological changes that alert the body and prepare it to deal with the situation (Lynn, 1966). The most obvious and immediate is a physical orientation toward the stimulus. For this reason, the orientation reaction has also been called the "what is it?" reflex. Sensory thresholds are lowered, ongoing physical activity is arrested, and muscle tone increases in preparation for action. A host of related physiological changes are involved in this complex response. Among these are an increase in the frequency of the electrical activity of the brain (EEG), constriction of the blood vessels in the limbs, variable changes in heart rate (usually a decrease) and respiration (ordinarily, deeper but less frequent breaths), and a sudden sweat-gland response (EDR). The orientation response was discovered quite by accident by some of Pavlov's students.

Whenever Pavlov entered a room to observe his students' latest experiment with a salivating dog, the animal turned toward Pavlov and stopped salivating (Lynn, 1966). That is, the dog oriented. What began as an inconvenience came to be studied as an important phenomenon in its own right. The process of orienting gradually developed as a key topic in Russian psychology. For historical reasons, it was only relatively recently that Western psychologists turned to the study of this response.

Sokolov (in Lynn, 1966) came to distinguish between the orienting reaction to a novel stimulus and the defensive reaction to a stimulus with threatening characteristics. American psychologists had long studied a response, similar to the defensive reaction, which they called the "startle reaction." If a gun is fired just behind your head, your response will be far more dramatic than if the window shade snaps up. In the startle reaction, an animal freezes, attacks, or runs away. The physiological changes are generally quite similar to those of orientation (and really just an extreme form of it) but, according to Sokolov, can be distinguished on the basis of the blood-flow pattern in the scalp. Orientation yields vasodilation of the forehead arteries, while the defensive response is signalled by forehead vasoconstriction. (See Chapter 5.)

If a stimulus is repeated a number of times, the orientation response will gradually subside. This decrease in response size is called habituation. The defensive reaction also habituates but at a slower rate. A number of models of the physiological changes underlying habituation have been proposed (see Lynn, 1966; Groves and Thompson, 1970), but these are beyond the scope of this book.

The habituation rate is frequently used as a dependent measure in psychophysiological research. Subjects might listen to a series of tones presented at regular intervals. The number of tones sounded before the EDR disappeared would be called the habituation rate. With the use of this procedure, for example, schizophrenics have been found to habituate more slowly than normal subjects (Zahn et al., 1968).

The great historical appeal of studying EDA has resided in the ease of its measurement and the melodrama of its appearance. The student first entering a psychophysiology lab today is as overwhelmed by the clarity of the SCR as were the early researchers. Here at last is a change that can be seen with the naked eye, giving us a peek into the hidden world of inner experience.

We have seen that EDA is, first and foremost, the product of sweat-gland activity—specifically of those sweat glands which are primarily responsive to psychic stimuli. Further, the magnitude of the EDR tends to be proportional to the intensity of the subject's experience. Finally, different EDA measures appear differentially responsive according to the *kind* of stimulus or internal state. SCL and SSCRs are not interchangeable measures of "sympathetic arousal."

We can expect that in the next few years the distinctions between these measures will be spelled out more precisely. Perhaps by starting with the notion that such differences are biologically meaningful, we may even begin to forge biological categories of behavior and experience. For example, instead of starting with the ill-defined category of "emotion" and asking which EDA measure reflects it, we can start with the fact that SCL and SSCRs are independent and try to catalog the behaviors and experiences that elicit changes in each. Once the categories of situations that affect SCL and SSCRs are established, we can then ask what all these situations have in common. Thus can we move closer to a science that is truly based on the human animal.

5

The Cardiovascular System

While the sweat gland may appear biologically trivial at first sight, no one would underestimate the critical importance of the cardiovascular system. The heart literally maintains life by constantly recirculating the blood. Even the earliest anatomists were certain that the heart was a very important organ; they just weren't sure what it did.

History

The ancient Egyptians believed that the heart was the seat of emotion. Philosophers as late as Aristotle attributed to the heart most of the functions that we now know are associated with the brain. This ancient belief survives in our language to the present day, as when we speak of a person with a broken heart or one whose heart is not in his work.

The study of the heart, like the study of everything else, lay dormant through the Middle Ages. The first great advance beyond the ancients came in 1628, when William Harvey argued that the blood circulated throughout the body, the same blood being recycled time after time. So impressed was Harvey with his observations of the complexity of this system that he attempted to reintroduce the ancient notion of the blood as the seat of the soul. This never really caught on again, but Harvey's elaborate series of experiments and observations still stand as an impressive example of the scientific method.

Just about 100 years later, a British clergyman named Stephen Hales devised a method for the measurement of blood pressure, or the force with which the heart pumped the blood. Using a clever device made of several brass tubes and the windpipe of a goose, he found that, when the artery of a mare was cut, her blood spurted about eight feet in the air. Scientists have since computed that a human's blood would rise about five feet if the same technique were used. Fortunately, other, less intrusive methods of measuring circulatory force have been devised since that time.

An Italian criminologist named Cesare Lombroso was one of the first to suggest that blood-pressure measurements were useful in studying psychological processes. More specifically, Lombroso believed that if blood pressure measurements were made while a criminal suspect was interrogated by the police, it would be possible to determine whether or not the person was telling the truth. (See Chapter 10.)

It is now widely accepted in medical practice that stress and tension are often associated with increases in cardiovascular function.

With the aid of portable measuring devices, observations have been made of increased heart rate (HR) and/or blood pressure (BP) in many stressful real-life situations. Indeed, the use of such portable machines has often been crucial for diagnosis of heart problems that cannot be seen in the relative tranquility of the doctor's office. Gunn et al. (1972), for example, tell of one patient whose abnormally high heart rate (paroxysmal atrial tachycardia, to be exact) appeared only in measurements during a contract bridge tournament, with his wife as his partner. Some years later, this same patient had a heart attack and died during a similar bridge tournament.

Daily heart rate measurements of one normal subject over the course of a year found that his resting heart rate peaked on Saturday and Monday—a finding that is not difficult to interpret in terms of a general concept of anxiety or excitement. Other situations in which cardiovascular increases have been seen include driving a car, donating blood, being interviewed by a psychiatrist, preparing for a ski jump, landing a plane on an aircraft carrier, and working in a brokerage house while the stock market is open (Gunn et al., 1972).

Increases in cardiovascular function are also observed, of course, during the muscular strain associated with physical activity. One of the more interesting examples of this phenomenon was in Masters and Johnson's (1966) studies of sexual activity. For women, at least, the increase in HR appears to be related to the intensity of the orgasmic experience.

Studies of sexual activity also point to the importance of local changes in blood flow. Genital erection is largely controlled by increased blood flow to the penis and clitoris. The "sex flush" frequently observed during sexual excitement is also a product of increased blood flow to the skin. The innocent blush of embarrassment is nothing more than a dilation of facial arteries leading to increased circulation and a warming of the skin.

Emotion and Arousal

In early psychophysiological research, measurements of the cardiovascular system were often taken as indices of arousal—much as EDA measurements were. But where the stimuli used in EDA studies were generally relatively mild (for example, hearing the word *prostitute*), cardiovascular measurements generally proved responsive only to more extreme stimuli.

For example, one series of studies showed higher HRs and BPs right before class examinations (Brown and Van Gelder, 1938). A. E. Nissen (1928) found BP increases from two patients sitting in the dental chair when their dentist walked into the room. In what must be one of the more extreme studies in psychology's checkered history, Landis (1926) induced three of his colleagues to undergo a two-day fast without sleeping. Each subject was then given the strongest electrical shock he would stand for as long as he would permit it. The physiological reactions to the shock included marked sweating, gasping, nausea—and BP increases.

Needless to say, the concept of overall activation in the cardiovascular system, like the concept of activation for other physiological systems, is a reasonable first approximation. But the concept of patterning of cardiovascular responses in different states was the next step.

In a classic study in 1953, Albert Ax directly confronted the issue of whether one emotion could be distinguished from another on the basis of its physiological concomitants. (See Chapter 2.) Specifically, he measured the cardiovascular, electrodermal, respiratory, and muscle systems. One of the major problems in studying emotions is that it is extremely difficult to produce them on demand in the laboratory. Ax's machinations to cause his subjects to become first angry and then afraid bear repeating.

Forty-three normal subjects were recruited for a study of "hypertension." A number of electrodes were attached to the subject and he was told that his only task was to lie down quietly while a nurse took his blood pressure once a minute. The subject was meanwhile chattily told that the equipment operator was sick and that filling in for him was a man who had just been fired for incompetence and arrogance. After a brief rest period, during which measurements were made, this stooge operator called from the next room that he was having some trouble with the recordings. He and the experimenter then switched places and the stooge proceeded to live up to his reputation for being obnoxious; he criticized the nurse, pushed the subject around roughly while "checking the connections," and told the subject sarcastically that the problems were his fault because he was late. For a total of about five minutes he abused the subject for not cooperating, for moving around, and for anything else he could think of. The experimenter then returned and apologized for his assistant's rude behavior. This deception appeared quite effective in inducing anger—more than one subject spontaneously suggested that "that guy deserved a punch in the nose."

Another rest period intervened before the induction of the second condition, fear. (In the same study, another group of subjects had this order reversed—fear was followed by anger.) In this case, a shock of gradually increasing intensity was given to the subject's little finger until he complained. The experimenter acted alarmed and frantically ran around the room, cautioning the subject that he must remain perfectly still for his own good. For the next five minutes, this charade continued—at one point the experimenter even pressed a button that caused sparks to fly around the room. Needless to say, the threat of accidental electrocution produced fear. One subject kept screaming, "Please take the wires off. Oh! Please help me," throughout the entire period. Another prayed, while a third later reported, philosophically, "Well, everybody has to go sometime. I thought this might be my time."

The elaborate methodology of this experiment suggests why studies of emotion are not particularly common. A growing concern with the ethical implications of deceiving subjects would make such a study inconceivable today. In any case, two different patterns of physiological response were observed as people experienced the two emotions. The fear pattern appeared related to the chemical action of the hormone adrenaline (epinephrine); the anger pattern was more closely related to noradrenaline (or norepinephrine) action. In a recent extension of this study, Weerts and Roberts (1976) found similar patterns of physiological response when people simply imagined being in situations that made them angry or fearful.

The major cardiovascular finding was that diastolic BP increases and HR decreases were more common for anger than fear. Among the other findings, SCL was more responsive to anger, while SSCRs were more responsive to fear. In terms of the Kilpatrick (1972) data, this suggests a greater cognitive component to the anger in this situation. This, in turn, reminds us that, even in this elaborate experiment, lying quietly throughout all these melodramas may have caused a different pattern than we would have seen had the subject been allowed to punch the stooge in the nose.

The substantive lesson of this particular experiment is that at least some emotions can indeed be distinguished physiologically on the basis of cardiovascular and other psychophysiological reactions. Once more, we see the observation of an overall pattern of physiological response across systems as the key technique.

Overview of Cardiovascular Measures

Like every other major physiological subdivision of the body, the cardiovascular system is one of awe-inspiring complexity and responsibilities. The heart muscle and the blood vessels work together to meet the ever-changing demands of our organs and to serve as a network of supply and communication—transporting nutrients, wastes, hormones, and drugs. This system is vital to survival but often frustrating to the physiologist whose task is to chart the many interactions within it.

For convenience, we can subdivide the general features of our cardiovascular plumbing as follows:

Heart Rate—How fast the heart pumps.
Contractile Force—How hard it pumps.
Cardiac Output—How much it pumps.
Blood Pressure—The force with which the liquid moves.
Blood Flow—Localized measures of the distribution of blood.

Clearly, since we are talking about the closed plumbing system of the body's circulation, all of these factors are interrelated. We can also subdivide these factors still further. For example, cardiac output is the product of heart rate and stroke volume, while stroke volume is the product of contractile force and venous return. Blood pressure, on the other hand, depends on both cardiac output and peripheral resistance (the characteristics of the tubes through which the blood flows).

Note that all of these measures are interdependent, and yet each is subtly different from the others. Schwartz (1971), for example, showed that, despite their intimate relationship, phasic measurements of heart rate (HR) and blood pressure (BP) are not highly correlated.

Within the limitations of current technology, HR, BP, and blood flow (BF) are of the most relevance to psychophysiology. Contractile force and cardiac output are difficult to measure from the surface of the body, although recent advances in the measurement of contractile force will be discussed later in this chapter.

As in the study of EDA, there is an important distinction to be made here between *tonic* measurements of activity over a relatively extended period of time (like the number of heartbeats in one minute) and *phasic* measurements of short-term adjustments to the immediate situation (for example, intervals between two or three successive beats of the heart). In general terms, we might say that tonic measurements of HR and BP give us an overall picture of the body's state of mobilization. The biological significance of phasic changes in HR and BP are more controversial (Obrist, 1976).

The actual distribution of blood to the organs depends on their relative needs. More localized measures of circulation within the cardiovascular system

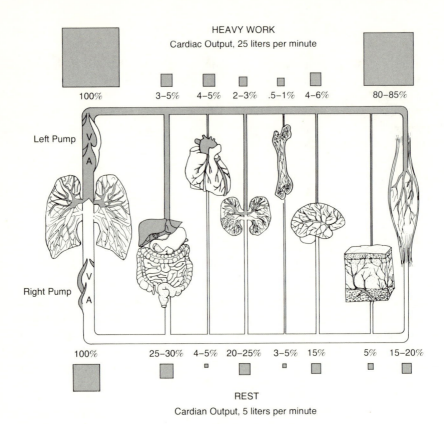

Figure 5.1 *Blood Distribution During Work and Rest.* This schematic drawing shows how the arterioles and capillaries are arranged in parallel-coupled circuits between the arteries *(top)* and the veins. The cardiac output may be increased five times from rest to strenuous exercise. The figures indicate the relative distribution of blood to the various organs at rest *(lower scale)* and during exercise *(upper scale)*. During exercise, the circulating blood is primarily diverted to the muscles. The area of the black squares is proportional to the minute volume of blood flow. (After P. O. Astrand and K. Rodahl, *Textbook of Work Physiology.* Copyright 1970. By permission of McGraw-Hill Book Company.)

have an important place in psychophysiological research. Figure 5.1 schematically illustrates the relative distribution of blood to various organs during exercise and rest.

Not surprisingly, the major effect of exercise is to increase cardiac output dramatically and to channel most of this increase to the muscles and the skin. Note that the change in total cardiac output may mean that the decreased share of the blood is offset; the brain, for example, gets more blood in absolute terms during work than rest, despite the fact that its share of the total pool decreases by a factor of 3. Similarly, the reservoir of blood in the stomach and kidney are depleted only slightly in absolute terms, despite their major decrease in terms of a share.

Peripheral blood-flow measures are concerned with these sorts of effects, usually in the limbs. When the activity of any organ increases, local metabolic requirements are met by increasing blood flow. This is accomplished primarily by action of the smooth muscles, in the arteriole walls throughout that organ, working to produce vasodilation. This peripheral vasculature appears to be entirely under SNS control. Vasoconstriction, or reduction of the arteriolar diameter, corresponds to sympathetic activation, while vasodilation represents a relaxation of sympathetic control.

Again, this might be explained in evolutionary terms: In the emergency fight-or-flight situations that the SNS responds to, it makes biological sense to cut down on peripheral circulation. A cut on the hand or foot, then, would not lead to as much bleeding.

Changes in peripheral circulation may also respond to changes in environmental temperature. When you pick up an ice cube in your left hand, vasoconstriction occurs *in that hand* to minimize its cooling effects on the blood. Conversely, under normal circumstances, constriction in the hand would lead to a local drop in skin temperature of the hand.

As we discuss the cardiovascular system, it may sometimes seem that physiological differences between the various measures are better understood than the physiological implications of observing one kind of response rather than another. But it is only by concentrating on a biological framework—and patterns of activity within that framework—that we will ever begin to make some sense out of nature's wisdom.

Physiological Basis

The heart is the most important muscle in the body. We rarely think of this fist-shaped organ as a muscle, but that is precisely what it is. Its function is to maintain blood circulation—supplying oxygen and nutrients to all bodily tissues while removing metabolic wastes. Nature has been wise enough to design the heart and brain in such a way that we are not *consciously* responsible for its operation; your heart continues to beat as you read this page or focus your concentration elsewhere.

Let us stop and consider the work done in a lifetime by this one-pound muscle. Assuming an average heart rate of about 70 beats per minute (BPM), the heart beats over 100,000 times a day, or more than 2½ *billion* times in an average life of 70 years. In the course of this same day, 1800 gallons of blood are pumped, for a lifetime total of about 46 billion gallons. The force required to pump this much blood, if it could be harnessed in a single instant, would lift a 10-ton weight ten miles. These imagination-defying statistics only remind us again of the striking capabilities of even a run-down human body.

Across species, we could say in a crude way that the normal resting HR varies with both the size and normal activity patterns of the animal. A rat has a resting HR of 400 BPM, a human baby, one of about 140 BPM; an elephant's is 25 BPM, and a whale's is estimated at about 5 BPM.

Experiments on decapitated criminals in the eighteenth century led us to estimate that the average person has about five quarts of blood, which is continually recirculated through the body. It travels through a fine network of tubes; blood rich with oxygen leaves the heart through the aorta, wends it way to target organs through arteries and arterioles, then passes through the capillaries, whose walls are only a single cell thick and allow transport of nutrients and removal of wastes from the organ, and finally returns through venules and veins to the heart itself. If all the capillaries in the normal adult's body were laid end to end, they would stretch from Boston, Massachusetts, to Hoboken, New Jersey, and back over 150 times (something on the order of 62,000 miles). The heart continues to recycle the blood through this labyrinth, never tiring and never faltering in the thankless task of keeping us alive.

Not only must the cardiovascular system cope with this unrelenting demand for nutrition but it must also make appropriate adjustments whenever the needs of a certain organ rise. A simple yawn and stretch requires massive reallocation of resources as blood rushes to the appropriate muscle groups. And the heart must also nourish itself, via the coronary circulation. Yet no matter how much we overstress and underexercise ourselves, it just keeps on pumping.

Figure 5.2 is a simple diagram of the heart muscle, while Figure 5.3 presents a schematic view of its role in circulation. Note in Figure 5.2 that the heart is

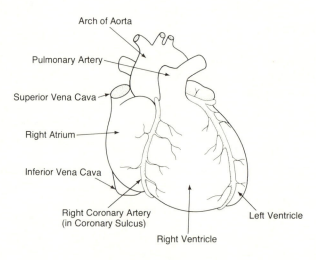

Figure 5.2 *The Heart.*

actually composed of four chambers that act as two pumps in tandem. In the systemic circulatory system, blood rich with oxygen is passed out of the heart from the left ventricle, through the arterial system to target organs where nutrients are removed and wastes added, then through the veins and back into the right atrium. The *pulmonary* system is concerned with passing this now oxygen-deficient blood through the lungs. And so blood passes from the right ventricle, through the pulmonary artery (the only artery in the body that carries oxygen-deficient blood), through the capillary system of the lungs, where wastes are removed and oxygen replaced, and back out the pulmonary vein to the left atrium.

This circulation through the body is maintained, of course, by a regular cycle of events in the heart itself. This cycle is divided into two major sections: systole, or the contraction of heart muscle, and diastole, or its relaxation. In the systolic phase, blood pressure peaks as blood is forced from the heart. During diastole, blood pressure reaches its lowest value as the valves of the ventricles

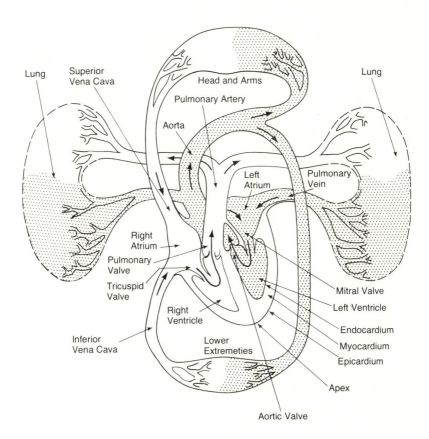

Figure 5.3 *Schematic View of the Circulatory System.* (See text for details.)

snap shut to prevent blood from spurting backwards. The opening and shutting of these and other valves make the familiar *lub-dup* sound of the heart beating in the chest. The *lub* sound corresponds to the sudden closure of the atrioventricular valves accompanied by a contraction of the thick muscular walls of the arteries. *Dup* is the sound of the sharp closure of the aortic and pulmonary valves. When these sounds are abnormal, one is said to have a heart murmur, which usually indicates that the valves are not closing properly. A skilled cardiologist may be able to diagnose specific problems with these valves on the basis of listening to the heart sounds through a stethoscope.

The body contains many checks and balances to determine the complex rhythm of the heart. The internal pacemakers of the heart, the sinoatrial (SA) and atrioventricular (AV) nodes, are primarily responsible for its rhythmic beating. They are subject to an elaborate network of higher control centers, the most important being via the sympathetic and parasympathetic branches of the autonomic nervous system. Stimulation of sympathetic fibers strengthens and accelerates the heartbeat, while parasympathetic activation slows HR.

The local control of factors like the pacemakers, the sensitivity of heart muscle fibers to circulating hormone levels, and mechanical influences from the diaphragm and rib cage, then, is supplemented by higher control centers. Ultimately, of course, the coordination of the cardiovascular system to meet tissue needs is overseen by the brain. The variety of connections to the CNS makes the remainder of the system appear simple.

Cohen and MacDonald (1974) have suggested six functional categories of CNS connections to conceptually organize the data. These include a "defense" pathway originating in the medulla, an "exercise" pathway originating in the motor cortex, and a "postural adjustment" pathway originating in the cerebellum, as well as several more traditionally accepted pathways through the medulla. The precise details are rather complex. Again, the most important lesson from our point of view is that cardiovascular adjustments reflect brain processes and that no cardiovascular measure is simply "peripheral."

Heart Rate and the EKG

One major advance in the study of cardiac function was the discovery of the electrocardiogram, or EKG, by Einthoven in 1903. (The abbreviation EKG, based on the original German, is preferred to the anglicized ECG. One explanation of this is the possible confusion of the abbreviation ECG and EEG in a life-or-death medical situation.)

The EKG is a recording of the electrical events associated with the muscular contraction of the heart. Figure 5.4 illustrates the conduction pathways in a normal, healthy heartbeat; the impulse begins at the SA node and spreads through the atria, causing the AV node to fire. These impulses are rapidly

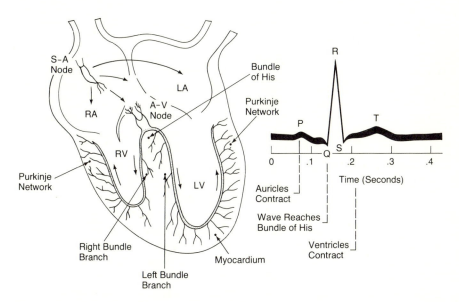

Figure 5.4 *EKG Wave-Form and Electrical Events in the Heart.* (See text for details.)

transmitted through the bundles of His and the Purkinje system, and the ventricles then contract. Figure 5.4 also illustrates the normal EKG wave-form recorded from the limbs for a single heartbeat and notes how the topography of the wave corresponds to these electrical events.

In a clinical diagnostic setting, the EKG may be recorded from as many as twelve different pairs of leads—half on the chest and the other half from the limbs. Each of the pairs of leads detects a potential electrical difference across the sides of the heart, and each gives subtly different information about both the placement of the heart in the chest and the actual mechanisms of its beating. A diseased heart may show peculiarities of wave-form on one or more of these different recordings, and this is one valuable weapon in the arsenal of the cardiologist.

Cardiac arrhythmia is the generic term for these unusual firing patterns. About 5% of the population exhibits cardiac arrhythmias at some time. Some arrhythmias are quite harmless, and others indicate a pathological state.

From our previous discussion, it should be obvious that the EKG can also be used to determine the precise portion of the cardiac cycle into which a given event falls. The S-T and T portion of the cycle represent systole (when BP is at its peak), while the T-P and P waves correspond to diastole. One implication of this fact for psychophysiology will become clear when we discuss John and Beatrice Lacey's suggestion that systole and diastole have different implications for the reactivity of the brain.

Traditionally, most psychophysiologists have used the EKG to measure heart rate, that is, the frequency of ventricular contractions. This is usually assessed on a beat-to-beat basis by an electronic circuit called a cardiotachometer, which measures the length of time between two successive QRS complexes (or ventricular firings) and converts this to a rate. Thus, if one second elapses between beats, we say a person's phasic HR for that beat was 60 BPM. If only half a second expires before the following beat, that person's phasic HR has jumped to 120 BPM. The phasic rate does typically vary from beat to beat but not quite as dramatically as in our example.

Figure 5.5 illustrates a typical EKG recording from a subject at rest, along with a cardiotachometer's display of phasic HR.

The HR recorded in this manner usually—but not always—corresponds to the pulse rate or number of pressure waves per minute propagated along the peripheral arteries. We are all familiar with taking the pulse at the radial artery in the wrist, although any major artery in the body can be used.

In certain sorts of abnormal or pathological conditions, the two values will not correspond. One of the more interesting instances of HR not matching pulse rate occurred in studies of the ability of certain yogis to stop the heart. This capability, if it in fact existed, would be of immense interest to Western medicine, since it would undercut some of its most central beliefs about the cardiovascular system. It has been observed that Eastern mystics are not always eager to prove their powers in a profane technological setting. Nevertheless, several tests have been performed in India on yogis who claimed to have this ability.

In 1961, Wenger, Bagchi, and Anand published results of tests of four yogis who claimed cardiovascular control, two of whom said that they could stop their hearts. Using a breathing exercise that involved a great buildup in abdominal muscle tension, they achieved variable degrees of control, although none came close to actually stopping the heart. What was interesting was that some of these exercises did lead to gradual disappearance of the pulse at the radial

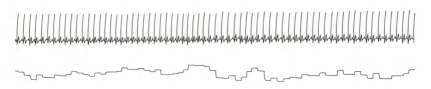

Figure 5.5 *Cardiotachometer Recording.* The cardiotachometer gives a continuous display of phasic HR by measuring the time between the last two beats of the heart and converting that figure to a rate in beats per minute. The upper tracing is the EKG; the lower tracing is the cardiotachometer output.

artery. That is, if someone took the yogi's pulse, it did appear that his heart was stopped. But the EKG told a different story.

More light was shed on this topic in studies of Swami Rama, an Eastern mystic visiting the Menninger Clinic several years ago (Green, Green and Walters, 1971) to give a demonstration of his bodily control. Using a similar breathing exercise, the Swami increased his HR in one beat from 70 BPM to over 300 BPM. The experimenters stopped him after about 20 seconds because they were concerned about the Swami's health. A cardiologist later examined the EKG and suggested that the Swami had gone into atrial flutter—a condition in which the atria fire more frequently than the ventricles and in which the heart is beating so quickly that no blood is pumped out. Again, the pulse would disappear under these conditions. Of course, the ability to produce atrial flutter at will is almost as amazing as the claimed ability to stop the heart, and the Swami became something of a celebrity on the psychophysiology circuit.

The average resting HR for an adult is around 70 BPM. Average rates slower than 60 BPM (bradycardia) or faster than 100 BPM (tachycardia) are generally taken as signs that there may be some pathology in the cardiovascular system. During exercise, the HR may climb as high as 200 BPM, with a gradual drop-off in the recovery period after exercise ends. If one exercises frequently, the characteristics of the cardiac muscle may be altered, so that the heart does not have to beat so fast to supply the muscles with oxygenated blood. Although cardiac output remains constant for the athlete, he comes to have a lower HR for both exercise and the resting state (Astrand and Rodahl, 1970).

Blood Pressure

Another common measure of cardiovascular function is blood pressure, or the force built up in the arteries as the blood encounters resistance in the peripheral circulation. As we mentioned before, BP varies with each beat of the heart: peaking during systole, at the contraction of the heart, and reaching its minimum during diastole, as the heart muscle relaxes before the next beat. Both BPs are usually expressed together, as systolic "over" diastolic. Systolic BP will, by definition, always be greater than diastolic. The units of measurement are mmHg (millimeters of mercury), a standard physical yardstick for the measurement of pressure. The normal resting BP for an adult is somewhere around 130/70 mmHg, depending on age and physical condition. Some researchers also discuss *pulse pressure*, which is the difference between systolic and diastolic —in this case, 60 mmHg.

A person is said to have hypertension (high blood pressure) when his resting BP exceeds approximately 140/90. This is a major health problem in our stressful society: About one-fifth of all Americans have high blood pressure at some time in their lives, and more than half of these will ultimately die from it.

About 90% of the cases of hypertension are termed "essential hypertension," meaning that there is no known physiological deficit and that it is generally assumed to be caused by psychological stress.

The most direct measurement is accomplished by actually inserting a pressure-sensitive transducer into a major artery. This surgical process, called cannulization, tends to be painful and somewhat dangerous. It is certainly not a procedure that is suitable for everyday use in the laboratory or the doctor's office.

Clinical blood pressure measurements are therefore made with the use of a sphygmomanometer, a more indirect and somewhat less accurate procedure. The use of this method depends on the discovery, in 1906, by a Russian physician named Korotkoff that the pulse of an artery can be detected through a stethoscope or microphone pressed on that artery when peripheral circulation is interfered with. The sounds produced are referred to, fairly enough, as Korotkoff sounds.

Typically, an inflatable bag is attached around the upper arm or leg. Air is then forced into the bag until the Korotkoff sounds disappear, indicating that the blood is no longer circulating and that the pressure in the inflatable cuff is greater than maximum, or systolic, BP. The bag is then slowly deflated until the first Korotkoff sounds appear with each beat of the heart. The pressure in the bag at this point, read from an attached pressure gauge, is called systolic BP, although it is clearly somewhat lower than true arterial systolic BP. The bag is then deflated until the Korotkoff sounds disappear altogether. This is a sign that the flow of blood is no longer interfered with, and thus the pressure exerted by the cuff is less than the diastolic BP. Compared to direct arterial measurements, this technique consistently underestimates both systolic and diastolic BP by about 10 mmHg. Further, it is very easily affected by beat-to-beat differences in BP, and thus a single determination is not enough to draw any firm conclusion (Tursky, 1974).

Although this use of the sphygmomanometer is quite adequate for diagnostic screening, the psychophysiologist is more likely to be concerned with phasic moment-to-moment changes in BP with a given task. The difficulties in getting such a measure without performing surgery on the experimental subject are enormous. The earliest solution involved inflation of a cuff to a point midway between systolic and diastolic BP and then recording changes in the air system of the apparatus. This measure of "relative blood pressure" is still used in professional lie detection but has a number of problems. Aside from the discomfort caused the subject, the measure tends to be confounded by changes in the volume of the arm; it is thus, to the purist, not really a measure of BP.

A number of automated methods now exist for "tracking" BP—cuffs inflate automatically in response to Korotkoff sounds detected by a microphone strapped to the arm. One such system is described in Appendix C.

Among the factors that determine BP are HR, contractility, and stroke volume (that is, characteristics of the pump) and peripheral resistance (that is, characteristics of the pipes, for example, their elasticity). It should be remembered that BP refers to *arterial* pressure. The circulatory system works on the basis of a pressure gradient, with the pressure dropping along each step of the way. By the time blood returns to the heart in the major veins, the pressure is only 1 or 2 mmHg.

One of the major physiological mechanisms for homeostatic maintenance of BP at reasonable levels is the presence of baroreceptors in the aortic arch and the carotid sinus. (The carotid is one of the major arteries supplying the brain with blood.) As pressure increases, these afferent receptors increase their rate of firing and act on centers in the medulla to bring about reflex slowing of the heart and dilation of the arteries, thus lowering BP. In extreme cases, this reflex has been brought into play among a few people whose collars were too tight (the carotid arteries go through the neck on either side), ultimately cutting blood circulation to the brain, particularly in older people whose arteries are less resilient than those of younger folks. John and Beatrice Lacey (1976) have suggested that the baroreceptors may also have an effect on other CNS areas, a hypothesis to which we shall return below.

BP, then, is another of the major gross measurements of global cardiovascular function. Its mechanisms of control are different from, but intertwined with, those of HR.

What Does the Heart Respond To?

While the sweat glands on the palms and soles of the feet respond primarily to psychic stimuli, HR and BP are more biologically fundamental processes that are not so easily identified with strictly psychological variables. In recent years, psychophysiological research on cardiac function has been dominated by the work of John and Beatrice Lacey at the Fels Research Institute and that of Paul Obrist and his colleagues at the University of North Carolina Medical School. The resolution of these often conflicting views involves some rather complicated issues, which are discussed at greater length in Appendix C (see "Two Views of Cardiac Function"). Here, we shall simply sketch in the broad outlines of their work.

The Laceys were among the first to systematically examine the simplistic concept of global arousal—a well-chosen target. They emphasized, instead, the idea of "directional fractionation": that different fractions of the total somatic response pattern may respond in opposite directions (1959). Beyond this emphasis on examining patterns of physiological response, however, they contended that cardiovascular increases *cause* decreases in brain function.

In the earliest studies, Lacey (1959) demonstrated that, for most people, a task like solving a mental arithmetic problem led to a classical arousal reaction in which both HR and SC increased. The same people, when they listened to a series of tones, showed HR decreases along with SC increases—thus, an example of "directional fractionation." As more tasks were discovered to show similar patterns, Lacey (1963) went on to argue that "environmental rejection" (thinking) led to phasic HR increases, while "environmental intake" (attention to external events) led to phasic HR decreases. Still later, Lacey (1967) emphasized the presumed basis of this observation: HR and BP increases increased baroreceptor (pressure-sensitive receptors in the aortic arch and carotid sinus) firing, which provided feedback to the brain and decreased its activity.

The intake/rejection distinction has had a tremendous impact on psychophysiological theory. Mangelsdorff and Zuckerman (1975), for example, invoked the Lacey formulation in explaining the results of a naturalistic experiment conducted during the height of popular protest over the Vietnam War. One part of this study involved presenting the same photographic slide, with two different captions, to two different groups of subjects (each group composed of equal numbers of ROTC cadets and non-ROTC college undergraduates). A war atrocity picture was labeled for one group as "a Vietcong massacre of civilians"; for the other group, the same picture was called "an American massacre of civilians." Phasic HR responses distinguished the two groups: the "Vietcong" label yielded HR decreases, the "American" label yielded HR increases. (Unlike other aspects of the study, this segment revealed no differences between ROTC and non-ROTC students.) Mangelsdorff and Zuckerman suggested that the HR deceleration indicated attention to the "Vietcong" massacre, while the HR increase of the group that saw the "American" scene reflected "sensory rejection." This study does far more than simply provide an example of the utility of the Lacey position. It reminds us again of the critical role of the brain in cardiovascular response. After all, the only difference between the two groups was in what they *thought* the pictures represented.

Direct tests of the Lacey hypothesis have yielded mixed results (see Appendix C). It has been attacked most vigorously by the Obrist research group. In his 1975 Presidential Address to the Society for Psychophysiological Research, Paul Obrist (1976) termed phasic HR effects "biologically trivial" and aired his skepticism about the productivity of concentrating on these small, transient responses.

The Obrist et al. (1970) theory of cardiac-somatic coupling stresses more commonsense notions of cardiovascular function—namely, the heart beats faster to supply more blood to tissues that need it. In an impressive series of studies on humans and lower animals, HR and EMG have covaried directly. That is, when muscle tension increased (thus increasing muscular demands for O_2 and nutrients) HR also increased; when EMG decreased, so did HR. HR and EMG are seen in this view as concomitant changes produced by the same CNS mechanism. It is not that one causes the other; rather, it is that the body is built in such a way that the two ordinarily change together.

Thus, the HR decrease observed when a person attends to the world around him is merely an indication, for Obrist, that our individual is sitting quietly.

Cardiovascular increases seen in mental arithmetic are a sign that a person tenses his muscles when he tries to solve a problem.

More recently, Obrist (1976) has stressed the importance of distinguishing between situations of "passive coping" and "active coping." In passive coping, the organism has little control over the environment—as, for example, when a person in a classical conditioning paradigm receives periodic electric shocks regardless of his actions. Under these conditions, the heart is under the control of the vagus nerve of the PNS and cardiac-somatic coupling occurs; that is, HR provides an index of bodily activity, as discussed above. Active coping occurs when a person's actions influence the environment—for example, when a person can avoid electric shocks by pressing a button. Here, the response of the heart seems to be under SNS control; large-magnitude tonic HR increases are observed that do *not* directly reflect somatic responses.

Whatever the final verdict on the Lacey and Obrist views, both the intake/rejection distinction and the passive coping/active coping distinction represent the kinds of biologically based categories of psychological events that are likely to be important in the psychophysiology of the future. Note also that both of these views go far beyond the simple arousal approach in their search for meaningful patterns of physiological activation.

Sexual Arousal

Sexual arousal is a whole body pattern of response involving muscular, respiratory, and cardiovascular adjustments. During the physical activity of intercourse, HR and BP increase dramatically, as they would during any other form of exercise. But the cardiovascular changes that are most distinctly sexual involve peripheral vasocongestion. (Katchadourian and Lunde, 1975.) Under ordinary circumstances, blood flow into an organ (via the arteries) and out of that organ (via the veins) is approximately the same. Vasocongestion involves an increased influx of blood that remains in the tissue, making it swollen, red, and warm. Genital erection is the most dramatic example of vasocongestion.

Both the penis and the clitoris contain cylindrical bodies of erectile tissue. During sexual excitement, the arteries dilate and excess blood is trapped in a series of compartments giving rise to the characteristic genital response. This initial vasodilation appears to be under the control of the PNS, unlike vasodilation elsewhere in the body, which represents SNS relaxation. Massive SNS activation, as in extreme anxiety, can prevent this PNS-controlled vasodilation. In later phases of sexual arousal, the SNS may come to dominate. Thus, sexual performance depends on a complex interaction between the antagonistic branches of the autonomic nervous system.

There are a number of possible psychophysiological techniques which can be used to measure penile erection (Zuckerman, 1972). Probably the most reliable and simplest to use employs some variation on a strain gauge. A strain gauge is simply a device that changes its electrical resistance when it is stretched. This can be attached, like a rubber band, around the penis. Since erection yields increases in circumference as well as increased penile length, the degree of erection can be measured as a varying electrical resistance by the polygraph. In addition to automatic recording, this procedure permits the observation of relatively small changes in circumference.

Aside from the pioneering work of Masters and Johnson (1966), the major measurement of penile erection has been in the sleep laboratory. Fisher et al. (1965) found that 95% of all REM periods were accompanied by erection in the male. (See Chapter 7.) This basic finding has been verified by many sleep researchers. One can, of course, also use this type of device to study reactions to various sexual stimuli. Freund (1963), for example, found the expected variation in the reactions of homosexual and heterosexual males to a series of pornographic slides that included something for every taste.

Recording female genital arousal is somewhat more problematic. The most successful techniques developed to date depend on the fact that female sexual excitement includes increased vaginal blood flow as well as clitoral erection. Blood flow is measured indirectly, either as a temperature change or via photoplethysmography (see below). Shapiro et al. (1968), for example, described a system in which two heat-sensitive thermistors are imbedded in a vaginal diaphragm. More recently, Sintchak and Geer (1975) developed a vaginal probe, resembling a tampon, which contains a photoplethysmograph. Figure 5.6 illustrates sample recordings from this device taken while a woman watched an erotic and a "neutral" movie. Hoon, Wincze and Hoone (1976) described an entire pattern of sexual arousal (seen in response to a videotape of sexual foreplay) involving not just vaginal blood volume changes but also systolic and diastolic BP increases and increases in forehead skin temperature.

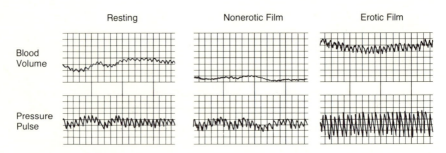

Figure 5.6 *Sample Recordings from a Vaginal Photoplethysmograph.* (Copyright © 1975, The Society for Psychophysiological Research. Reprinted with permission of the publisher from "A Vaginal Plethysmograph System," *Psychophysiology*, 1975, 12, 115, by G. Sintchak and J. H. Geer.)

Skin Temperature

The temperature of the skin is largely a function of peripheral circulation. Vasoconstriction, a decrease in diameter of peripheral arteries caused by SNS activation, lowers skin temperature. Vasodilation, an increase in the diameter of peripheral arteries caused by SNS relaxation, raises skin temperature. Measures like BV and PV (see below) are also responsive to peripheral circulatory adjustments, but there is no simple relationship between them (Plutchik, 1956).

There is evidence that the arteries and the capillaries (which connect arteries to veins) can contract independently (Plutchik, 1956). The color of the skin depends primarily on capillary action, its temperature on arterial action. Warm, pale skin suggests that the arteries and arterioles are dilated, while the capillaries are not; cold blue skin indicates strong contraction of the arteries, while the capillaries are dilated. Because an increase in capillary diameter has little effect on blood volume, the words *vasodilation* and *vasoconstriction* are generally used to refer strictly to arterial action.

The fingers and toes are generally slightly colder than any other skin surface. Their absolute temperature depends on many factors, only a few of which reflect distinctly psychological processes. Skin temperature responds first and foremost to changes in environmental temperature. Such adjustments are regulated by CNS control centers in the hypothalamus. The hypothalamus governs thermoregulatory sweating as well as peripheral circulation, and these mechanisms may interact to determine skin temperature.

But many studies have indicated that, within normal ranges of room temperature, skin temperature does respond to psychological stress. Mittleman and Wolff (1939), for example, found systematic skin temperature changes as people discussed their lives. Such emotions as embarrassment, depression, and anxiety were associated with drops in finger temperature; erotic excitement and relaxation, among others, yielded higher finger temperatures.

This study and many other skin temperature studies have concentrated on people with Raynaud's disease: pathologically cold hands and/or feet. Attacks occur either after exposure to cold or in an emotional situation. The condition is much more common in women than men and may be genetically linked. (Treatment of Raynaud's disease with biofeedback will be discussed in Chapter 10.)

In general, women do have colder hands and feet than men, although it is relatively rare that it reaches the pathological extremes of Raynaud's disease. Some researchers have speculated in evolutionary terms that the poorer peripheral circulation of females was necessary to insure a more stable blood supply to the internal organs during pregnancy. Other researchers have stated that they don't have a clue why this should be true, if indeed it is.

One reason that skin temperature has not been emphasized in psycho-physiological research is the extreme difficulty of accurate and unbiased recording. Most frequently, a thermocouple or thermistor (the voltage of a thermocouple and the resistance of a thermistor vary systematically with temperature changes) is taped to a finger. Given the very small magnitude of skin temperature changes (usually less than 1° F), there are many problems with this procedure. Even minor variations in air currents in a normal room may create difficulties.

Some of these problems may be solved by the use of radiometric devices that measure heat radiation without touching the skin surface. An elaborate electronic device that looks something like a TV camera is aimed at the subject. (These devices are now most commonly used in a medical setting to detect pathological tissue growths.) Temperature gradients are displayed on a picture tube as different color bands. A Polaroid snapshot can be taken of the result for later analysis.

Some work on facial thermography was recently conducted at Boston's Erich Lindemann Mental Health Center (Schwartz and Logue, 1977), using this system. A striking sex difference emerged, with women having colder noses and cheeks, relative to the rest of their faces, than men. Across all subjects, there was evidence that the mouth area was warmer during "happy thoughts" than during "sad thoughts." Since thermography is sensitive to blood flow in relatively deep muscle structures as well as more superficial blood flow, this finding may be related to the same research group's findings on facial musculature changes in the emotions (see Chapter 8).

Plethysmography

The plethysmograph measures changes in the volume of a limb or organ caused by variations in the amount of blood contained in it. The earliest approach involved sealing the finger, for example, in a rigid airtight container. This container was attached by tubing to an "oncometer," which contained a sensitive diaphragm whose responses to changing pressure could be mechanically or electronically recorded.

This same principle was applied in one early study of blood flow to the brain. A laborer who had lost a small section of his skull in an accident was studied. Increased blood flow to the brain caused the scalp to bulge over this spot, because his brain was otherwise sealed in the tight container of his head. And so a cork was pasted over the hole in his skull and its deflections were electrically recorded (Shepard, 1906).

At present, a more common method of assessing digital blood flow is photo-plethysmography (see Appendix C). In one such system, a light is shone through a digit while a photosensitive plate on the other side of the finger records how much light got through. As the density of the tissue increases with greater blood flow, less light is registered coming out of the finger.

More technologically sophisticated procedures are needed for study of problems like blood flow to different brain areas. One recent procedure involves injection of a radioactive isotope into the cerebral circulation (through the carotid artery). Changes in blood flow to different brain areas for different sorts of tasks have been observed using this technique (Risberg and Ingvar, 1973). For example, increased blood flow to the frontal region has been observed in abstract reasoning, while speech leads to increased flow in the motor areas and "language" centers of the dominant hemisphere. This finding is quite consistent with contemporary notions of localization of brain function. Clearly, this is a very intrusive technique and one that cannot be performed in most psychophysiology labs.

One can, of course, talk about relatively tonic and phasic changes in blood flow. Phasic changes are called pulse volume (PV) measurements and have to do with beat-to-beat variations in the force of flow (filtered to avoid confounding with slower baseline changes). More tonic measurements of change over time are called blood volume (BV) measurements. Both measures tend to show vasoconstriction in response to psychic stimuli. Measurements of skin temperature will tend to show similar responses, because one effect of vasodilation is to warm the organ in which it occurs.

It should be noted that all of these commonly used techniques give us information about *relative* blood flow rather than absolute. The latter can be assessed only by venous occlusion plethysmography.

A sample plethysmograph recording was shown in Figure 5.6. Though this reproduction actually illustrates a recording of sexual arousal from the highly specialized vaginal photoplethysmograph, the wave-forms are very similar to those which would be seen in any plethysmograph recording. (In Figure 5.6, the PV channel is labeled "Pressure Pulse".) The BV and PV recordings are simply different electronic transformations of the same electrical signal. PV is recorded at a higher sensitivity and with more filtering of low frequencies than BV. The result is that the PV recording is more responsive to beat-to-beat variations in the pumping action of the heart, whereas BV is a more tonic measure of the overall engorgement of the body part with blood.

One of the more critical findings regarding localization of blood flow has to do with Sokolov's distinction between orienting and defensive reactions to stimuli. As we noted earlier (Chapter 4), Sokolov has found that novel stimuli of mild intensity led to an orienting or "what is it?" reflex, while more intense stimuli may yield a defensive reaction. The major physiological difference between the two is that the orienting response is characterized by vasodilation of arteries on the forehead (at the bifurcation of the temporal and frontal arteries), whereas the defensive reaction yields vasoconstriction at the same site. Both types of stimuli yield vasoconstriction in the digits.

Cook (1974) notes that American studies based on group trends have often failed to substantiate Sokolov's basic claim. However, she points out a number of studies indicating that, if within-subject analyses are done, the findings hold. For example, Hare (1973) found that subjects who expressed fear of spiders were more likely to show cerebral vasoconstriction to spider pictures than subjects who expressed no such fear. Thus, whether or not the defensive reaction is observed depends on whether a given individual perceives a given stimulus as threatening.

Peripheral measurements of BV and PV have been most intensively studied in relation to the orientation/habituation problem. However, there have been a number of other interesting findings. Kelly, Brown, and Shaffer (1970), for example, reported that forearm blood flow distinguishes patients hospitalized for anxiety from other psychiatric patients and normal controls. Although HR also distinguishes the groups, forearm blood flow measurements correspond more closely with clinical improvements seen when a patient takes tranquilizers.

Local adaptive responses have also been observed. Zimny and Miller (1966) showed that a cold stimulus applied to a finger causes the blood vessels of that finger to contract.

According to one theory, less adaptive local changes in the vasculature lead to the pain of migraine headaches. The migraine attack typically begins with a nonpainful phase of sensory disturbances (for example, flashing lights), which is characterized by vasoconstriction of the scalp arteries. This is followed by painful vasodilation of the external carotid artery (Dalessio, 1972). Biofeedback studies of training for voluntary control of peripheral circulation suggest that this may be a useful clinical technique for relieving migraine (see Chapter 10).

6

The Respiratory
and Digestive Systems

As you might guess from the brevity of this chapter, measurements of the respiratory and digestive systems have not been as widespread or as theoretically important as EDA, HR, or BP. Respiration, the rhythm of breathing, is one of the oldest psychophysiological measures. But the relative crudity of convenient respiratory measures, along with certain historical incidents discussed below, have kept respiration from being taken seriously. It has now fallen so far out of favor for study in its own right that respiration is not even indexed in Greenfield and Sternbach's (1972) exhaustive *Handbook of Psychophysiology*. The gastrointestinal tract, on the other hand, rates a chapter of its own. Thus, these two sets of measurements have a reputation for being less important than other psychophysiological responses.

The Respiratory System

Stoerring (1906) was among the first to study respiration as a function of psychological state. He suggested that the inspiration/expiration ratio (I/E ratio), in which the respiratory cycle is timed for each phase and an overall ratio computed, be assessed in various situations. Benussi (1914) claimed that the I/E ratio provided an objective index of lying. Although the accuracy of this measure was disputed by later experimenters (Burtt, 1921; Landis and Wiley, 1926), respiration remains one of the key procedures in modern-day lie detection (see Chapter 10).

Other early researchers attempted to manipulate emotional experience while measuring respiration. Rehwoldt (1911) found that his subjects showed the fast and deep breathing of emotion when they recalled or imagined some emotional experience. Blatz (1925) induced fear with a trick chair that suddenly fell over backwards while his subject sat on it. Lengthening respiration and increases in HR were observed. Riddle (1925) found that poker players increased their rate and extent of breathing during a game. She also reported moderate correlations between a player's rating of his "desire to win" a given hand and his respiratory patterns.

Considerable enthusiasm was generated by Feleky's (1914, 1916) report that he could distinguish six primary emotions—pleasure, pain, anger, wonderment, fear and disgust—on the basis of I/E ratios. Interestingly enough, this list of basic emotions is virtually identical to one that emerged from recent studies of facial expression and emotion (see Chapter 8). However, failures to replicate Feleky's work with respiratory measures, which had involved only a single experimental subject in a single session for each emotion, led to a more guarded view of their value.

The respiratory system consists basically of the nose, the mouth, and the

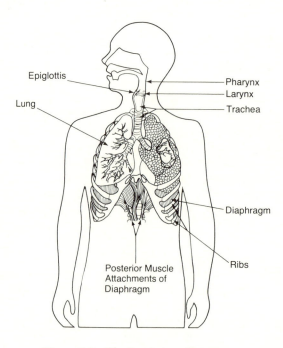

Figure 6.1   *The Respiratory System.*

passages to and from the lungs (see Figure 6.1). The main respiratory apparatus consists of the diaphragm and the intercostal and abdominal muscles—all part of the striped ("involuntary") musculature. Yet breathing involves an unusual combination of voluntary and reflex control. Trying to commit suicide by holding your breath would be one frustrating way to demonstrate this curious mixture. Although we can control inspiration and expiration within normal limits, a respiratory center in the medulla checks the carbon dioxide content of the blood and initiates a powerful respiratory reflex when necessary. Similarly, the normal rhythm of breathing goes on without our awareness or active involvement. But smoking a cigarette implies active control of inhaling and exhaling. Speech and singing, too, involve complex voluntary adjustments in our breathing pattern. A cough, laugh, or sneeze represents common respiratory adjustments that may be voluntary or involuntary. The structure of brain mechanisms overseeing respiratory adjustments reflect the complexity of respiration's many functions.

Functionally, the air that flows through the lungs in inspiration supplies oxygen to blood flowing through the capillaries of the lungs. Simultaneously, carbon dioxide and other poisonous metabolic wastes are passed from the blood and removed from the body in expiration. There is a simple linear relation between the amount of muscular work a person does and the rate of oxygen absorption (Krogh, 1941). This rate varies from .2 l/kg/hr (liters per kilogram of body weight per hour) in rest to 4 l/kg/hr in extreme exertion. This direct relation between overall demands of the body and breathing led many to adopt respiration as a promising measure of the arousal of the organism (Woodworth and Schlosberg, 1954). But the gradual disillusionment with the arousal concept was one major factor in respiration's decline as an index of emotion.

The oldest method for recording respiration involved a direct measurement of the volume of air with each inhalation and exhalation. The gases expelled were sometimes collected for chemical analysis. Respiration was usually measured from the variations in a pressure-sensitive transducer as the air of breathing passed by. Clearly, this method implies a closed system covering the nose and mouth. Its inconvenience was probably taken to the extreme in a study by Bartlett (1956), in which nose-clamps and mouthpieces were attached to individuals about to engage in sexual intercourse. Somehow the subjects managed to perform so that an orgasmic respiratory peak was detected. But it is probably safe to assume that this cumbersome apparatus introduced some artificial constraints.

A less precise but easier method involves taping a thermistor near the nose. Air is warmed by the body before it is exhaled, and so the increased temperature of each exhalation is easy to distinguish from the lower temperature of the inhalation.

More commonly, respiration measurement depends on changes in the girth of the chest and abdomen with each breath. A stretchable strain gauge can be strapped around either site in such a way that the expansion of the body is

displayed on the polygraph as a changing resistance. [Grossman (1967) argues
that thoracic and abdominal contraction may vary independently under certain
conditions, and so the researcher who is seriously interested in respiration must
measure both simultaneously.] Since the basic tightness of the belt varies from
subject to subject, this method, like the use of a thermistor, does not give
reliable data on the absolute volume of air inhaled or expelled. It does give a
quite reasonable record of variations in the rate or amplitude of breathing, as
seen in Figure 6.2. This record can then easily be analyzed for measures like
the number of breaths per minute, the relative amplitude of breaths under
various conditions, or even scored more intuitively for "respiratory irregulari-
ties" (for example, Schwartz, 1971).

Most psychophysiologists today measure respiration only to monitor for artifact. A simple sneeze or cough wreaks havoc in the psychophysiological lab;
electrodes may slip slightly as the subject jerks in the chair, large muscle potentials may appear with the movement, a sweat-gland response occurs, and so on.
And so in many psychophysiological studies, particularly those concentrating
on autonomic nervous system measurement, respiration is monitored routinely
as an "extra channel." The respiratory data are not analyzed separately, but are
merely used to tell the experimenter which parts of his experiment do not
belong in the final analysis.

A similar application has arisen in the field of cardiovascular biofeedback (see
Chapter 10). It is well known that a person can raise his heart rate by hyperventilating. Experimenters who were interested in showing learned control of heart
rate were not interested in simply forcing their subjects to breathe faster or
slower. In many HR biofeedback studies, breathing was simply monitored and
subjects who engaged in gross respiratory maneuvers were instructed to use a
different strategy (for example, Hassett, 1974). Studies aimed directly at the

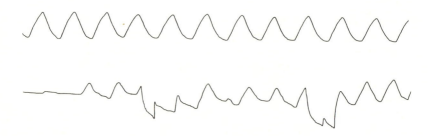

Figure 6.2 *Sample Strain Gauge Recording of Respiration.* Two respiration
records from the same subject. The upper tracing shows the regular pattern of
inhalations (ascending line) and exhalations (descending line) of normal rest. The
lower tracing was recorded during a period of talking and laughing.

question of the relation between heart-rate biofeedback changes and respiration have generally showed that the two can be separately manipulated (see Vaitl, 1972).

A few have continued to use respiratory measures as a more global indicator of metabolic state. Wallace, Benson and Wilson, (1971), for example, reported that respiratory rate and the volume of air breathed decreased dramatically during Transcendental Meditation. Decreased oxygen consumption was one of the most dramatic findings in a whole bodily pattern of relaxation, which they christened "a hypometabolic state." Sleep researchers also monitor breathing patterns throughout the night.

On the whole, it appears that respiration may be the most underrated variable in current psychophysiological research. The admitted crudity of simply monitoring chest expansion could be somewhat offset by simultaneous abdominal measurement. Using this sort of system, Svebak (1975) found that measurement of respiratory patterns under resting conditions enabled him to predict which women (but not which men) would laugh the hardest as they watched highlights of a Norwegian version of "Candid Camera."

The Digestive System

Anyone who has ever stood up in front of a large audience and felt a wave of nausea wash over his body knows how intimately the gastrointestinal (GI) tract is tied to our emotional lives. But, although we are often inconveniently aware of the stomach's responses to psychic stimuli, this has not been a major area of research for psychophysiology. For these complex changes deep inside the body are not easily detected at the body's surface. Unlike the powerful electrical potentials of the muscular contraction of the heart, the electrical changes involved in stomach contraction are difficult to detect and interpret. Further, many subjective symptoms are induced by shifting chemical concentrations within the GI tract. Thus they have been studied, using quite complicated and specialized apparatus, almost exclusively in the confines of the physician's office. Some physiological changes have thus far completely eluded our technological know-how. For example, Wolf and Welsh (1972) comment, "There are essentially no methods for studying [gastrointestinal] blood flow in the intact human."

Nevertheless, there have been some pioneering studies of gastrointestinal response. Even this primitive research has indicated once more the complexity of bodily responses and the unwillingness of human physiology to conform to our simple descriptions. For example, Cannon's (1927) notion of the either/or action of the SNS and PNS has been contradicted even in the most basic case of nausea. This unpleasant experience simultaneously combines decreased motor activity and secretion of gastric juices (reflecting vagal inhibition and thus an

SNS-like response) with increased salivation (a PNS response). Thus, both branches of the autonomic nervous system work together to produce the final experience.

The digestive system (illustrated in Figure 6.3) is usually broken down into two parts. The GI tract includes all those structures through which food passes from beginning to end. As food travels through this system, it is gradually broken down into nutrients that can be absorbed into the blood stream and wastes that can be moved through the body. The other part includes all those organs that contribute chemical juices necessary for the digestive process.

Similarly, we can distinguish between two kinds of physiological changes in the GI tract that we are able to record: chemical and motoric (that is, muscular). Basic observations about both were first made through the study of patients with gastric fistulas—artificial openings from the stomach to the surface of the body. These may be created surgically (as for feeding a patient whose throat is blocked) or in accidents. On June 6, 1822, a Canadian trapper named Alexis St. Martin was standing too close to a friend who was firing a shotgun. The resulting wound healed as a permanent opening from his stomach to the belly surface near his navel. The attending physician, William Beaumont, saw a tremendous opportunity to study gastric function in the unfortunate trapper and provided many of our fundamental ideas about the process of digestion through his observations (1833). More importantly for our purposes, he observed changes in the appearance of gastric tissue that were correlated with St. Martin's understandable emotional turmoil.

More recent observations on patients with gastric fistulas (Wolf and Wolff, 1947) confirmed and extended Beaumont's theories. The fistula patient "Tom" showed increased HCl secretion in the stomach and increased motor activity in aggressive states of anger and resentment. Fright and depression, on the other hand, led to corresponding decreases in gastric function. Wolf and Welsh (1972) point out that such attitudinal links to stomach function are likely to vary from one individual to the next. Just as one person responds to depression by overeating while another depressed person may feel nauseated and stop eating almost entirely, so the response of the GI tract to similar states will be quite variable in different subjects.

Important as these findings are, they obviously do not provide a methodology for the study of normal human gastric function. Although some complex clinical procedures exist for studying the chemical changes in the GI tract, they are quite expensive and often uncomfortable for the patient. Further, because they are generally not suitable for analyzing transient responses to psychic stimuli, they are not readily adapted for psychophysiological research. The study of the motor activity of the stomach has attracted considerably more attention.

There are several methods of monitoring the stomach's rhythmic contractions in the normal subject. Those most frequently used require the subject to swallow some transducer. This may be a small balloon that remains connected

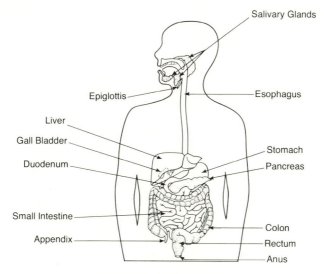

Figure 6.3 *The Digestive System.*

to a pressure-sensing device. As the stomach expands and contracts, it exerts a variable pressure on the balloon. More sophisticated systems involve swallowing an electromagnetic device or even a pressure-sensitive transducer connected to a miniaturized radio transmitter. Clearly, the larger the device, the more unpleasant the experience for all concerned. There is also the nagging suspicion that such intrusive methods may create abnormal patterns of activity.

A more promising development is that of the electrogastrogram (or EGG), which relies on electrical changes at the surface of the body reflecting stomach contractions. Russell and Stern (1967) suggest placing an active electrode about one inch above and two inches to the left of the navel. The standing electrical potential (on the order of .5 mV) between this electrode and a reference site on either leg will reflect gastric motility. This procedure compares favorably with other recordings of gastric motility, although the information yielded is not precisely identical.

Despite the limitations of the current technology for recording gastric response, some fascinating observations have been made. We shall use some research on gastric motility to illustrate how psychophysiological observation may provide a clue for framing hypotheses in behavioral psychology.

When the stomach is relatively empty, rhythmic contractions begin to produce the pangs of hunger that tell us it is time to stop for a cheeseburger. Using the balloon-swallowing technique, Stunkard (1959) studied the relation of periodic stomach contraction to the subjective experience of hunger. Stunkard would simply ask his subjects at regular intervals whether they were hungry or not and would then compare their answers with the record of stomach contractions. He found that subjects of normal weight did indeed feel considerably hungrier when their stomachs were contracting. However, overweight subjects did not show this relation.

At first glance, this looks like just one more piece of data in the confusing puzzle of human behavior. But Stanley Schachter, a social psychologist at Columbia University, put this finding together with some discoveries about brain lesions and eating to suggest the following hypothesis: While normals respond to *internal* cues in the perception of hunger, obese people are more sensitive to the *external* cues of the environment. He proceeded to test this idea in a long series of clever experiments which are summarized in his book *Emotion, Obesity and Crime* (1971). For example, in the first study he told normal and obese (15% or more overweight, according to actuarial tables compiled by the Metropolitan Life Insurance Company) subjects that they were "tastetesters" for some new low-calorie crackers. Each subject was provided with several bowls of crackers along with elaborate scales for noting their texture, sweetness, and so on. They were to eat as many crackers as they wanted in the process of rating these characteristics. As you may have guessed, the time-consuming rating scales were a ruse; Schachter was simply interested in seeing how many crackers the fats and thins would eat. To control their biological level of hunger, he requested all subjects not to eat for several hours before the experiment (telling them that other foods could disturb their sensitive taste buds, with a single anchovy pizza disabling them for weeks). For half of each group, he then provided roast-beef sandwiches so that they could fill themselves up. Just as he predicted, the normals who were full of roast beef ate fewer crackers than the hungry normals, responding to the internal cues of hunger. But the overweight subjects were unaffected by what they had already eaten; they munched away at the same rate despite their recent meal.

Schachter went on to demonstrate this same kind of attention to external cues among the obese in many different situations. Obese people ate less when they made the transition to tasteless institutional food; overweight Jews were more likely to fast on Yom Kippur than their biologically tied thin friends. Conversely, in the presence of tempting delicacies, the fats were always the first to give in.

Schacter's experiments offer more than an explanation of why some of us are chubbier than others; psychophysiological methods provide far more than an end in themselves for understanding the biological underpinnings of behavior. Psychophysiological findings may serve to suggest hypotheses that are strictly behavioral. The cleverness of this research is not in pinpointing a physiological difference (hunger as a response to stomach contractions) in two groups but in going beyond that, to see a possible behavioral implication (different eating habits) of the physiological difference.

7

The Eyes

The eyes are our single most important source of information about the world around us. The complicated visual apparatus provides us with a continuous picture of our ever-changing world. The process by which rays of light induce chemical changes in the retina, ultimately yielding our conscious visual experience, is one of the most fascinating stories in sensory neurophysiology. Gregory (1966) provides an excellent introduction to this topic.

As psychophysiologists, our primary interest is in observable responses of the eye to psychological events. These include pupillary diameter, eye blinks, and eye movements. These measures have a special place in psychophysiology in that no special equipment is required to observe them. No matter how carefully I look at you, I cannot see your heart beat or your blood pressure go up. But I can notice the various adjustments of your eyes. Hess (1975) rather poetically calls the pupil "A piece of the brain sticking out of the human body for all the world to see and evaluate."

In this chapter, we shall consider three major aspects of the visual system. This discussion will serve as a bridge between the primarily autonomic measures we have presented thus far and the higher-level voluntary responses that will be considered in the next few chapters. Pupil size is controlled by the antagonistic action of SNS and PNS. Eye blinking might be likened to respiration in that it is ordinarily an automatic involuntary process that we are unaware of but can easily be brought under conscious control. Finally, the muscular adjustments involved in eye movements are somewhat "more voluntary" than eye blinks in that they are more frequently under conscious control. Thus, they can serve as an introduction to the voluntary musculature (see Chapter 8).

The Pupil

Overview

The pupil is an opening in the iris through which light is admitted to the retina. The pupil will dilate if you sit in a dark room, making the most of the light available, or constrict as you watch people walk by on a sunny beach. The pupil also helps to focus a visual image by constricting for near vision.

These fundamental facts are not the whole story of pupillary response, of course, or the measure would be of little interest to the psychophysiologist. Confucius said: "Look into a person's pupils, he cannot hide himself." For centuries, Turkish rug merchants have carefully watched their customers' eyes as they display their wares. Pupillary dilation is taken as a sign of interest in a given rug, and the merchants bargain accordingly. When we speak of a person whose "eyes are wide with fright," we are referring not only to the position of the eyelids but also the characteristic dilation of the pupils to strong emotions. Psychologists long ago noted these changes not only in stressful situations but also in the presence of far milder psychic stimuli. Bumke (1911) noted that even a mild handshake elicits pupil enlargement. More dramatically, if a subject counts the beats of a metronome, his eyes can be seen to contract and dilate to its monotonous rhythm.

But, as we shall see, it is important to continually remind ourselves of the primary function of the pupil: to regulate the amount of light entering the eye by adjusting its diameter. This simple fact may account for a number of observations. Grinspoon (1971) notes, for example, that many marijuana smokers and law enforcement agents firmly believe that pupil dilation is one effect of the weed. But systematic research has shown that, in itself, marijuana has no effect on the pupil's diameter. This myth seems to be based on the fact that, in our society, people so frequently choose to smoke marijuana in dimly lit rooms. Their pupils then dilate to admit more light. Thus, what may seem like a "psychic stimulus" may have another, far more direct explanation.

The diameter of the human pupil can vary from 1.5 mm to 9 mm, responding to changes in illumination in as little as .2 seconds (Lowenstein and Loewenfeld, 1962). Pupil diameter is determined by two sets of antagonistic muscles in the iris. Decreases in size are controlled by the sphincter pupillae, mediated by the parasympathetic nervous system (PNS), while increases in diameter result from the action of the dilator pupillae under the control of the sympathetic nervous system (SNS). Hess (1972) also stresses the possibility of more direct control of pupillary diameter by the central nervous system, but only the autonomic pathways are firmly established.

The two sets of antagonistic muscles are in a constant interplay. As in most ANS-mediated responses, it thus becomes difficult to deduce whether a given response represents activity of one branch of the ANS or depression of its antagonist. For example, when an ophthalmologist wants to dilate the pupil to observe the retina, he uses atropine to block PNS constrictor mechanisms rather than pharmacologically inducing SNS activity. Under more normal conditions, a pupil dilation could result from either cause.

In addition to the relatively large changes in pupillary diameter typically observed by the psychophysiologist, there is a constant undercurrent of activity called "pupillary unrest" or "hippus." This refers to the fact that pupillary diameter is never entirely constant. These continual miniature readjustments have generally been ignored by psychological researchers because of measurement difficulties.

Pupillary diameter is usually measured by simply photographing the eye (see Appendix D). Various devices also exist to convert the diameter to a continuously varying voltage for display on a polygraph.

Pupillometrics

It is impossible to talk about modern psychophysiological research on pupil diameter without talking about researcher Eckhard Hess of the University of Chicago. Hess is a rather controversial character who tells the whole story of "pupillometrics" (a term he coined for an article in *The Saturday Evening Post*) in his delightful book, *The Tell-Tale Eye* (Hess, 1975).

One night as Hess lay in bed paging through a book of animal pictures, his wife casually remarked that he really should read in better light, because his pupils were dilated. This casual remark started him thinking. The next day, he presented his research assistant, James Polt, with a group of pictures of majestically scenic landscapes and then watched Polt's eyes. When Polt came upon the ringer in the group, a picture of a young woman in a state of undress, his pupils suddenly dilated, and Hess shouted the midwestern equivalent of "Eureka!"

They proceeded to launch the first of a series of studies of pupillary dilation to a series of photographs. In 1960, Hess and Polt published the first of these observations comparing the pupillary responses of four men and two women. They discovered that the males' pupils dilated when they saw a scantily clad woman, while the females' pupils dilated at the sight of a similarly undressed man. In later studies, "aversive" scenes of affliction and deformity led to pupillary constriction. These and other observations led Hess (1972) to conclude that positive affect yielded sympathetic-like pupil dilation, while more negative emotions were accompanied by the parasympathetic-type response of constriction.

A number of studies were launched that seemed to support this distinction. Hess, Seltzer, and Shlien (1965) demonstrated that self-professed male homosexuals showed relatively greater dilation to pinups of men than of women, while a comparable group of heterosexuals showed greater dilation to the female pictures. Atwood and Howell (1971) went so far as to show that prison inmates who had been convicted of molesting young girls gave their greatest dilations to pictures of the young.

Hess's enthusiasm over these discoveries knew no bounds. As Rice (1974) remarks, the search of academic psychology for a reliable way of knowing what people *really* think and feel is comparable in intensity only to the Crusaders' quest for the Holy Grail: "Whoever found it would certainly win fame and fortune, if not tenure." And Hess was sure he had it: a culture-free way to look inside people's heads without having to rely on their erratic verbal reports. He became a consultant for Interpublic, a major force in the field of advertising. The original theory was that expensive advertising campaigns could be pretested by simply noting whether the latest commercials yielded the promising pupil dilation or the telltale thumbs down of pupillary constriction. There was even a rumor, thoughtfully passed on by *Psychology Today*, that federal intelligence agencies investigated the effects of interrogation on pupil size.

Hess (1975) details four studies in which verbal reports of advertising effects (the traditional procedure) are directly compared to pupillary responses to see which was a better predictor of later sales figures. In three of these four cases, the pupillary prediction is indeed better (the fourth was a tie). However, in only one of the four studies was *either* prediction statistically significant. In that one study, both the verbal reports and the pupillary responses were effective at the .05 level.

As other university and applied researchers flocked to the field of "pupil-lometrics," many of Hess's formulations came under attack. One problem with his method involved a failure to standardize fixation points. We noted above that major changes in pupil size are caused by changes in brightness. Janisse and Peavler (1974) give the following example of possible problems in the original Hess research: Suppose that a picture of a shirtless male is presented to groups of both sexes. If the women who are subjects tend to stare at his dark pants, the pupils will dilate slightly. If the men, on the other hand, stare at his far brighter face, the pupil will constrict in response to this additional brightness. On the basis of these and other sorts of criticisms, several reviews of the evidence (Goldwater, 1972; Janisse, 1973) conclude that the like/dislike distinction cannot be made by observing pupil size.

It does appear to be true that many different sorts of sensory stimuli produce dilation, the SNS-type response. Further, the degree of dilation is related to the intensity of the experience. In this, the pupillary response resembles the sweat-gland response (see Chapter 4). Indeed, Hess (1972) reports a strong but not perfect correlation between pupillary dilation and sweat-gland activity. He suggests that future researchers might concentrate on the precise relation between the two, their *pattern* of activation, for further insight into their biological relationship.

Precisely this was done in a recent study of schizophrenia (Patterson, 1976). Pupillary constriction in the light/dark reflex was compared to the recovery limb of the SCR to a series of tones. Those schizophrenics whose pupils constricted slowly consistently had fast SCR recovery limbs. Conversely, patients with fast pupillary constriction had slow SCR recovery limbs. Patterson discusses the implications of this finding for theories of the physiological basis of schizophrenia.

Pupillary dilation has also been observed as a concomitant of mental effort. If you stare into a mirror and then try to multiply 57 times 6, you will notice a slight increase in pupillary diameter. More difficult problems produce greater dilation. This fact has been used in various practical studies of performance. Janisse and Peavler (1974), for example, reported a study for the telephone company in which one of the authors compared two different methods of having information operators look up telephone numbers. They found that the method described as more difficult and as causing greater fatigue also produced wider pupil dilation.

In general, the field of pupillometrics contains many provocative findings, but we shall have to see which ones stand up to the acid test of time. Tryon (1975) documents the many physiological and psychological variables, ranging from political attitudes to the wavelength of visual stimuli, that affect pupillary diameter. Experiments will have to be designed very carefully indeed in order to disentangle all these factors.

Eye Blinks

> [Let us] . . . spare a thought for the eyelids: their regular blinking action . . . to maintain the film of moisture on the cornea, their swift and involuntary closure to protect the eyes from danger, and their involuntary closure to save us from unwanted sensation. Would that we had been provided with equally effective earlids (Wilman, 1966).

Psychophysiologists have paid relatively little attention to studying eye blinks. This is partially due to a lack of a standard recording technology. A number of ingenious devices, ranging from a thread glued on the eyelid and attached to a mechanical counter to special glasses containing a light source and a photoelectric cell, have been used in isolated studies. But more traditional and less intrusive electrical recordings have not been widely accepted: Subtle movements of the eyebrows and cheek musculature associated with blinking are obscured by the corneoretinal potentials generated when the eye reflexively rotates upward during a blink. Many researchers therefore continue to rely on some variant of simple observation.

There are several different kinds of eye blinks. Most familiar are voluntary closings of the eyelids for a relatively short time. These tend to be of relatively long duration and have not in the past been of major interest to the psychophysiologist.

Reflex blinking, the second type, can be elicited by many stimuli, from a speck of dust in the eye to a sudden loud sound. This protective action of the eyelid has figured prominently in studies of classical conditioning. Conditioned eyelid closure has been found by pairing some neutral stimulus with puffs of air directed at the eye, electric shock, and loud tones (Kimble, 1961). However, this research is not a major focus of interest for the psychophysiologist because it concentrates on the learning process; reflex blinking is treated as just one more built-in reflex of the organism, no different from the knee jerk. Since this reflex is one of the last to disappear under anesthesia, surgeons sometimes use it as a rough guide of anesthesia depth. But, like the classical conditioning literature, this phenomenon is not of major interest to the researcher interested in physiological clues to normal human consciousness.

Of considerable potential interest to the psychophysiologist, however, is the third type of periodic blinking. For the literal-minded, the phrase "in the blink of an eye" refers to roughly .35 seconds, this being the measured duration of periodic blinking (Adler, 1965). The rate of periodic blinking varies widely from person to person but appears fairly stable for a given individual under constant conditions. Because not all blinks are complete closures, not all experimenters have defined blinks in exactly the same way. Further, many of the recording techniques may have interfered with the blinking process. Thus it is difficult to talk in the abstract about true average blinking rates. With these disclaimers in mind, we shall now discuss true average blinking rates. In a classic study of eye blinks, Ponder and Kennedy (1927) found a mean rate of 7.5 blinks per minute. This figure is misleading, however, in that the rates for individuals ranged from 1 per minute to 46 per minute.

The neurophysiology of periodic blinking is not well understood (Hall and Cusack, 1972), although it does appear to be controlled by the CNS via the VIIth cranial nerve (the facial nerve). Nor is its functional value entirely clear, despite the oft-repeated belief that blinking maintains corneal moisture. Criticizing this view, Ponder and Kennedy (1927) argued that, before six months of age, infants do not blink at all. Further, they recorded the blink rate of subjects in a hothouse (very low humidity) and a steam bath (high humidity) and found no difference.

Individual differences in blinking rate constitute one potential source of data for the psychophysiologist. More attention has been paid in the past to a search for "general laws" of blinking. It is quite clear that an individual's rate changes with his psychic state. A number of experimental and real-life observations convinced Ponder and Kennedy (1927) that this rate reflected the "degree of mental tension." For example, in courtroom observations, they noted that a witness's blink rate doubled from the time of questioning from his own attorney to cross-examination by the opponent.

Hall and Cusack (1972) provide an excellent critical review of the entire eye blink literature. After setting up a list of criteria for adequate studies (including statistical corrections for unusual distributions and individual differences, adequate attention to contaminating variables, and an operational definition of blinking), they found to their chagrin that not a single study was "adequate." Nevertheless, they finally revised the theory of Kennard and Glasser (1963) to argue that blinking appears to be curvilinearly related to attention: Excessive boredom or extreme emotion increases blinking, while adaptive levels of attention are indicated by intermediate blinking rates. Whether this formulation stands the test of further research or not, it does appear that the unconscious and involuntary rate of eye-blinking is lawfully related to underlying psychological processes.

Eye Movements

Overview

The constant muscular adjustments of the eye are intimately involved with the visual process. As you read this page, your eyes jump constantly from one phrase to the next. If you move your head slightly to one side as you read, the image of the book will remain steady as your eyes suddenly shift their position. If you hold the book further away, your eyes will move slightly apart to adjust their focus.

The earliest investigations of eye movements were based on direct observation. Neurologists and ophthalmologists learned over the centuries that important clues to nervous system damage could often be gleaned from eye movements. To the present day, simple observation of the gross movements of the eyes continues to be an important tool in medical diagnosis. And, as we shall see in this chapter's later discussion of cerebral asymmetry, such basic techniques can also be useful in the study of normal psychological function.

But staring into another person's eyes, while fine for lovers, is not always adequate for more detached scientific investigation. Very subtle eye movements simply cannot be detected in this fashion. More systematic attempts to record eye movements began with direct mechanical linkages. Delebarre (1898) developed a primitive contact lens made from a plaster cast of an artificial eye. A cup formed from the cast was then fitted over a subject's anesthetized eyeball. A hole was cut over the pupil, and the entire bulky device was connected by a series of rods to a permanent recording system. Clever as this system was, given the technological limitations of the time, the discomfort caused by the system precluded the possibility of recording under anything even approximating normal conditions.

A less intrusive set of methods came with the application of photography to the problem. Very simply, a series of pictures of eye position is taken. (See Appendix D.)

Such techniques were often applied to very practical problems of eye movements in driving, industrial settings, and so on. An entire literature devoted to eye movements in reading appeared (Tinker, 1958). Investigators soon found that reading was done in "chunks." The eye did not move smoothly from one word to the next but jumped from phrase to phrase. The simpler the reading material, the larger the jump. Some of these discoveries were instrumental in developing "speed reading" techniques, whose principle is simply to digest the material in larger chunks.

Recent technological advances have allowed some researchers to answer questions that were previously unthinkable. Lambert, Monty and Hall (1974) described an elaborate computer-controlled eye-tracking system that imposes virtually no artificial constraints on the subject and permits a very precise specification of eye position. McKonkie (1976) used this system to coordinate the appearance of a page of text with a subject's eye movements. He was interested in determining how much information the eye takes in as it focuses on a given point. His computer system enabled him to surround normal text

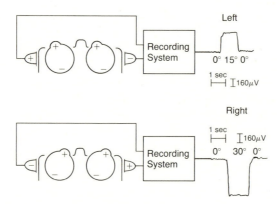

Figure 7.1 *The Electrical Basis of the EOG.* The eyeball is like a miniature battery. As it rotates, the poles of this "battery" come nearer to the respective electrodes positioned around the eye. The change in electrical potential is recorded, giving information about the angle of rotation. (After Shackel, 1967.)

with a series of nonsense words—wherever a subject looked, he would see a perfectly normal portion of the text, but it would always be surrounded by nonsense words. By manipulating the length of the normal portion of the text, McKonkie discovered that different types of information are acquired at different distances into the periphery. The eye encodes meaning only 4 to 6 characters to the right of a fixation point, for example, but word-length patterns are detected up to 14 characters away and used for guidance of the eye to its next fixation point. Sophisticated systems of this sort may ultimately be useful in the diagnosis and treatment of reading disorders.

A far simpler technique, which enables one to determine eye position when the lids are closed, is the electrooculogram, or EOG. This procedure is a direct recording of the electrical potentials generated by eye movement. The first researchers to use this method believed that they were recording the action potentials of the muscles that move the eye in its socket. Mowrer, Ruch, and Hiller (1936) demonstrated that the earlier researchers were in fact recording a potential difference from the eye itself: Even when the muscles were not employed (for example, when the eyes were moved passively), the EOG appeared.

Figure 7.1 illustrates the anatomical basis of the EOG: The cornea is electrically positive relative to the retina. The orientation of this corneoretinal potential shifts as the eyes change their position. (See Appendix D.)

Kinds of Eye Movements

Using the EOG and other recording techniques, researchers have discovered several different characteristic patterns of eye movements. Figure 7.2 represents typical electrooculograms for various conditions.

First consider the recording of lateral eye movements (from left to right) that correspond to reading a newspaper. Here we see the typical fixations and saccades of normal vision. The eye focuses on a particular spot and remains fixated there between .25 of a second and 1 second. This stationary position of the eye is seen in the lateral EOG as a horizontal line; the potential remains constant as the eyes hold a position. They then jerk suddenly to a new fixed position in a saccadic movement lasting .02 to .10 of a second—represented here by a vertical line indicating a change in potential difference between the sides of the eyes. This subject reads a column of newsprint in about five chunks. You can see the subject retracing his steps on line 3—returning to a phrase that he skimmed too quickly.

This pattern of fixations and saccadic movements is maintained when a subject looks around the circumference of a circle. Instead of smoothly following its contours, both lateral and vertical eye movements are characterized by jerks from one fixation point to the next. Contrast this with the relatively smooth EOG record that results when the subject follows a finger tip drawn around the

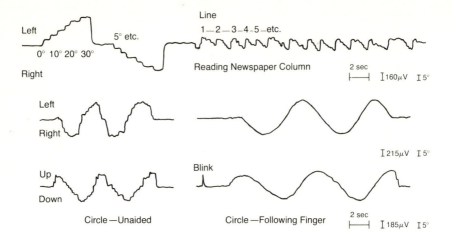

Figure 7.2 *Sample EOG Recordings.* (After Shackel, 1967.) For "circle-unaided," the subject tries to scan smoothly around a circle by himself; for "following finger," his eyes follow a fingertip drawn around the circle.

circumference of the same circle. *Pursuit* movements involve the automatic following of some moving figure in the environment. As in this example, they are typically far "smoother" than the stop-and-go jerks of the eye evaluating a stationary object.

The *compensatory* movements of the eyes (which correct for changes in head position) are also relatively smooth. These can easily be observed by having a friend stare at your finger and move his head slightly while you watch the eye movements. Important as the mechanisms of compensatory eye movements are to the normal individual (since, without them, any small shift in position would make the world jump around), they are quite troublesome to the psychophysiologist. Since the EOG is based on the standing corneoretinal potential, the same electrical record is observed whatever the cause of the eye movements. Thus the EOG from a person who looked off to one side would be identical to that from a person who continued to look straight ahead but turned his body so that the eyes were now off to one side.

The movements of experimental subjects are rarely so dramatic, but one is always left with the problem that eye movements are confounded with head movements. The most common solution to this problem is to keep the head from moving. Typically, the subject is asked to bite into a stationary board covered with wax for the duration of the recording. This is clearly a rather artificial situation, and more sophisticated approaches involve more freedom of movement with simultaneous recording of head position (Tursky, 1974b).

In addition to the eye movements discussed thus far, there is an entire category of continual smaller eye movements termed *physiological nystagmus*. If the sensitivity of the recordings in Figure 7.2 were increased, you would see that even during fixation, the eye is continually darting back and forth. Some kinds of nystagmus are clinical signs of underlying pathology. Others are essential for normal vision.

The latter was elegantly demonstrated in a series of experiments by Dichtburn and Ginsborg in 1952. (See also Yarbus, 1967.) Using a contact lens with a miniature projection system, they managed to stabilize an image on the retina, thus canceling out physiological nystagmus. Such images tend to fade in and out of view after a few seconds. That is, the retina responds to change rather than to stability. Miniature eye movements provide the ever-changing picture of the world that is, paradoxically, necessary to make it seem stable.

All of the types of eye movements discussed here are conjugate; that is, both eyes move in the same direction at the same time. As mentioned earlier, there are also eye movements of convergence and divergence, in which the eyes move closer together or farther apart to focus at different distances. Any child who has entertained his friends by walking around staring cross-eyed at his nose is aware of this possibility. Most psychophysiological recordings are of the more normal binocular EOG, in which the two eyes act together.

Hemispheric Asymmetry

As we indicated in Chapter 2, the two hemispheres of the brain have specialized to take on rather different functions. In addition to the contralateral wiring of the human nervous system (left side of the brain controls the right side of the body, and vice versa), it appears that different modes of thought may be based on biological differences between the halves of the brain. For the right-handed person, the left hemisphere is primarily involved in verbal, logical thinking, while the right hemisphere is more concerned with spatial, intuitive thinking. (Lefties are more complicated in that they usually have "mixed cerebral dominance," in which functional differences between the hemispheres are not so clear-cut. We shall therefore limit our discussion to right-handed people.)

The basic distinction is based on many sources of evidence (Ornstein, 1972), ranging from the behavioral limitations of brain-damaged people to such sensory asymmetries as differences in hearing from the right and left ears. Of special relevance here is Kinsbourne's (1972) suggestion that the direction in which a person's eyes move as he considers a question reflects which cerebral hemisphere he is using. To test this hypothesis, he asked subjects questions that emphasized verbal or spatial information. Lateral eye movements (LEMs; also called conjugate lateral eye movements, or CLEMs, because the two eyes move together) were predominantly to the right for verbal questions and to the left for spatial questions.

This is quite consistent with the general idea of contralateral control. Electrical stimulation of the left hemisphere frequently produces eye and body orientations to the right, and vice versa. Kinsbourne hypothesized that predominant activation of either hemisphere leads to a kind of electrical "overflow," which then stimulates the body and eye orientation centers on the same side. Despite the relative crudity of this physiological explanation, several other experimenters have verified the basic finding of LEMs to the right for verbal questions and LEMs to the left for spatial questions (for example, Galin and Ornstein, 1974).

Schwartz, Davidson, and Maer (1975) went one step further by combining right- and left-hemisphere functions in their questions. They combined the traditional spatial and verbal categories with emotional (presumably right-hemisphere) and nonemotional content. Thus they compared the extremes of verbal-nonemotional (VNE: strictly left-hemisphere) content with spatial-emotional (SE: strictly right-hemisphere) content, as well as the two intermediate (mixed-dominance) categories of verbal-emotional (VE) and spatial-nonemotional (SNE) questions. Their findings, too, were consistent with the idea that right LEMs indicate left-hemisphere "activation," and vice versa.

For example, when a subject considered the VNE problem, "Make up a sentence using the words *code* and *mathematics*," he typically moved his eyes to the right. But when the same subject tried to answer the SE question: "If you were crossing a street from west to east, and a car coming from the south smashed into you, which leg would be shattered first?" he was more likely to look to the left as he considered his response. LEMs to the two intermediate categories were almost equally split between left and right.

Of course, the direction of one's gaze can be influenced by a host of extraneous factors, from something out the window to something in the eye. A number of studies are presently being conducted to isolate some of these factors. Gur, Gur, and Harris (1975), for example, suggest that, if the experimenter sits directly in front of the subject, task differences are less likely to appear than if the movements are recorded by a TV camera while the experimenter sits behind the subject.

Bakan (1971) suggests that differences between people can also be detected in LEMs. An artist, being a more spatial thinker, might tend to answer all questions with a left LEM (indicating greater overall reliance on right-hemisphere thinking), while a lawyer, presumably a more verbal, logical type of person, would be expected to show predominantly right LEMs. Subsequent research (Galin and Ornstein, 1974; Hassett and Zelner, 1977) has not borne out this hypothesis.

One would not expect every LEM to correspond exactly to the underlying theory. On the average, however, different sorts of questions do seem to yield consistently different LEMs. In short, a psychophysiological response measure as simple as the direction in which a person's eyes move as he answers a question can give us valuable information about fundamental biological processes.

Sleep

Every night, all of us pass on to another world inside our heads. In his dreams, the quiet office worker may stand up to his boss, run from a monster, and discover the love of his life, all within a single night. The 90 minutes or so that we spend dreaming each night is so intense, so satisfying, and so real that primitive peoples believed that dreams held the key to the future. To the present day, any paperback bookstore will have a collection of volumes to help people to interpret their dreams.

This important portion of mental life was virtually disregarded by psychologists for many years. How, after all, could one study such an ephemeral phenomenon? Indeed, how could we even be sure, in the scientific sense, that dreams exist?

The first answers to these questions came, like so many discoveries, by accident. Eugene Aserinsky, a graduate student at the University of Chicago around 1950, was doing a study of the movements of sleeping infants. He would watch sleeping infants for hours, carefully noting their cycles of thrashing around the crib. During these tedious observations, he noticed that in addition to periodically thrashing around, the infants often began rolling their eyes back and forth beneath their closed lids. Several similar observations were buried in the archives of sleep researchers, but Aserinsky wisely decided to pursue the observation by studying adults. He quickly discovered that older people, too, pass through several periods of rapid eye movement (or REM) during each night's sleep. More importantly, he found that if an adult was awakened during REM, he tended to report that he had just been dreaming. The same person, if awakened when his eyes were not tracing these telltale patterns (non-REM or NREM) was relatively unlikely to report a recent dream.

In a short article in *Science*, Aserinsky and his mentor, Kleitman (1953), reported their dramatic discovery to the scientific community. Here at last was an objective physiological index of man's rich inner life. And so the field of sleep research was born.

Aserinsky's and Kleitman's basic findings were soon replicated in laboratories around the world. At regular intervals throughout the night, even subjects who swore they had never dreamt in their lives suddenly began moving their eyes back and forth in short bursts of activity. The correlation of these REM periods with dreaming is not perfect, but it is an impressive one nonetheless. In a review of sixteen studies of this topic, Snyder and Scott (1972) found that dreams were reported after REM awakening between 60% and 89% of the time, with a median value of 74%. The values for NREM dream reports were far more variable, but the median was only about 12%. Further, in every single study, dreaming was reported more frequently after awakening from REM than NREM. Many of the differences in experimental opinion about the exact relationship can be attributed to the difficulty of deciding just what qualifies as a dream. Just about everybody will mumble something if you suddenly wake him up and ask what he was dreaming about. Most researchers specify some sort of coherent narrative as the critical characteristic of a dream, but differences in the application of this criterion have led to healthy differences of opinion about the precise relationship.

It is widely agreed that each of us passes through five to seven REM periods in a normal night's sleep. About 23% of the sleep time of a young adult is devoted to REM. Newborn infants spend up to half of their 16-hour sleep time in REM, but the figure declines to the adult average by the age of 3 (Roffwarg, Muzio, and Dement, 1966). REM periods are characteristic of the sleep of all mammals. There is evidence that in animals, too, REM is tied to dreaming. In their excellent introduction to the sleep literature, Luce and Segal (1966) report on experiments of Dr. Charles Vaughn at the University of Pittsburgh, in which monkeys were trained to press a lever whenever they saw a slide. During REM sleep, these same animals unconsciously began pressing the bar as if to signal the complex visual imagery of their dreams.

REM sleep is not only common, it may be essential. Dement (1960) attempted to deprive people of REM sleep by awakening them whenever their eyes began to dart back and forth. In the first night of the study, a subject might have been awakened seven times. But by the fifth night, as many as 30 awakenings might be required to avert REM. It was as if these subjects were "trying harder" to enter the critical REM state. When these people were finally allowed to sleep undisturbed, their proportion of REM time increased, as though they were paying off a physiological debt. This pioneer study suggested that REM-deprived subjects also became nervous and irritable, a finding that has not withstood the acid test of replication. But the body's attempt to make up for lost REM has been observed time and time again.

Early sleep researchers likened REM to the movements of the eyes while watching a film. The idea that REMs mimic normal waking eye movements to follow the action in a dream has, however, been discredited by studies using more sensitive recording procedures (Jacobs, Feldman, and Bender, 1972). REM represents a quite complex pattern of eye-movement activity that remains fundamentally the same in different individuals, despite dramatic differences in dream content.

REM sleep is now seen as a fundamental biological process, intimately tied up with our inner lives. But why did Mother Nature design us to dream? This question remains unanswered. Psychoanalysts find the key to our personalities in what we dream about. At the other end of the spectrum, pioneer Nathaniel Kleitman (1960) has written, "The low grade cerebral activity that is dreaming may serve no function whatsoever." Perhaps the attitude of most scientists toward questions of this sort is best typified by the response of one researcher to the question, posed by a TV interviewer, "What is the function of sleep?" He smiled quizzically and answered, "I don't know. What's the function of being awake?"

8

The Muscles

The muscular system is our biological key to the outside world. If you write a poem, cast a vote, or throw a dish at a loved one, it is the muscles of your arm that turn the thought into action. If you step on the brake, walk to the store, or kick an assailant, it is the muscles of your leg, acting in concert with the entire body musculature, that enable you to do what you think is right. In each case it is the brain that "decides" what to do. Under ordinary circumstances, we learn what the brain has decided in another person only by observing the movements of his muscles—either in speech or action.

We take all this for granted. It is so obvious that it never enters our minds—until we see someone who has been paralyzed by an accidental injury. Then we are reminded of our absolute and total dependence on the biologically commonplace. How minor an inconvenience blindness or deafness seems, compared to loss of the ability to contract our muscles.

The behavioral psychologist directly observes nothing but the movement of muscles—for that, after all, is what overt behavior is. For many situations, these observations are quite sufficient. The biologically oriented psychologist could record the muscular activity that a rat exerts every time he presses a bar, but if we merely want to see if the animal will work for food, this measurement would be an extravagance. But suppose we are interested in predicting *when* the rat will press the bar. Or suppose that we want to know about the occasions when the rat begins to press the bar but "changes his mind." The biological recording of muscular activity becomes critical.

History

As we discussed earlier, it was Luigi Galvani who first discovered the critical role of electrical energy in muscle movement. For it was he who chanced upon the fact that introduction of a small current into the body yields a muscular response. Galvani also demonstrated that, conversely, a normal muscle movement is accompanied by a detectable change in electrical activity. Almost a century and a half elapsed before the technology of medical recording became sufficiently advanced to effectively record the electrical potentials associated with normal human muscular function.

Edmund Jacobson was one of the most important figures in making electromyography (EMG), the recording of electrical potentials associated with muscular contraction, useful to psychologists. Jacobson is best remembered as the father of "Progressive Relaxation," a systematic technique for inducing rest that is still used in psychotherapy. Simple relaxation was an important medical tool in those pretranquilizer days. Himself an insomniac, Jacobson knew all too well that rest meant much more than just lying down. And so he developed the Progressive Relaxation techniques. The basic principle involved practice in relaxing specific muscle groups, which led to a growing "muscle sense"—that is, an awareness on the patient's part of his muscular state. (Technological shortcuts to this same goal are now available in the form of EMG biofeedback; see Chapter 10.)

In the course of his studies of rest and relaxation, Jacobson looked for objective measurements of muscle tension. In early studies, he relied upon the magnitude of the knee-jerk reflex as an index of overall relaxation. Later he moved on to direct recording of the EMG and was responsible for technological as well as substantive advances in understanding this complex measure.

One of his early observations was that when a subject was completely relaxed his "mind was a blank." This observation was extremely relevant to one of the most controversial psychological theories of his time, the peripheral view of thinking. In its more extreme forms, as popularized by John Watson, the father of Behaviorism, this view defined thought as a "general term to cover all subvocal behavior" (Watson, 1919). In his never-ending attempt to make covert processes observable, Watson wanted to argue that all mental phenomena are in some way related to the activity of the skeletal musculature. Thus, when a person was thinking, he was merely talking to himself very quietly.

Naive as this view now sounds, it had one undeniable advantage over opponent theories of that period: It could be tested and thus proved right or wrong.

As is so often the case with psychological theories, however, the test was easier said than done. Given the technology of the time, it was extremely difficult to record the electrical activity of the muscles of the larynx. And when it was recorded, it was virtually impossible to eliminate the contamination of reflex swallowing movements and other clearly nonvocal laryngeal functions.

In one of the more innovative studies of this period, Max (1935) studied the hands of deaf mutes, reasoning that, since they spoke with their hands, the muscular movements that accompanied thinking (if Watson was correct) could be recorded from this more accessible site. And indeed he found that muscular action potentials in the hands during problem solving were far more common in deaf mutes than in normals. Max (1937) also contended that finger movements were more common during dreaming for deaf mutes, but more recent investigations using modern techniques suggest that these are found equally in normals (Stoyva, 1965).

Other studies of this period also suggested some links between muscular activity and thought. When a person imagines tensing his right arm, for example, muscle tension is greatest in the right biceps (Jacobson, 1938). Further, if one imagines lifting a heavy weight, the accompanying muscle tension in the forearm is greater than if one imagines lifting a lighter object (Shaw, 1940), just as it would be if the two weights were actually lifted.

To the contemporary psychophysiologist, these findings come as no surprise: The body acts as an integrated whole. If the brain thinks about a given act, preparatory muscle movements generated by the brain are to be expected. The mistake of Watson's simplistic approach is to identify the thought only with its peripheral manifestations. For contemporary techniques of measuring activity in the central nervous system can show the origin of thought in the brain.

Before the refinement of EMG recording techniques, a number of other measures of "muscle tension" were employed. These ranged from Jacobson's knee-jerk measurements to the recording of the muscular forces used in various tasks (Davis, 1932). Morgan (1916), for example, measured the force with which a subject struck the keys of a typewriterlike device under varying conditions. The point to be made here is that the term "muscle tension" has often been used rather loosely in psychological research, particularly in the older literature. One must be careful, therefore, when comparing studies. Clearly, the EMG provides a measure of electrical activity associated with muscular contraction that is far more direct than these older methods.

Many of the early studies of the EMG were based on the arousal theory. Muscle tension was taken as a general index of a person's alertness during the performance of mental or physical work. From this point of view, it seemed useful to search for the one muscle that provides the best index of overall level of muscle tension. Nidever (1959) and Balshan (1962) argued that the limb musculature provided the most basic information under resting conditions. But Nidever found that this fundamental factor shifted to the head and neck mus-

cles when his subjects undertook a serial learning task. This contrasts with Voas's (1952) finding that muscle tension is focused in the arms during mental exertion.

But, as Goldstein (1972) points out, such a search is a pointless one. The very fluidity with which we move proves that the muscles of the body do not stand in constant relation to one another. What we should be interested in, then, is the *pattern* of muscular responses in a given task. We must expect that our biological flexibility will be manifested as different patterns of muscular exertion under different conditions. An excellent example of the value of this approach will be seen in the work of Schwartz and his colleagues on patterns of activity in the facial musculature during emotion, to be discussed later in this chapter.

While psychologists have emphasized the action of large muscle groups during complex behavior, clinical kinesiologists have used EMG recordings to diagnose muscular dysfunction. Some of the most exciting work in this area has been done by J. V. Basmajian (1967) on single motor units, the anatomically fundamental building blocks of muscle groups. Using miniature electrodes placed under the skin, Basmajian (1963) has developed feedback techniques that enable people to gain a remarkable degree of control over these miniature muscles. This single motor unit training (affectionately abbreviated as SMUT) has proven particularly useful in the development of artificial limbs. The operation of motors in the limb can be controlled by the amputee's direction of the single motor units.

Typical Responses

Thus far, we have been using the term *muscle tension* rather loosely. What the electromyogram actually records is the total series of action potentials that cause muscular contraction. There is some evidence that in the range of nonstrenuous situations typically encountered in psychology experiments, the relationship between the actual force exerted by a muscle and the EMG is linear (Goldstein, 1972).

Figure 8.1 illustrates an actual recording from the corrugator muscle over the eyebrow under conditions of rest and contraction (compare Figure 8.4). Note that during muscular contraction the amplitude and frequency of the spikes increase dramatically.

In the early days of electromyography, scoring such a record was a gargantuan task involving the physical counting of the number of spikes and computing their relative amplitude. Techniques pioneered by Jacobson (1951) now allow this to be done electronically. For any given time period, the total area under the curve can be computed as illustrated in Figure 8.1. The wave is first rectified (that is, positive and negative signs of voltages are ignored and only the

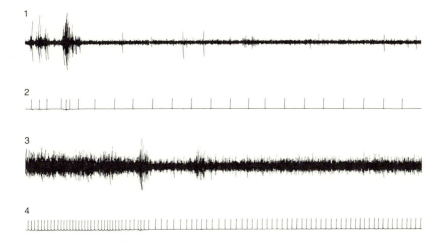

Figure 8.1 *Sample EMG Recordings.* "Raw" EMG (lines 1 and 3) and integrated EMG (lines 2 and 4). Note that when magnitude of raw signal increases, frequency of integrator firing also increases. Recorded from corrugator muscle. (Courtesy of Patricia Salt.)

absolute value is computed) and then integrated (that is, the area under the curve is determined). In our illustration, the integrating circuit continuously measures the "buildup" of voltage until some predetermined value is reached. The integrator then resets automatically and begins anew. The total measure of muscular activity can then be seen by simply counting the number of times the integrator resets.

It is difficult to reconstruct the actual wave-form from its integrated summary because the integration reflects a complex interaction of the frequencies and amplitudes of the waves. However, total muscular contraction is reasonably reflected by the summary, making the wave-form a relatively minor concern.

Physiological Basis

A muscle is a mass of tissue that consists of millions of separate muscle fibers bound together and acting in concert. Each muscle fiber is a fine thread only about .1mm in width but up to 30 mm long. When stimulated by an electrical action potential, this fiber will contract, decreasing its length by as much as one-half. Muscle fibers are functionally grouped together into motor units. The number of fibers in each motor unit depends on the muscle type. Muscles concerned with very fine motor adjustments (like those concerned with the position of the eye) may have as few as 10 muscle fibers to a motor unit, while

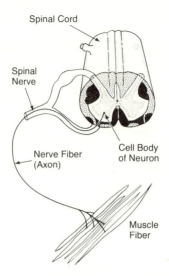

Figure 8.2 *A Single Motor Unit.*

the cruder postural muscles may have up to 3000 muscle fibers connected into a motor unit. A muscle, then, consists of a group of motor units.

Figure 8.2 illustrates the anatomical organization of a simple motor unit. Each motor unit is controlled by a single motoneuron (nervous system cell) located in the spinal cord for the body muscles and in the brain stem for the muscles of the head. An axon then leads from the cell body to a series of muscle fibers.

Muscle contraction results from a large number of motor units acting together. The total amount of muscular contraction is a function of both the number of motor units activated and their frequency of firing. In the normal case, the nerve impulses are staggered, so that fluid motion results from many different motor units acting at different times. In some diseases, the motor units act in near-perfect synchrony, resulting in tremor or twitches as the nerve impulses act.

The surface EMG is a direct measure of the firing of motor units that causes contraction. Since it is recorded from the skin, the picture is a bit more complex than that. Motor units at differing depths may be differentially attenuated. But, as we have shown, the total electrical activity bears a good relation to the amount of muscular force exerted.

If two electrodes are carefully placed over a specific muscle group, the electrical activity will most closely correspond to the contraction of that muscle. Figure 8.3 illustrates the major muscle groups of the body. Probably the most frequently recorded sites from the body are the trapezius (the back of the neck)

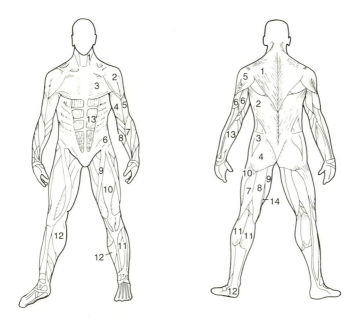

Figure 8.3 *Major Muscle Groups of the Human Body. Front view:* 1. sternocleidomastoid; 2. deltoid; 3. pectoralis major; 4. biceps; 5. triceps; 6. external oblique; 7. brachioradialis; 8. flexor carpi ulnaris; 9. sartorius; 10. quadratus femoris; 11. anterior tibial; 12. gastrocnemius; 13. rectus abdominis. *Back view:* 1. trapezius; 2. latissimus dorsi; 3. gluteus medius; 4. gluteus maximus; 5. deltoid; 6. triceps; 7. biceps femoris; 8. semitendinosus; 9. gracilis; 10. vastus lateralis; 11. gastrocnemius; 12. Achilles' tendon; 13. flexor carpi radialis; 14. semimembranosus.

and the brachioradialis (on the lower arm). As noted earlier, the specific muscle groups chosen for a given study ideally reflect the kinds of activity that one would expect for the specific experimental task. We can then determine empirically just what the pattern of activation in these groups is.

Emotion and Arousal

Recently, psychophysiologists have returned to the study of the facial musculature in emotional states. More than a century ago, Charles Darwin (1872) argued in *The Expression of Emotion in Man and Animals* that facial expression held one of the keys to the puzzle of finding objective indicants of our rich emotional lives. Specifically, he argued that various facial expressions were built into the organism to reflect different feelings. An angry Bantu looks very

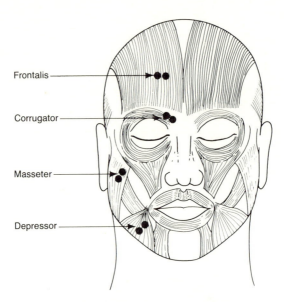

Figure 8.4 *Major Facial Muscles and Recording Sites.* Electrode placement for recording from four major facial muscles. (Courtesy of Gary E. Schwartz.)

much like an angry New Yorker. Many psychological studies of the ability of observers to pair expressions with the underlying feelings followed (Woodworth and Schlosberg, 1954). Summarizing recent research, Ekman (1971) concluded that there was indeed uniformity of facial expression across cultures, at least for the following basic emotions: happiness, sadness, anger, fear, surprise, and disgust.

In the last few years, research at Boston's Erich Lindemann Mental Health Center has begun to relate such expressions to electrical changes in the facial musculature (Schwartz et al., 1976). Figure 8.4 represents these muscle groups as well as the precise electrode placement in these studies.

In the general paradigm for this research, subjects are asked to imagine various sorts of experiences while they sit quietly in a darkened room. Early studies found that subjects who, like the children in *Peter Pan*, were asked to "think happy thoughts" showed increased electrical activity in the depressor muscle, with a corresponding decrease in corrugator activity (compared to a neutral "baseline" period). When the same subjects generated sad imagery, integrated EMG increased in both the frontalis and corrugator muscles. These changes precede any overt change in facial expression and also allow a finer discrimination of expressions than simple observation. That is, preliminary data suggest that the EMG recording is sensitive to very subtle muscular changes that cannot be seen by the naked eye.

In further work with patients suffering from clinical depression, this research group found that the depressed patients were not as good as a normal control group at thinking happy thoughts—at least as judged by their EMG response. Their sad and angry images, on the other hand, were as sad and angry as anybody's. Finally when both groups "imagined a typical day," the EMG of normal subjects resembled their happy patterns, while the depressed patients had a much more depressing pattern of muscular activity.

Approaches like this emphasize the ability of EMG to respond to very subtle changes. Note also the emphasis on patterns of muscular activity in these studies. No single muscle group, by itself, defines a facial expression; rather it is the interplay of many different muscles.

9

The Brain

In a sense, all of psychophysiology is the study of the brain. If a person gives an SCR to an obscene word, it is the brain that classifies the word as obscene and directs the SNS to respond. When a witness's eyeblink rate increases during cross-examination, it is the brain that classifies the situation as stressful and responds accordingly. For every situation, the brain coordinates unique patterns of physiological response. The brain is the master organ; we are our brains.

Now we come to direct recordings of the neutral activity of the brain. As the brain is the most complicated and least understood organ, recordings of its electrical activity are quite complex.

History

Many of our present ideas about brain function can be traced back to Franz Gall, the father of phrenology. At the beginning of the nineteenth century, Gall announced that the brain was made up of twenty-seven separate organs, each of which was responsible for one of the basic faculties of man. He further claimed that, by studying the pattern of bumps on a man's skull, one could see how well each of these organs was developed and thus predict his personality. A man with a bump on his left temple, for example, might be expected to have an overdeveloped sense of acquisitiveness that would be seen in his Scrooge-like dealings with his neighbors. In his own day, Gall was condemned by religion. Today he is condemned by science: Skull shape does not conform to brain shape and his whole classification scheme has been discredited.

But the seed of the idea of brain localization had been planted. Although our current knowledge rejects the idea that each discrete brain area controls a specific behavior, there is no question that we can talk about at least some localization of brain function. Anatomical connections from the eyes, for example, travel a well-defined path from the retina to occipital cortex on the back of the head. Indeed, one of the major thrusts of current research on the brain is the attempt to discover just how localized various sorts of functions are.

In 1875, a British surgeon named Richard Caton first showed that it was possible to record the electrical activity of the brain of a living animal. Caton, like Gall, was interested in demonstrating that different areas of the brain were involved in different activities. Using equipment that was remarkably insensitive by modern standards, Caton was able to show characteristic electrical changes on the surface of the sensory cortex of a rabbit when a light was shone into its eyes. He also noted a regular pattern of background electrical activity when the animal was not being exposed to the light.

It was more than fifty years before similar observations on humans were reported. An Austrian psychiatrist named Hans Berger (1929) discovered that "brain waves" could be recorded from the surface of the human skull. In a series of experiments performed during neurosurgery, Berger was able to show that some of these electrical potentials did originate from the brain and were not simply a reflection of the activity of the scalp musculature. Further, he found that the electrical characteristics of these signals were related to his subject's state of mind. The most prominent waves were relatively large-voltage (approximately 50 microvolts) synchronous waves with a characteristic frequency of about 10 cycles per second. He christened these the "alpha" waves and contrasted them to higher-frequency "beta" waves that appeared as a subject became more alert.

For electrodes, Berger used relatively large pads soaked in saline and attached to the forehead and the back of the skull. He believed that he had discovered a physiological response measure analogous to the electrocardiogram. Just as the EKG provided an index of the overall state of the musculature of the heart, he argued that the *electroencephalogram* (EEG) gave an index of overall activity in the brain.

Later researchers demonstrated that the EEG was qualitatively different from the simpler measures of autonomic nervous system activity that had preceded it. The periodic beating of the heart and associated electrical changes is simplicity itself compared with the awesome complexity of the EEG. Intuitively, we might expect the code of the brain to be infinitely more complex than the contraction of a muscle. The EEG lives up to these expectations and more.

Not only is the specific site of brain activity critical in interpreting the waves but the complexity of the wave-form almost defies researchers to make some sense out of it.

Berger's contemporaries were skeptical of his report, and it was not until Adrian and Matthews performed a dramatic demonstration of EEG recording at the 1935 meetings of England's Physiological Society that the phenomenon was widely accepted. Dr. Adrian himself was connected to a recording machine and showed that the larger alpha rhythms tended to stop when he opened his eyes.

The years that followed were exciting ones for brain-wave researchers. Although they were hampered by the financial limitations of a bleak economic period, they plumbed the depths of the brain with enthusiasm, capitalizing on major advances in amplifier electronics and applying them with tremendous inventiveness. Reports of EEG research from that era were just as likely to include circuit diagrams of equipment as to include sample EEG records.

Berger's preliminary observations of the distinctive EEG correlates of epilepsy were verified by Gibbs, Davis, and Lennox (1935). The same year, Kornmüller demonstrated conclusively that recording from different skull sites yielded different wave-forms. In 1936, Walter showed that brain tumors typically caused abnormally slow waves in the surrounding tissue and that the EEG could be used to help locate them. After an interruption by World War II, EEG research continued to expand. In 1949, the first issue of *Electroencephalography and Clinical Neurophysiology*, an international publication devoted entirely to brain-wave research, was published.

The progress since then has not always been smooth. The possibility of recording brain activity in waking, experiencing people led scientists to new heights of optimism about the potential for understanding mind-body relationships. Some even foresaw a day when we could "read minds" simply by looking at a pattern of brain waves. Countless investigations of EEG correlates of intelligence, personality, and behavior were initiated. The results, for the most part, have been disappointing.

In the first review of EEG literature in the English language, Jasper (1937) prophesied: "Attempts to identify (EEG) characteristics with equally vague psychological processes such as 'attention,' 'consciousness,' 'thought processes,' and various complex attributes of 'personality' serve . . . only to add to the present confusion in psychological terminology." The thousands of studies conducted since that time have validated this gloomy prediction in some ways and set its limits in others.

There are over 10 billion separate nerve cells in a man's brain, woven in a tight latticework of reciprocal interconnections. Even the most precise EEG recordings inevitably detect the chatter of hundreds of thousands of these cells, muted and distorted by the skull. As Margerison, St. John-Loe, and Binnie (1967) put it, "We are like blind men trying to understand the workings of a factory by listening outside its walls."

Overview of EEG Measures

Some of the most exciting current work in physiological psychology involves electrical recording from isolated neurons in the brain. This single-cell recording, as it is called, is an intrusive technique involving the implantation of electrodes into brain tissue and thus is normally limited to lower animals.

The psychophysiologist's commitment to the study of brain function in humans ordinarily means, of necessity, recording from the surface of the scalp. The term EEG is sometimes used to refer to direct cortical recording or even to subcortically implanted electrodes, but we shall reserve it here for surface recordings.

Tomorrow's psychophysiology may be able to record from structures deep inside the brain without resorting to surgery. All electrical currents produce magnetic fields, and the electricity of the nervous system is no exception. Very weak magnetic fields are generated by the brain's complex electrical rhythms. At M.I.T., Cohen (1972) has been doing research on the recording of these weak magnetic fields.

With detectors situated about 5 cm above the scalp, he has been able to record this magnetic activity in a heavily shielded room. This is no mean feat. The actual fields are on the order of 10^{-9} gauss. This is roughly $\frac{1}{100,000}$ of the random magnetic background noise of an urban environment. Thus, magnetoencephalography now demands unusually elaborate and expensive equipment. However, by virtue of eliminating scalp electrodes and their electronic limitations, this method may provide information on the brain's electrical activity that is not accessible to more traditional methods.

Today EEG remains the most promising and least understood of the tools in the psychophysiologist's arsenal. One of its most striking features is its spontaneous, autonomous character. Only in death do the regular electrical oscillations of the brain cease; even deep coma and anesthesia are signaled by characteristic brain wave patterns. Most EEG research has involved the analysis of these spontaneous rhythms.

Near the end of this chapter, we shall turn to more sophisticated techniques: average evoked potentials (AEP) and the contingent negative variation (CNV). Each of these measures involves "averaging" the spontaneous rhythms. The basic principle is that, if a stimulus is repeated a number of times, small-magnitude transient changes in the EEG can be observed by canceling out the background electrical activity.

But let us return now to the analysis of spontaneous rhythms. The simplest kind of approach involves simply looking at the brain-wave record and forming a clinical impression, as discussed later in this chapter. This technique is most useful for the dramatic changes of such pathological states as epilepsy. The study of more subtle changes as a function of psychological states begins with a consideration of the frequency and/or amplitude of brain waves.

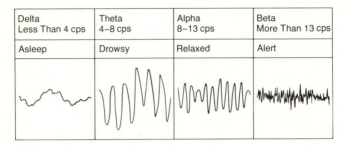

Delta Less Than 4 cps	Theta 4–8 cps	Alpha 8–13 cps	Beta More Than 13 cps
Asleep	Drowsy	Relaxed	Alert

Figure 9.1 *Brain Waves Classified by Frequency.* The behavioral labels for each frequency band represent the very gross distinctions typically discussed in arousal theory.

You will recall that Berger (1929) gave the name "alpha" to relatively large-voltage synchronous waves of roughly 10 Hz that appeared primarily in the occipital regions of the skull when a person was in a state of relaxed wakefulness. He contrasted it with what he called "beta" waves—low-voltage asynchronous waves of higher frequency that appeared to accompany states of relative alertness. As more researchers verified the appearance of these waves, *alpha* came to refer to all EEG activity in the 8-13 Hz band, while *beta* referred to all waves with a dominant frequency greater than 13 Hz. Berger's early observations about the relationship of beta waves to alertness have been generally confirmed, at least on a simplistic level; waves of higher frequency have usually been taken as a sign of greater arousal (Lindsley, 1951).

Two other major frequency bands—theta (4–8 Hz) and delta (less than 4 Hz) have been added to Berger's original dichotomy. Idealized diagrams of these four major categories are presented in Figure 9.1. It should be emphasized that these represent a relatively arbitrary grouping of brain-wave frequencies rather than physiologically distinct categories. Further, their relationship to "mental alertness" is a rather loose one, with many exceptions. Theta, for example, frequently accompanies emotional distress in adults. Finally, these classifications do not apply equally at all ages; the alpha rhythm does not appear until early adolescence.

Nevertheless, these are the major traditional categories of brain-wave frequencies. At any given moment, the average adult may show a brain-wave pattern that is not a simple example of any of these frequency bands. Fourier analyses, described later in this chapter, are frequently employed to determine which frequency bands are dominant.

The other major characteristic of the spontaneous rhythms of the brain is their amplitude—that is, the magnitude of the electrical changes. These are not independent of frequency by any means. The higher-frequency beta waves are typically only one-tenth the magnitude of the slower alpha waves in the same subject.

Typically, frequency and amplitude measurements were combined in the first attempts to consider EEG changes more systematically. For example, one of the most common dependent variables in EEG research is "% time alpha," or percentage of time in alpha. The apparent precision of this term is somewhat deceptive. As we have seen, *alpha* refers simply to waves of 8–13 Hz. But virtually every complex wave-form will include some activity in this band. Therefore, the "presence of alpha" must be defined in terms of some minimal amplitude, defined absolutely or relatively. In the absolute method, some arbitrary cutoff is imposed—for example, any 8–13 Hz wave with an amplitude of 30 microvolts is "alpha present"; by implication, a wave of the same frequency of 29.9 microvolts or less is scored as "alpha absent." The relative method defines the cutoff point individually for each subject. Typically, a person rests for five minutes at the beginning of the experimental session. His mean peak alpha amplitude for this period is determined. This might be 60 microvolts for one subject and 45 microvolts for another. Alpha is said to be present for each subject when his 8–13 Hz activity exceeds some fixed proportion (for example, one-third) of this total. Thus, in our example, Subject 1 would be said to have "alpha present" whenever his 8–13 Hz activity exceeds 20 microvolts; for Subject 2 in the same study, 15 microvolts would be the cutoff point. This technique is a first step in removing individual differences to isolate different responses in a given task. Clearly, it is less appropriate when one is interested in studying difference between subjects. Today's sophisticated EEG researchers usually try to measure several frequency bands at the same time and discuss the overall pattern of electrical activity.

"Alpha blocking" is another of the more popular traditional EEG measures. This refers to a sudden dramatic decrease in alpha amplitude which typically occurs upon stimulus presentation. For example, if a light is shone in a person's eyes, he ordinarily will show alpha blocking in the occipital regions of the skull. As in the case of "% time alpha," the precise definition of a "sudden dramatic decrease" may vary from researcher to researcher. Further, it should be noted that the term is somewhat ambiguous. When alpha is "blocked," the spontaneous brain rhythms do not disappear. Rather 8–13 Hz activity is replaced by higher or lower frequencies.

Thus, while frequency and amplitude analysis of the EEG is a step in the direction of precision, it is far from the final answer. More elaborate (and costly) techniques for EEG data analysis will be discussed after we consider the physiological bases of the EEG.

Physiological Basis

To the present day, the primary thrust in electroencephalography has been an empirical one—comparing the EEGs of different individuals and different psychological states. The vast majority of researchers have been concerned with its physiological bases only in the crudest sense. The research interest that this topic has generated has been concentrated on explaining the synchrony of the alpha rhythm. Since the surface EEG reflects the activity of many hundreds of thousands of cells, such explanations have emphasized mechanisms by which large masses of cells act in concert.

Before turning to these hypotheses, we must note that a few skeptics have asserted that alpha has little or nothing to do with true cortical potentials—that it is an artifact. Kennedy (1959) argued that alpha rhythms were produced by the mechanical pulsation of a gel (here, the brain) which in turn caused differential electrical pulsations. In other words, it is the brain sloshing around in the skull that produces alpha. Recordings of similar rhythms from structures deep inside the brain (Andersen and Andersson, 1968) tend to undercut this theory.

In a similar vein, Lippold and Novotny (1970) have reported a series of elegant experiments which, taken together, argue that occipital alpha is merely a reflection of corneoretinal potential changes (recorded in EOG) caused by tremor of the extraocular muscles. In reply, Shaw, Foley, and Blowers (1970) presented the case of a 27-year-old woman who showed characteristic alpha rhythms that blocked during a mental arithmetic task despite the fact that she had had both eyes removed (because of complications from bilateral glaucoma).

The fact that curarized animals (whose extraocular muscles are paralyzed) are traditionally used in studies of alpha-generating mechanisms and do in fact show such cortical rhythms also argues against eye movements as the sole basis for this phenomenon.

There have been a number of more serious physiological hypotheses concerning the CNS mechanisms that might underlie alpha activity. Lindsley (1956) argued that fluctuations in the excitability of many individual neurons become synchronized. Bard (1961) implicated basic cellular metabolic processes. Eccles (1953) felt that reverberating chains in the cortex are responsible for alpha.

Perhaps the best-documented view is that of Andersen and Andersson (1968). After a thorough review of neurophysiological literature, they concluded:

> Experiments with ablation of the cortex with persisting thalamic rhythmic activity, deafferentation experiments through acute or chronic isolation of the cortex, surface or general cooling and the effects of local injection of different drugs point to thalamic rhythmic activity as the essential generator of the rhythm. This does not mean that the cortex itself has no capacity for rhythmic behavior but that the rhythmic tendency is so much stronger in the thalamus that this structure is normally the pacemaker.

These researchers, it should be noted, suggested that various thalamic areas project to different cortical sites for the generation of alpha. One allied trend in cerebral psychophysiology is a greater concern with the psychological implications of assessing EEG patterns taken at a given recording site.

Cerebral Localization

Berger's (1929) original observations were based on the belief that the EEG reflected the overall activity of the brain. There has been some tendency among psychophysiologists to implicitly accept this view. That is, as long as the electrodes were attached to the skull, their precise location wasn't very important. This in turn implicitly implies an acceptance of the "holistic" view of brain function, as opposed to spotlighting specific localized functions.

When Gall proposed his system of phrenology it was, as Edmund G. Boring (1950) put it in A *History of Experimental Psychology*, "an instance of a theory which, while essentially wrong, was just enough right to further scientific thought." For, in addition to calling attention to the anatomy of the cerebral cortex, Gall revived the idea of localization of function and extended it to complex mental processes.

In the century and a half since, the concept of localization has been in and out of favor several times. The studies of Pierre Flourens in the early nineteenth century favored a more holistic view. On the basis of what now appear to be faulty observations, he concluded that complex mental functions were represented diffusely throughout the brain. This notion of "equipotentiality" held sway over Western medicine until 1861, when Paul Broca presented his observations on brain-damaged patients to the Paris Anthropological Society. He exhibited the postautopsy brains of several stroke victims who had lost the ability to speak and showed that they had a relatively well-defined lesion in the left hemisphere. Similar clinical observations by Wernicke and others revived the concept of localization of function in the brain. At about the same time, experimental demonstrations by Fritsch and Hitzig that electrical stimulation of certain well-defined cortical areas elicited quite specific muscular movements in the dog further supported the localized view.

In 1905, Pierre Marie reexamined the brains presented by Broca and argued that his conclusions, too, were based on faulty evidence—that the brain lesions were far more extensive than Broca had realized. Once more, the holistic view, that the brain acts as an integrated whole, was on the ascent. Karl Lashley's extensive work in the first half of this century on the effects of brain lesions on maze learning in the rat lent support to the holistic position. Lashley's data indicated that the degree of impairment of learning depended on the total amount of cortical tissue destroyed, not on the specific site of damage. He formalized the notion of equipotentiality—any part of cortex, he argued, can take over the function of any other part. However, even Lashley gradually came to accept some subdivision of cortical labor.

The question today is not whether there is localization of function in the human brain but, rather, how much. Among the most influential of current researchers is the Russian neurophysiologist, A. R. Luria. Luria (1973) has proposed that the brain is organized into functional units that coordinate com-

plex mental activity. There may be considerable plasticity within the organiza-
tional levels of each unit, but the units themselves are tied to specific cortical
areas. Others continue to argue for more localization or less.

Everything about human behavior tells us that the brain is not a formless
mass of cells; it must be coherently organized to permit the complex range of
human activities. At this point, we are just beginning to understand the language of the brain. Perhaps, for example, cerebral specialization is not a simple
matter of anatomically localized cells but has to do, rather, with patterns of
neural firing (John, 1972; Bartlett and John, 1973). In another hundred years
our present views of localization of function will surely seem as crude as Gall's
phrenological maps do today.

It is here that EEG studies have a unique contribution to make. For, crude
as the record of underlying physiological activity now is, it reflects the function
of the normal human brain. Virtually all of our current ideas about localization
of function are based on studies of lower animals or brain-damaged patients.
(For excellent introductions to this research, see Gardner, 1974; Rose, 1976.)
Studies of localized EEG function can supplement and extend this data.

Anatomically, the cortex is usually divided into four major sections, or lobes,
as illustrated in Figure 9.2. At the very least, it is clear that stimulation in different sensory modalities is differentially represented in the lobes of the brain.

Occipital cortex is concerned with the processing of visual stimuli. This has
been the most popular recording site for psychophysiologists because alpha of
the largest amplitude is typically found in occipital cortex. Temporal cortex is

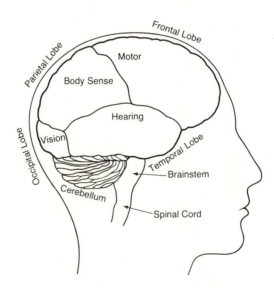

Figure 9.2 *The Lobes of the Brain.*

more concerned with the auditory system. Thus, if one is interested in EEG reactions to a series of tones, temporal recording is probably more appropriate than occipital. Somatosensory cortex is a small area around the central sulcus, an indentation that separates the frontal and parietal lobes. It is here that the sensory information from our touch senses is received and motor commands to the body are sent out.

The left and right sides of the brain are also somewhat different. Although there is much redundancy in the two halves of the brain, in general the human nervous system is based on a contralateral design: the left hemisphere of the brain controls the right side of the body and the right hemisphere controls the left side of the body. Thus, one would expect that, if the right fist were clenched, EEG changes would be most noticeable in the left hemisphere and vice versa. This is in fact the case. Finally, there also appear to be more psychological differences between left- and right-hemisphere function. In right-handed people, for example, linguistic functions seem to be located in the left hemisphere, as Broca originally suggested. We shall return to these facts in a later discussion of recent research on hemispheric asymmetry.

There is considerable evidence that EEG changes on the scalp reflect the activity of underlying areas. Gastaut (1952), for example, discussed what is now called the sensory-motor rhythm over somatosensory cortex. This rhythm is similar in form to occipital alpha. However, the somatosensory rhythm is blocked when a person moves his limbs, while occipital alpha is more responsive to visual attention.

Thus, although we do not know the precise source of EEG rhythms on the cellular level, we do know that the rhythms recorded from different spots on the skull will be differentially responsive, depending on the recording conditions. Studies of EEG localization offer hope for helping us to understand just how the brain is organized. Knowledge of the nature of this biological division of labor will, in turn, help psychologists develop biologically meaningful behavior categories.

Electrode Placement

We know that simultaneous recordings from different skull sites can be quite different. When we place that simple fact against the backdrop of the localization controversy, we can see that it is especially important to understand the fundamentals of electrode placement in electroencephalography.

As in all psychophysiological recordings, two electrodes must be placed on the body to form a complete circuit. In the case of EEG, there are two major possibilities. In *bipolar* recording, both electrodes are placed on the scalp. Each of these electrodes will then be detecting the electrical activity of the brain and the resulting EEG will reflect the potential difference between these two conflicting electrical signals. Monopolar recording involves placing one electrode on the scalp and the second on an "electrically neutral" site—most frequently, one or both of the earlobes. At first sight, monopolar recording seems preferable; one would assume that only one site of brain activity is recorded. However, there is reason to believe that bipolar recordings provide more localized information (Lindsley and Wicke, 1974). At the present time, the relative virtues of monopolar and bipolar recording are still a matter of debate.

Nevertheless, a precise system for specifying electrode location has been largely agreed upon. In early EEG research, the placement of electrodes was often summarized simply with reference to the underlying lobe of the brain—for example, right occipital. To avoid confusion between laboratories, the International Federation of Societies for Electroencephalography and Clinical Neurophysiology adopted the "10–20 system" for specifying electrode placement. Figure 9.3 is a diagram of electrode placement under this system.

Use of this system is based on precise measurement, for each subject, of the distance from the nasion (depression at the bridge of the nose) to the inion (a hard bone on the back of the head) and from the left to right auricular depressions (slight valleys just in front and above the lobes of the ears). Electrodes are then placed either 10% or 20% of these distances along the skull. Further diagrams and explanations of the 10–20 system appear in Appendix F. But several points must be made here so that we can refer to electrode placement in various studies.

Note that the letters preceding each number refer to underlying brain areas: O for occipital, P for parietal, F for frontal, T for temporal, and C for the central fissure. Odd numbers are assigned to left hemisphere sites and even

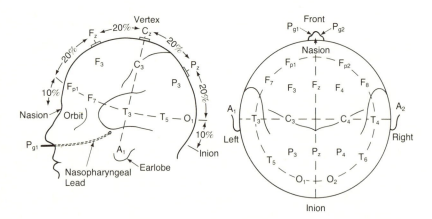

Figure 9.3 *The Ten-Twenty System.* Electrode placements on the surface of the scalp. F = frontal, C = central, P = parietal, T = temporal, O = occipital. Odd subscripts, left side of head; even subscripts, right side of head; Z, midline. (After Jasper, 1958.)

numbers to the right hemisphere. The letter Z refers to sites directly on the top on the head—on a straight line from the nasion to the inion. Thus, C_z refers to the spot precisely in the middle of the top of the head. This common recording site is also called the vertex. Use of this system reminds us that we are not recording, as Berger thought, the "EKG of the head." Rather, different brain areas respond differentially.

EEG Analysis

More than half a mile of polygraph paper may be covered with the brain's complex squiggles in the record of a single night's sleep. How can we reduce this mountain of data to manageable proportions?

We have already briefly discussed the basic rhythms of the EEG (delta, theta, alpha, beta) and principles of frequency and amplitude analysis. Now let us backtrack a little to consider clinical EEG interpretation.

Figure 9.4 illustrates a variety of normal and pathological EEGs. In a clinical setting, probably the most important application of EEG is as a diagnostic aid for petit mal epilepsy. This condition may be difficult to assess behaviorally, as its symptoms—momentary losses of concentration, slurring of speech, and so on—may be relatively minor. The EEG can be particularly helpful in these cases in evaluating the effectiveness of various antiseizure medications for a given individual.

The clinical recording of EEG typically involves a fairly standard set of electrode sites and behavioral tasks, including hyperventilation and photic driving, in which seizure activity is artificially induced by flashing a rhythmic light in the patient's eyes. Given the dramatic brain wave changes associated with epilepsy, clinical electroencephalographers have not always felt the need for precise standards of normality and abnormality.

For some researchers, then, reading an EEG became more of an art than a science. Encouraged by the dramatic success of the EEG in pinpointing brain malfunction in epileptics, these researchers sought to discover the physiological problems of those with psychological wounds. Their lack of physiological precision was compounded by a lack of behavioral precision, as studies were launched on EEG correlates of psychosis, alcoholism, criminality, and so on. But alcoholism, criminality, and psychosis were defined differently in different studies. And the physiological correlates were often a simple idiosyncratic estimate of "abnormality." It comes as no great surprise, then, that hundreds of such experiments have led to no real consensus on the question of "mental abnormality" and the "raw" EEG.

Consequently, many researchers felt the need for a more precise approach than simply looking at the EEG record. Many techniques have been proposed and more are continually being discovered. Shagass (1972) provides a brief

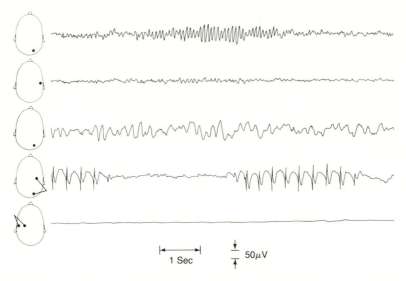

Figure 9.4 *Typical Electroencephalograms.* (The small "heads" to the left of each record show electrode placement.) The first two records were simultaneously recorded from a normal adult at rest. Note the large magnitude alpha waves that appear only in the occipital (upper) recording. The third channel illustrates an occipital recording from a normal child. Alpha is not present in young children. The next record shows the dramatic spiking associated with a petit mal epileptic seizure. The last line shows the electrically quiet record of "cerebral death" (although this patient's heart was still beating, he was clinically dead). (Based on Gary Vander Ark and Ludwig Kempe, A *Primer of Electroencephalography.* Roche Laboratories, Division of Hoffman–La Roche, Inc., 1970.)

introduction to several of the more popular systems. Our purpose here will merely be to provide an overview of possible approaches. Broadly, we must first distinguish between single-site and multiple-site approaches.

For the single-site approach, we are interested in separately considering the records for different brain areas. (This may be based on monopolar or bipolar recording techniques.) The critical distinction is that we wish to consider only one channel of information at a time. In the more complicated case of multiple-site analysis, we are concerned with phasic relations between two or more brain areas, so simultaneous recording of several EEG channels is a prerequisite.

Again, the simplest form of a single-site analysis is the clinical method of visual inspection of the record for salient features. A greater degree of precision is possible if we analyze the total activity in different frequency bands. Thus, we may filter the EEG so that only 8–13 Hz activity (alpha) appears on a second polygraph channel. As discussed above, we can then define some minimal amplitude as representing "true alpha" and electronically or manually record the percentage of total time that alpha (or any other wave band) exceeds this amplitude.

More precise methods attempt to consider the amplitude of activity across a wide spectrum of frequency bands. Such methods typically rely on the mathematical principles of the Fourier series. Almost 200 years ago, Fourier demonstrated that any complex wave-form is mathematically identical to the sum of a series of sine waves of varying amplitude and frequency.

The highly complex wave-forms of the EEG can be reduced, then, by a Fourier transformation to a series of sine waves of different frequencies and amplitudes. A power spectrum analysis provides a "picture" of the relative power (which depends on the amplitude of the component sine waves) at various frequencies. The actual mathematics of this process is rather complex and requires the use of high-speed digital computers. The critical point for our purposes is that a power spectrum analysis gives a far more complete description of the EEG than a simple measure of percentage of time of activity in any given frequency band. In effect, it is an overall summary of activity across a wide range of frequency bands.

Research by Lykken, Tellegen, and Thorkelson (1974) on the genetics of resting EEG provides a nice illustration of this technique. In this study, the EEG power spectra of monozygotic (identical) and dizygotic (fraternal) twins were compared. (The assumption in this, as in most other studies of human behavioral genetics, is as follows: If genetically identical twins are more similar on a given trait than genetically different twins, the trait is believed to be heritable.) As part of a larger study on hypnotic susceptibility, the twins were asked to close their eyes for three-minute periods at the beginning and end of a one-hour experimental session. As you can see in Figure 9.5, the similarities between monozygotic twins were quite striking. Indeed, these twins were almost exactly as consistent with each other as they were with themselves (that is, pre- and post-tests compared). This illustration also shows that the dizygotic twins were not at all consistent. All told, the heritability of six different EEG parameters averaged to 0.82. (In this same study, the heritability of resting HR was found to be 0.67).

But let us return to our survey of techniques of analysis. The use of computers also makes possible several other approaches analysing relative activity in different frequency bands. The most frequently used of these are period analysis (or the "zero cross method") and autocorrelation techniques. But, at least for the present, the most popular techniques in EEG research are filtering for different frequencies and power spectrum analyses.

Multiple-site analysis involves several levels of complexity beyond the measures described above. This is encouraging; we know that the chatter of several billion nerve cells acting to coordinate our mental lives is a complex matter requiring a complex approach. If the EEG consisted of a series of straight lines,

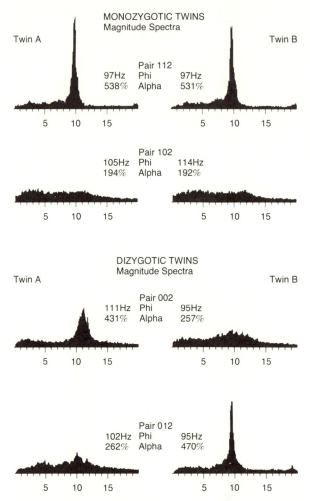

Figure 9.5 *EEG Power Spectra of Monozygotic and Dizygotic Twins at Rest.* Note that monozygotic twins have
very similar records; dizygotic twins do not. This suggests
that resting EEG parameters are heavily influenced by
heredity. Phi is the median frequency within the "alpha
bump"; alpha is defined here as the total proportion of the
power within a 3Hz band centered on phi. (After D. Lykken
et al., 1974.)

it might be much easier to "understand," but it would not promise to open the
doors of our mental life.

    Among the most promising multiple-site methods are those developed by the
Russian workers Livanov, Gavrilova, and Aslanov (1966). Recording from up to

fifty electrodes simultaneously, they calculated 1225 correlation coefficients (between all possible pairs of electrodes) to determine which brain areas seem to act in concert—that is, the precise areas in which the EEG was relatively synchronous. Among their key findings: In normal individuals at rest, most brain areas are not synchronized. However, during solution of a mental arithmetic problem, many different cortical areas become synchronous, particularly in the frontal cortex.

The technical demands of recording fifty simultaneous channels of EEG and analyzing all the possible interrelationships are truly formidable. But it is likely that many advances in understanding the convoluted functions of the human brain will require just this kind of daring and willingness to embrace complexity rather than be intimidated by it.

Sleep

For the normal individual, only the cyclical changes of sleep have freely whispered their secrets to the electroencephalographer. About one-third of our lives (or twenty-three full years if we live to age 69) is spent in sleep. And yet it was only with advances in the EEG (and eye movements, as discussed in Chapter 7) that this vast chunk of human existence began to receive serious scientific attention.

Our previous discussion of REM sleep and dreaming has already suggested that there are different kinds of sleep. While the casual observer may see nothing more than an inert body for eight hours or so, the electroencephalographer can plot our nightly progression through relatively distinct sleep stages. As early as 1862, Kohlschutter demonstrated that the loudness of a sound required to wake the sleeper varies systematically over the course of the night. But the discovery of four sleep stages awaited the age of electroencephalography.

Figure 9.6 illustrates typical EEG recordings from the occipital lobe for the four stages of sleep as outlined by Dement and Kleitman (1957).

A person falling asleep characteristically moves progressively through these stages. Any disturbance, such as a sudden noise, tends to reverse the process by bringing the sleeper back to an earlier stage. Over the course of the night's rest, one moves back and forth between these stages, periodically emerging into the REM sleep of dreams, whose EEG is very similar to Stage 1. Each individual seems to have a characteristic pattern of movement through the stages.

There is some evidence that these different stages may be functionally different. Luce and Segal (1966) suggest, for example, that Stage 4 sleep, which typically is most common in the first few hours of sleep, serves the function of physical restoration. If you spent the day loading trucks, you are likely to spend a greater proportion of your sleep time in Stage 4 than if you spent all day reading A *Primer of Psychophysiology*. The research for precise behavioral dif-

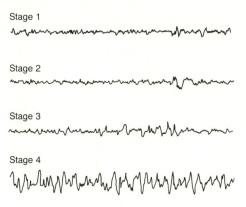

Figure 9.6 *EEG Stages of Sleep.* In Stage 1, seen first as a person lapses from wakefulness, alpha activity is gradually replaced by low-voltage changes in potential. Sleep spindles, which are irregular bursts of 12–14Hz activity, first appear in Stage 2 sleep. These spindles then continue along with large random delta potentials as high as 300 microvolts during Stage 3. Finally, in Stage 4 sleep, these large delta waves come to dominate the EEG.

ferences between these physiologically distinct sleep periods continues to occupy researchers in the field (Snyder and Scott, 1972).

EEG changes have also been detected in sleep-deprived subjects. After studying all night before a final exam, you are likely to find yourself suffering from occasional lapses of attention, or "microsleeps." For the few seconds that you blank out, the EEG also seems to be that of a sleeping man (Liberson, 1945). In this sense, the EEG appears to give an index of a person's "mental activation."

It was the clear-cut transition of EEG stages throughout sleep that led in the early 1950's to a resurgence of interest in "arousal theories" of human behavior (for example, Lindsley, 1951). However, throughout our consideration of human physiology, we have continually emphasized the importance of understanding each of the biological systems of the body on its own terms. Arousal is too simple a concept.

Hemispheric Asymmetry

In Chapter 7, we discussed biological differences between the two cerebral hemispheres and how lateral eye movements (LEMs) could be used as an index of differential employment of the two sides of the brain. We found evidence there that (for right-handed people) the left hemisphere of the brain was indeed more "active" during verbal tasks, while the right hemisphere had greater involvement in spatial tasks. As a dependent measure of hemispheric involvement, LEMs have the virtues of simplicity but the disadvantage of a rather tenuous physiological rationale for inferring brain use. Clearly, the use of EEG recordings of the two hemispheres during similar tasks would give us greater confidence than the LEM results.

And so a number of studies of hemispheric asymmetry in the EEG have been undertaken. Typically, they use the rather simple measure of the relative amplitude of alpha over each of the hemispheres (ordinarily computed as a ratio). The presumption is that as a person activates part of his brain, the amplitude of alpha should *decrease*. And a growing number of studies have found exactly that relation.

In a partial replication of some earlier work (Galin and Ornstein, 1972) Doyle, Ornstein and Galin (1974) compared parietal and temporal recordings from the two hemispheres in a variety of tasks. Their results were quite consistent with the LEM studies. Imagining writing a letter, a verbal task, suppressed alpha over the left hemisphere, while memorizing a geometrical design, a spatial task, yielded right-hemisphere alpha suppression. In this study, the integrated power of activity in all major frequency bands was carefully analyzed. And the hemispheric differences appeared almost entirely in alpha, supporting its use in other studies.

Measuring occipital alpha, Morgan, MacDonald, and Hilgard (1974) found left-hemisphere suppression when their subjects thought of words beginning in *t* and ending in *s*, and right-hemisphere alpha suppression when the same subjects pictured an elephant in a swing. Dumas and Morgan (1975) found right-hemisphere activation in a facial memory task, while the left hemisphere was used while listening intently to boring passages from the *Congressional Record*. In this study, various degrees of difficulty of the tasks were found to have no effect on the asymmetry. Further, there were no differences in the relative responses of artists (who might ordinarily rely more on right-hemisphere processing) and engineers (characteristically left-hemisphere users). Just as in the LEM data, task differences produce major asymmetry effects, while differences between individuals are, at best, minimal.

Reasoning that music is also tied up with the right hemisphere, Schwartz et al. (1974) compared alpha suppression while subjects whistled, sang, and recited the lyrics of the same song. Consistent with their predictions, the verbal task of reciting the lyrics led to the greatest relative left-hemisphere alpha blocking, whistling blocked right-hemisphere alpha, and singing (which combines the verbal and musical aspects) produced an intermediate pattern.

Thus there is a considerable body of evidence that even a relatively crude measure of alpha amplitude is sensitive to differential activation of the hemispheres of the brain.

Averaged Evoked Potentials

Thus far, we have limited our discussion to the spontaneous EEG, that is, the regular electrical fluctuations of the brain. As we mentioned earlier, it is also possible to observe more subtle responses to well-defined events. The basic principle of the averaged evoked potential (AEP) is that averaging enhances any activity with a fixed relation to some event. If we were to add 200 random EEG samples, we should come up with a straight line. But if we add 200 EEG samples, each of which was taken after a light flashed, we should be able to see the small reactions to the light stimulus. From this point of view, the normal rhythmic fluctuations of the EEG are "noise" obscuring our signal—a subtle, small-amplitude response to the light flash.

An application of this principle can be seen in Figure 9.7. Here, an electric shock was repeatedly applied to a nerve on the right wrist. The recording was monopolar P3 (the left parietal cortex). The left column displays several responses to a single shock. In each case, the neural response to shock is obscured by extraneous electrical activity. But, as increasing numbers of responses to the shock are averaged, an identifiable pattern of response emerges.

Note that the time frame represented in this illustration is only 100 msec or one-tenth of a second. The total amount of time considered for most AEPs is

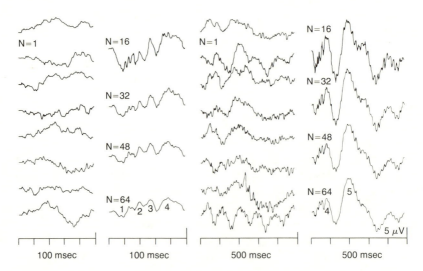

Figure 9.7 *Averaged Evoked Potentials with Varying Numbers of Stimulus Repetitions.* The first and third columns represent EEG responses to a single stimulus; the second and fourth columns represent AEPs after 16, 32, and 64 repetitions. Stimulus is right median nerve shock. Recorded from P3 (referenced to linked ears A1-A2). Positivity upward at scalp electrode. (After Goff, 1974.)

between 500 msec and 1 second. Note also that the concept of averaging neces-sarily implies a situation in which a response is repeated, time after time.

In Dawson's (1947) original study, the averaging was cleverly done by multiple-exposure photographs. The EEG response to stimuli was displayed on a cathode ray oscilloscope. Each response was individually photographed. When all the images from a series of stimuli were superimposed, the thickest lines in the summary picture represented the averaged response.

Since these classic observations, a number of more sophisticated techniques have been developed for recording the AEP. Signal averagers are specialized digital computers that automatically average the responses to a series of stimuli.

Several different terms are used to refer to the AEP. The most common is *averaged evoked response,* or AER. Both of these terms refer to exactly the same phenomenon. AEPs may also be named according to the sensory modality stimulated. Thus VER (or VEP) stands for a *visual evoked response,* typically to a series of light flashes. SER (or SEP) is the abbreviation for *somatosensory evoked response,* recorded after a series of electric shocks. Similarly, AER (or AEP) may stand for the *auditory evoked response* to any auditory stimulus. The abbreviation ERP also sometimes appears for *event related potential.* Or you may see CER for *cortical evoked response.* Again, all of these terms refer to the averaged electroencephalographic response to repeated stimulation.

The characteristics of any given AEP depend on the sensory modality stimu-lated, the physical characteristics of the stimulus, its context and significance, the area of the brain it is recorded from, and even the individual brain itself. Different components of the AEP are systematically affected differently by each of these sets of variables and their interactions. For example, Figure 9.8 illus-trates typical AEPs to a shock stimulus (labeled SER), an auditory stimulus (AER), and a visual stimulus (VER). The little 10–20 diagrams to the right of each AEP illustrate the magnitude of the various peaks as a function of elec-trode location. For the auditory AEP, for example, peak P3 is largest when recorded from C_z (the vertex). If the response to the same stimulus is recorded from parietal cortex, other central sulcus sites, or the posterior frontal cortex, the P3 wave will be only about one-half as big. In other cortical sites it will be reduced still further. This can be contrasted to the P3 peak to a visual stimulus, which is largest in the occipital area.

At first glance, this finding may appear to be inconsistent with our previous formulation of localization of cortical function. Although visual cortex is in-deed occipital, we would expect to find the greatest reaction to auditory stimuli in auditory, or temporal, cortex. However, P3 occurs approximately 160 msec after stimulus presentation, and evidence from other AEP studies has indicated that by this time the stimulus has already been detected by auditory cortex and is now "passed" to other brain areas for further analysis.

AEP analysis focuses on the various peaks in each response. Their latency, amplitude and slope may be considered. As suggested above, each peak is typi-

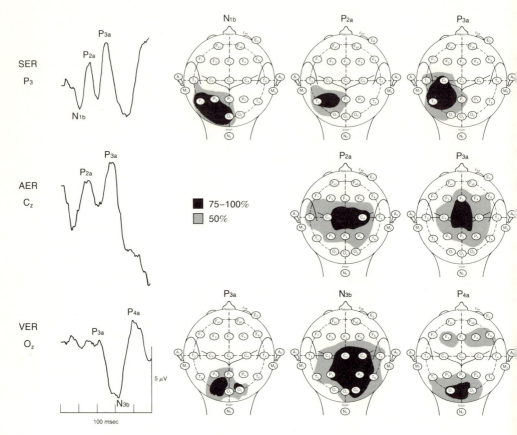

Figure 9.8 *Localization of AEP Peaks.* (See text for details.) (After Goff, 1974.)

cally "named." Although this may be as simple as numbering them 1, 2, 3, 4, more commonly they are separated into positive going waves (P) and negative going waves (N). Thus, above, P3 refers to the third positive going peak. In monopolar recordings, negativity usually, but not always, appears as an upward deflection, as in most psychophysiological recording. For bipolar recordings, one must specify the electrode that serves as a reference point (that is, negativity at which site).

Still another way of naming peaks is by referring to the approximate number of milliseconds that elapse between the stimulus presentation and the time when the peak typically appears. Thus the P300 wave, discussed below, is a positive going peak that appears approximately 300 msec after stimulus presentation. Since there is no firm criterion for deciding how great a deflection constitutes a "peak" (so P4 to one researcher might be P3 to another), this system, by specifying the time frame, has certain advantages for effective communication, and we

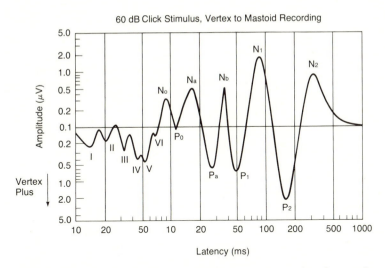

Figure 9.9 *Idealized Auditory Evoked Potential.* Mean data from eight subjects for identification of peaks. Note the logarithmic transformation of time scale, which makes the AEP shape seem somewhat unusual. (After Picton and Hillyard, 1974.)

will use it where possible. But, in reading AEP literature, one must be aware that the lack of standardization in reporting conventions requires that all the fine print be read before one tries to compare AEPs from two different laboratories.

Let us consider these temporal relations in more detail. Figure 9.9 represents a "typical" auditory AEP. (Note that the time scale is distorted to emphasize the early response components. Clearly a normal linear time scale would deemphasize the early peaks.) Picton and Hillyard (1974) and Picton et al. (1974) have clearly specified the neurological meaning of components of the auditory AEP. The first 8 msec of the response reflects the activity of the auditory and cochlear nuclei in the brainstem. From 9 to 50 or 60 msec, the reaction of auditory cortex is registered. It is also at this time that scalp muscle artifacts are most likely to appear. Thus, these first 60 msec or so of the AEP represent the brain simply "hearing" the stimulus. These early components of the AEP remain fairly constant, regardless of changes in the subject's state of consciousness or attention to the stimulus.

Later AEP components then reflect differences of a more psychological nature. For auditory stimuli, the later components are most prominent over frontal cortex, where some information processing occurs. For example, one may be asked to listen to a series of tones and classify them into two groups—the normal loud tones and occasional weaker ones. If one is required to attend to the faint tones by counting them, N90 (also called N1) and P170 (P2) will be enhanced for the faint tones. This is true despite the fact that early components of the AEPs in response to normal and quiet tones will be identical. Thus the later components are reflecting the brain's attempt to "pay attention."

Still later response components may reflect increasingly complex levels of psychological processing. For example, a subject may be asked to concentrate on listening to a series of tones spaced at regular intervals. Occasionally, a tone will be omitted from the series. When AEPs are computed for the omitted stimuli (that is, averaged from the point where the stimulus should have occurred), the brain's surprise is registered by an increased amplitude of a P450 wave.

The studies upon which these conclusions were based represent an infinitesimal fraction of the research presently being conducted on the AEP. Taken together, they are giving us the first clues in our understanding of how the brain makes sense of the world around us. Let us briefly consider three more recent studies that suggest the possibilities of the AEP measure.

The first, by Hillyard et al. (1973), further refines our understanding of timing in the auditory AEP. This study was directed at one of the fundamental problems in attention, what some psychologists have termed the "cocktail party phenomenon." This refers to our ability to attend to a single auditory message in a noisy environment. Although you may be surrounded by tipsy colleagues raucously recounting their favorite anecdotes, you can filter out the background noise and carry on a reasonably sensible conversation with a soft-spoken friend.

For an experimental analog of this auditory confusion, Hillyard put stereo headphones on his subjects and played tapes of two different sets of sounds to the right and left ears. Again, the subject's task was to pick out and count the tones that were different (here, in pitch) in a long series of such tones. Sometimes they had to concentrate on the tones presented to the left ear and sometimes on the different set coming to the right ear. The experimenters then separately averaged AEPs to the tones according to (a) which ear they were presented to and (b) whether they were "relevant," that is, differing in pitch.

Recording from C_z, they found that the N90 (or N1) peak was larger to all right-ear tones when one's task was to concentrate on the right ear and to all left-ear tones when the subject had to listen to the left. That is, this peak represented the brain's first level of filtering—deciding which stimuli were worth listening to. Later in the AEP, the P300 (or P3) wave differentiated the relevant from irrelevant tones within that ear. This represented a higher level of perceptual processing, where the brain decided whether a given tone was "normal" or not.

A criticism of some of the studies we have discussed here is that, whenever stimuli were differentially attended to, they also differed in certain physical characteristics (as above, the volume or pitch of the tones). To demonstrate that physically identical stimuli can yield different AEPs in the same subject, depending on their context, Johnston and Chesney (1974) presented the following stimulus array in a study of the visual AEP:

17
P B E
12

Note that the middle ambiguous stimulus is likely to be perceived as 13 in the context of a series of numbers, or as a B in the context of similarly written letters. Each subject was exposed to repeated presentations of this ambiguous stimulus in the two different contexts. AEPs were recorded from both frontal and occipital regions. While the occipital recordings were the same regardless of context, frontal AEPs depended on the context in which the stimulus was presented. As might be expected, these differences were found in relatively late portions of the AEP (beyond 160 msec). This study clearly demonstrates that AEPs, from the frontal cortex, respond to "meaning."

Finally, on a more methodological note, Rust (1975) demonstrated that genetic factors influence the AEP, just as Lykken, Tellegen, and Thorkelson (1974) showed the importance of genetic factors for the spontaneous EEG. The amplitude of various peaks was more similar for identical twins than fraternal twins, although the latency of responses did not seem to depend on genetic factors.

For many psychophysiologists, the AEP represents the most promising technique now available to us, reflecting as it does the brain processes underlying normal human behavior. Now let us consider another new event-related potential that averaging techniques have opened up to us.

Contingent Negative Variation

The CNV is a special kind of event-related potential that was discovered quite by accident by Walter et al. (1964). This group was studying the more traditional AEPs (as discussed above) in a reaction-time task: In their experiment, a light flash was followed at some fixed interval by a tone that signaled the subject to press a key. They had planned to look at the separate AEPs to each of the stimuli. At the same time, they were experimenting with the effects of different kinds of filtering on the AEP wave-form. As we discussed earlier, the EEG is normally recorded within a relatively narrow frequency band (see Appendix F)—shifts in potential of less than 1 Hz are almost always filtered out of the EEG record. Walter and his colleagues were allowing these very slow frequency drifts of potential to appear on the record when they noticed that a very slow increase in negativity at the vertex (C_z) appeared just before the button press.

They quickly shifted the focus of their research to this previously undetected negative wave. They soon found that, like the AEP, the components of the wave-form could be more clearly distinguished if the cortical response to several stimuli was averaged. Figure 9.10 illustrates individual responses to a series of stimuli and their average. [This may be slightly misleading, in that only about one out of every three normal subjects shows such dramatic changes in the raw record (Cohen, 1974). However, with the aid of averaging, the CNV is found in all normal subjects under these circumstances.] The Walter group soon found that the magnitude of this change was lawfully related to the speed with

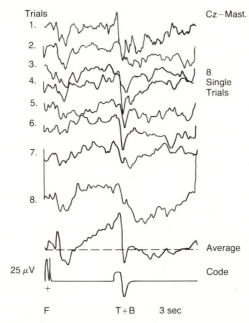

Figure 9.10 *Typical* CNV. The first eight tracings show individual EEG responses for each trial; the average CNV is then presented. The code at the bottom includes a calibration signal to the extreme left; F = light flash, T = tone, B = button press. (After J. Cohen, 1974.)

which the subject pressed the button—large-amplitude CNVs being found with the quicker reaction times. Walter et al. (1964) christened the CNV the "expectancy wave," since it appeared to be associated with the subject's anticipation of his button press.

The basic characteristics of the CNV were confirmed and extended in many subsequent studies. The basic paradigm of this research closely follows the above paradigm: An alerting stimulus (S_1) is followed after some fixed time period (usually a second or two) by an imperative stimulus (S_2) to which the subject must respond. Cohen (1969) demonstrated that this response need not be an overt motor action; he had his subjects think the word *how* to themselves when S_2 was presented. However, some specific response to S_2 is required.

The average amplitude of the CNV is about 20 μV, with a range of 10–50 μV. Given the small size of the response and its very slow frequency characteristics, very special precautions must be taken to avoid artifacts. (See Appendix F.) The greatest amplitude is usually observed by recording monopolar C_z, although its distribution over the scalp tends to vary from one subject to another (Cohen, 1974).

Factors that have been found to increase CNV amplitude include encouraging a subject to concentrate and telling him that he is "doing well." Embarrassment, worry, bad news, and other distractions tend to decrease CNV amplitude (Cohen, 1974). The actual psychological categories of events that elicit the CNV have been characterized as "expectancy," "conation," "motivation," and "attention" by various researchers. The words of Walter (1969) are particularly relevant in this context: "When you are dealing with a complex problem or a system which is open to a number of interpretations, people are nearly always right in what they assert and wrong in what they deny."

There are a number of recent research reports that suggest that the CNV may be useful for psychiatric diagnosis. Injuries to either cerebral hemisphere, for example, tend to decrease CNV amplitude, particularly on the side of the lesion. Even more encouraging is the finding that recovery of function from such injuries tends to be related to recovery of CNV amplitude (Cohen, 1974).

Deficits that are less clearly neurological are also associated with CNV variation. Antisocial psychopaths, for example, consistently have rather small CNVs. Obsessive and compulsive patients tend to maintain negativity even after an overt response is made (Cohen, 1974).

While the CNV is normally defined rather narrowly as the vertex negativity shift seen during the foreperiod of a reaction-time task, McAdam (1974) argues that it is in fact a special case of the "readiness potential" found by Kornhuber and Deecke (1965) to precede any voluntary act. For example, if a subject taps his fingers repeatedly, the averaged EEG preceding this response shows a very similar negativity shift. (EMG is ordinarily recorded to define the beginning of the voluntary movement.) These readiness potentials make their first appearance about one and a half seconds before the beginning of the movement, and show maximal amplitude over the cortical area involved. Thus, when the right finger is tapped, the largest negative shift appears over left motor cortex. Similarly, McAdam and Whitaker (1971) found the maximal readiness potential preceding the pronunciation of words over Broca's area (the cortical section—in the left interior frontal area of most right-handed people—associated with speech production).

It is clear that all of these recently discovered event-related potentials will figure in future attempts to unravel the mystery of the brain.

10

Applied Psychophysiology

We have now seen how each of the body's major systems functions, how it is currently measured, and what relevance it has to psychology. This basic knowledge may be expected to have a growing impact on some very immediate problems in the world beyond the confines of the academic ghetto. The puzzling problems of mental abnormality, for example, are just beginning to surrender their secrets to the psychophysiologist's tentative probes.

Here we shall discuss in detail two of the most important current applications of psychophysiological knowledge and methodology. Lie detection is one of psychophysiology's oldest applications; biofeedback is one of the newest. They represent quite different kinds of approaches.

The field of commercial polygraphy (a name that its professionals prefer to the more value-laden "lie detection") has grown up almost in spite of psychophysiological research rather than because of it. Commercial polygraphers and academics publish in different journals and go to different conventions. Their relationship is one of distrust founded on ignorance.

The academic is likely to complain that lie detection in the field relies on crude instruments and unproven methods to make life-or-death judgments. The polygrapher counters that his critics live in ivory towers and that lie detection serves a valuable social function in helping to bring criminals to justice.

The field of biofeedback (training people to control their physiological processes), on the other hand, grew directly out of what at first seemed rather esoteric academic controversies in learning theory. After researchers had demonstrated under very tightly controlled conditions that animals could regulate function in the autonomic nervous system, others saw the clinical implications. The enthusiasm of the applied biofeedback researchers often outstripped their concern for careful scientific controls. Nonetheless, the field remained firmly grounded in findings from the laboratories of experimental psychologists.

Lie Detection

Contrary to its public image, the major commercial application of polygraphy is not in criminal interrogation but in screening employees for businesses. In 1972, roughly 25% of all US firms asked at least some of their present and prospective employees to submit to lie-detector tests. A total of about 400,000 such tests were performed in that same year (*Time*, March 19, 1973). A more recent estimate (Lykken, 1974), puts the total number of annual polygraph examinations at "several million." The purpose of these tests may be as specific as finding out who has his hand in the till in a local hamburger stand or as general as seeing whether a prospective employee has an unsavory background.

The legal status of lie detection is presently in a state of flux. A review of state legislation as of 1971 (Romig, 1971) found that twelve states limit the use of lie-detection as a precondition of employment, although ten of these make exceptions for law-enforcement positions. Seventeen states, mostly in the South and including none of the above twelve, require a polygraph operator to be licensed. In the other thirty-three states, you can become a professional polygrapher merely by laying out a thousand dollars for the machine and putting your name in the yellow pages.

The professional associations of polygraphers favor national standards for certification. Still, there are no figures available on the backgrounds of the nation's 3000 or so current professionals.

Research scientists tend to be rather skeptical of the claims of these professionals. Like all good businessmen, the polygraph experts tend to advertise their successes and forget their failures. Most of them rate their success in the range of 95% to 98%, but this seems to be based on their impressions rather than on firm evidence.

The uncertain status of lie detection is reflected in the way it is treated under the law: Lie-detection results are not admissible evidence in a court of law. However, exceptions have been made. Some courts have ruled that if both prosecution and defense agree that a man accused of a crime should undergo such a test, the testimony of the polygraph operator may be accepted. Furthermore, any confession obtained as the result of a polygraph examination can be used in court. Thus the polygraph can be used as sort of a mental blackjack to coerce confessions: The operator may point to a mark on the paper and tell an ignorant defendant that it proves that he is lying. Indeed, many confessions are obtained in just this way. Whether they are valid or not is another question; many people have been known to confess to crimes that they did not commit.

The history of attempts to discover deception is a long one. One oft-repeated tale is of a prince who used the following method to investigate any crime in his area. All the suspects were rounded up and brought to his palace. They stood with their hands behind them and were told that in the next room was a sacred donkey that would bray when the guilty man pulled his tail. Each went in turn into the darkened room with the donkey and then returned to his spot in front of the prince. After all were finished and the ass had not made a sound, he ordered every man to put his hands out in front of him. The prince had dusted the donkey's tail with black powder, and the theory was that only the guilty man would have clean hands because only he would be afraid to pull the tail. (Sternbach, Gustafson, and Colier, 1962). Some experts see this as an analog to contemporary lie-detection methods in that the suspect's belief in the system is crucial to the procedure's success.

Cesare Lombroso, an Italian criminologist, was the first to suggest that modern physiological technology be applied to the problem of detecting deception. In the 1890s, he started taking blood pressures of suspects while they were being interrogated by the police and claimed that he could tell when these people were lying. Later, Benussi suggested that a person's breathing patterns could also give valuable information about a man's efforts to deceive. A small "sigh of relief" occurred after every tension-laden question, he argued (Larson, 1932).

In the 1920s, Leonarde Keeler began applying these techniques in his work with the Berkeley, California, Police Department. He was so successful that he left his job and formed a company to manufacture Keeler polygraphs—devices that simultaneously recorded a person's respiration, "relative blood pressure," and EDA.

The "relative blood pressure" is obtained by inflating an arm cuff to a point approximately halfway between systolic and diastolic pressures. This is the familiar sphygmomanometer (see Chapter 5), which reflects both volumetric changes in the arm and heart rate and thus is not comparable to modern laboratory BP recordings. Furthermore, this technique of maintaining the pressure of an inflated cuff can be both dangerous and painful unless the cuff is frequently deflated. This is a major factor in determining the relatively short length of the actual "lie detection" part of a polygraph examination.

EDA is measured with relatively crude equipment. Some researchers have argued that this may have a major influence on results, but an unpublished study by Gustafson (Orne, Thackray, and Paskewitz, 1972) found no significant difference between detection rates for a Stoelting Deceptograph (one of the more popular commercial devices) and more elaborate laboratory equipment.

There is no one set of physiological responses that can be reliably identified with the telling of a conscious lie. Rather, a polygrapher looks for signs of sympathetic-like activation or "arousal"—irregular breathing patterns, high heart rates and blood pressures, and possibly SRRs. He deals intuitively with many of the problems that plague the research psychophysiologist—the effects of a varying baseline, of differences between physiological measures and between people. Thus the polygrapher's final decision is based on an elaborate gestalt rather than a set of well-defined criteria. As such, it must be considered an art rather than a science. But note that, however intuitively this process proceeds, the professional depends on an overall *pattern* of activation rather than any single response.

Everyone will respond emotionally to the question: "Did you murder your mother?" The problem of the polygrapher, then, is to find other questions that will elicit comparable physiological responses in the innocent man but not in the guilty (Orne, Thackray, and Paskewitz, 1972).

Most people who work in the lie-detection field come from a law-enforcement background and already have considerable experience in the art of interrogation. If they receive any formal training, they are further versed in the standard procedures for performing a lie-detection test. The way this cross-questioning is conducted is crucial; indeed, some polygraphers have argued that they could determine whether a person was lying or not, even if the machine were broken. Like the sacred ass that the prince used to find his guilty man, the lie detector need only be believed in by the suspect to produce the truth.

Typically, a criminal interrogation takes place in a quiet, plainly furnished office. The polygrapher tells his victim that the lie detector is a scientific instrument designed to record physiological reactions. He stresses the fact that there is no point in trying to fool the machine and encourages the suspect to prove his innocence by telling his side of the story. He then reviews the subject's history with him, sympathizing with any crimes that he may admit to but stressing throughout that lying is the lowest form of degeneracy. This may sound almost comic, but the skilled interrogator is a formidable opponent.

They repeatedly go over the crucial parts of a defendant's story, the polygrapher casually mentioning that he might as well tell the truth now rather than be exposed during the examination as a liar. With the subject, the polygrapher formulates about a dozen questions for the actual lie-detection test. Some of these are nonemotional (for example, "Is your name John Smith?"); some are emotional but not relevant to the crime (for example, asking a person accused of murder whether he has ever used drugs); and several relate specifically to the crime in question. The theory here is that the innocent person will react equally to all questions accusing him of anything illegal, while the guilty will respond *more* to the questions concerning his specific crime. The polygrapher takes great pains to phrase the questions as specifically as possible in the criminal test: Rather than asking, "Did you ever steal anything?" he will ask, "Did you ever steal more than $100 from the Central Supermarket?"

This pretest interview takes about an hour to complete. Throughout this time, the polygraph itself has never been connected. Many people find themselves so unnerved by the threat of exposure that they admit to crimes during this period. For those who don't, the devices are then attached and a little demonstration is staged to convince the subject of the futility of any attempt to fool the machine. The person picks one card from a deck of cards and tries to conceal its identity from the operator. The operator then identifies the card— thus making the subject even more nervous about anything he hopes to conceal. The actual investigation then begins, the interrogator asking the dozen questions they agreed on, going over them several times.

If there is some bit of information known to the police that has not been released to the newspapers or the suspect, a "peak of tension" test may be performed. For example, if a certain amount of money has been stolen, the investigator can ask: "Was it $15 . . . $43 . . . $89 . . . $127 . . . $206?" If the correct amount was $127, for example, the polygraph record should show the guilty man getting more and more anxious as the true amount approaches and then relaxing as it is passed. Or they might ask: "Was Mrs. Smith killed with a gun . . . a knife . . . a letter opener . . . a length of rope?" If only the murderer and the police know that a letter opener was the true weapon, the innocent man should show no change in response for this as compared with other possible weapons.

There are many different systems for scoring the physiological data to determine whether or not a person has lied. Few of them can be specified quantitatively; all depend to some extent on the judgment of the polygrapher. Further, most professionals prefer to make global judgments based on all the evidence available and from the conduct of the suspect during the interview rather than strictly from his physiological responses. Thus, the whole procedure can be seen as one more method of police interrogation rather than as a strictly physiological test.

Preemployment interviews are conducted in a similar manner. Here, the goal of the polygrapher is to discover whether the prospective employee has an unsavory background, so the questions tend to be more general. Again, the final judgment is based on more than the polygraph record alone.

In short, as leading polygrapher Fred Inbau put it in testimony before the U.S. House of Representatives: "The technique is no better than the man making the diagnosis" (U.S. Congress, 1965). This is somewhat upsetting, given the lack of standards in the profession; as mentioned before, in most states anyone can buy a polygraph and set himself up in business.

If it is true that the individual polygrapher is vital to the success of the process, it is impossible to test whether lie detection itself works. It may work for one man and not for another. But then the question becomes: Did the successful polygrapher need the polygraph itself, or did he merely need to convince his subject that he would be caught if he lied? And how did he know that he was "successful," assuming that the device worked in the first place? Because the man he thought guilty confessed? Because the man he thought innocent was released on his recommendation?

The problems in evaluating the validity of lie-detection methods are at least as complicated as those in evaluating the outcome of psychotherapy. Who are legitimate subjects and experimenters? How do you define success? Further, as businessmen, the polygraphers who conduct the studies may have a vested interest in proving the standard claims of 90%-to-100% accuracy.

A large number of studies have been done to determine whether lie detection is valid or not. The results depend on who did the study and how they defined success. Consider the following example. Suppose 100 people are suspected of a theft. All 100 are given lie detector tests. All 100 appear to be innocent. According to the statistics used in some studies, this would give a success rate of 99%, because 99 of the 100 were innocent and appeared to be so. Thus, in this case, a 99% success rate is claimed despite the polygrapher's inability to provide a single clue as to who committed the crime (Orne, Thackray, and Paskewitz, 1972).

Statistics from the U.S. Army Military Police tell the following story. Of 4,622 men given lie detector tests, 1,302 appeared guilty of various crimes in the judgment of the polygrapher. Fifty-three percent of these later confessed. How many of these men falsely confessed, we will never know. For another 20%, the guilty verdict was supported by further evidence. But in 28% of the cases, the verdict of guilty was never substantiated by further evidence. Surely, at least some of these men were guilty of the crimes in question. But how many innocent men were subjected to further investigation, harassment, and even imprisonment on the basis of these tests? Again, we'll never know. Of the men whom the test declared innocent, 2.3% were later convicted on the basis of other evidence (Orlansky, 1965). How many guilty men were allowed to go free and the investigations discontinued because the lie detector said they were innocent? Another unknown.

For all criminal cases studied before the early 1960s (Orlansky, 1965), the polygraph was proven wrong in up to 2% of the cases. Usually, it was a case of a guilty man going free, but sometimes innocent men were convicted partly on the basis of this mistaken evidence. Two percent sounds like a very small figure, but it is no consolation to someone sent to jail because the lie detector lied. Furthermore, this is just the number of studied cases in which the polygraph verdict was *proven* wrong. The very fact that the test turns out a certain way often discourages the police from looking further into the case.

In short, we must agree with Dr. Jesse Orlansky, who concluded in a report to the Department of Defense: "Although the method of lie detection has been used extensively and is regarded favorably by its practitioners, the degree of its validity is still not known."

The few laboratory researchers who have ventured into the forbidden land of lie detection have addressed themselves to two basic questions: (1) How effective is lie detection? and (2) What variables affect the success of detection? In general, it is dangerous to extrapolate from their results to commercial procedures.

These efforts tend to use more elaborate equipment and concentrate on a single physiological indicator—usually EDA. Further, most studies are plagued by the very artificiality that makes them possible: Subjects are typically homogeneous groups of college students who are guilty of relatively little and have little to lose by being detected. Finally, the judgments are made not on the basis of a global impression of all the evidence, but strictly on the basis of well-defined physiological responses.

A description of several representative studies may give a clearer idea of both the strengths and the weaknesses of the laboratory approach. In 1959, David Lykken published a description of his "guilty knowledge" technique—a variation on the "peak of tension" test. Lykken argued that it is easier and more efficient to look for physiological reactions to details of a crime (presumably known only to the guilty party) than to try to determine when a person is lying. For this procedure, then, the interviewer simply presents a list of actual and fictitious details of the crime. The guilty man should respond differentially to the relevant items. The innocent man should respond more or less equally to all the alternatives.

His subjects were 49 college males. Two elaborate mock crimes, a murder and a theft, were acted out by some of the subjects. Some "committed" both crimes, some neither, and some just one. As Lykken describes the theft:

> S had to idle near the doorway of a different office until the occupant, a woman, left it to go to the washroom. S then hurriedly entered and riffled through the desk calendar until he found a page on which his own name had been entered. He erased the name and then searched through the desk until he found an article . . . which he had been instructed to "steal." Leaving the office, he hid the stolen property in a locker in the hallway.

Every subject was then interrogated about both crimes. One of the questions was: "The thief hid what he had stolen. Where did he hide it? Was it (a) in the men's room, (b) on the coat rack, (c) in the office, (d) on the window sill, (e) in the locker?" If a person had in fact enacted the theft, he should show an unusual response to the last alternative.

SRRs were the sole physiological measure. A person received a higher score for a large SRR to the relevant item. The guilty party was correctly identified for 44 of the 50 crimes. (Remember, some of these people committed more than one crime.) Of the 48 occasions when innocent parties were questioned, all 48 were correctly judged not guilty. Thus, the total detection rate was 93.9%.

In a follow-up study (Lykken, 1960), a more complicated scoring procedure was used to correct for the effects of faking responses to irrelevant items. The subjects were 20 professional people (psychiatrists, medical students, and the like) who were offered $10 to beat the procedure and given a 15-minute lecture on EDA and lie detection, including ideal strategies for escaping detection. All

20 people were correctly identified by the procedure. Lykken suggests that the "guilty knowledge" test may prove useful to the polygrapher in the field, provided certain facts about the crime are known only to the police and the guilty party—an assumption that might be rather difficult to prove in court.

Other researchers have considered variables that might affect more traditional lie-detection procedures. For example, in 1963, Gustafson and Orne designed an experiment to see whether a person motivated to beat the polygraph is more likely to succeed than a person who doesn't care. Half of their subjects were told that the experiment was designed to see how well people could keep information from the experimenter, that only people of great emotional control and superior intelligence would succeed, that they should try as hard as they could to "beat the equipment," and that they would be given a $1 bonus for success. The other half were merely told that it was a study of the physiological responses of normal people to a series of numbers and letters.

Each subject picked one of five cards, each of which was marked with a letter or a number. A few minutes later, a tape recording of the list of five cards was played. To minimize the effects of orienting (see Chapter 4), the first item was not scored. The average SRR to each character was then computed. In the motivated group, 12 of 18 college males gave the largest mean SRR to the figure they had chosen, while only 6 of 18 unmotivated subjects could be distinguished on the basis of their SRRs. This difference was statistically significant, and the authors concluded that the motivation to deceive works against a subject.

Again, note the differences between these studies and the use of the polygraph in a criminal investigation. EDA was the sole physiological measure and its scoring was purely objective, as opposed to the more global procedures of the man in the field. Criminal investigators tend to rely on patterns of cardiovascular and respiratory change, claiming that EDA is too sensitive to be used in such an emotionally charged situation (Barland and Raskin, 1973).

A more obvious and more critical difference is that the laboratory subjects are well-educated people who are participating in a psychology experiment; whatever happens, they will be free to leave when it is over. Contrast this with the attitude of a heterogeneous criminal group whose very survival may depend on the results of their examination. On the other hand, the laboratory situation does enable the investigator to decide the rules of the game and thus study a question like the effects of motivation.

Orlansky's (1965) review of such laboratory studies found a median detection rate of 92%. A more recent review by Orne, Thackray, and Paskewitz (1972) reported a median success rate of 80% for those studies using a mock crime and 73% for those using more neutral stimuli.

A study by Barland and Raskin (1975) attempted to bridge the gap between researcher and practitioner. Field techniques of polygraphy (including standard interrogation procedures, use of a Keeler polygraph, and typical scoring systems) were used to detect "mock thieves" and innocent parties. Fifty-three percent of the subjects were correctly identified, 12% were incorrectly classified (of these 9 people, 6 were found guilty despite their innocence) and 35% of the examinations were inconclusive.

There are a number of ways of trying to beat the polygraph (Barland and Raskin, 1973). It is possible that hypnosis and certain drugs may help to mislead the polygrapher. It is also possible that sufficient biofeedback training (discussed later in this chapter), may enable one to control physiological responses to the point where detection becomes impossible. These are all matters toward which future research must be directed.

There are two basic strategies for trying to fool the polygrapher. One is to eliminate all responses so that no item produces any response whatever. The basic principle here is that the person being interviewed should try to respond automatically to all the questions without really paying any attention. He should, instead, concentrate on the pattern on the wall in front of him or some other neutral object. Although some people claim success with this technique, in general it is very difficult to do; if achieved, it may make the interrogator suspicious, and it has been known to have exactly the opposite of the desired effect. Along these same lines, some criminals have been known to spray their hands with antiperspirant. Although this does indeed have the effect of reducing SR activity, it of course has no effect on the other physiological measures.

A far more useful technique is that of producing false responses to irrelevant questions. A skilled interrogator may see through this strategy, but it may lead the polygrapher to the wrong conclusion if employed at just the right moments.

A variety of procedures may be used to produce false responses. Purely mental exercises are the most difficult to detect: Whenever you want to produce a response, merely try to multiply two long numbers in your head or think angry or sexy thoughts. If you can appear to maintain your concentration throughout, this should work for most people. Another alternative is to tense some muscle group without the experimenter's knowledge. People typically press their toes against the floor, cross their eyes, or push the tongue against the roof of the mouth whenever they wish to produce a false response. The trick here is to hide this movement from the interrogator.

Pain also produces the physiological responses characteristic of stress, and some people have gone so far as to hide a thumb tack inside one shoe so that a foot pressed against it would produce a false response. Again, the alert interrogator will check to make sure that such means are not being employed.

Our conclusions about lie detection, then, are not as clear-cut as one might hope. In the hands of the skilled operator, the polygraph is highly successful, but not infallible, in differentiating the liar from the man who tells the truth. In the hands of the unskilled operator, the lie detector may be a real menace to civil liberty.

Lykken (1974) argues that the use of lie detection for preemployment screening is far more insidious than its use in criminal cases (for which he recommends his "guilty knowledge" test). He presents a fairly elaborate mathematical analysis to show that, since relatively few people would be expected to lie in the business setting, many more innocent people will be hurt by its failures.

From a more theoretical point of view, the study of lie detection has a considerably more direct lesson. First of all, the very term *lie detector* is something of a misnomer. No one claims that there is a unique pattern of physiological responses associated with deception. Perhaps the term *emotion detector* or *arousal detector* would be more accurate.

We must also remember that the professional employs many techniques that are almost irrelevant to the actual physiological data and that, when he does read the physiological record, he looks for a *pattern* of physiological activity. Experimental support for this practice comes from a laboratory study by Cutrow et al. (1972). Nine separate psychophysiological variables (breathing amplitude, breathing cycle length, eye-blink rate, eye-blink latency, finger pulse volume, heart rate, SRRs from the palm, SRRs from the forearm, and voice latency) were measured in a typical laboratory lie-detection paradigm. While each of these measures separately distinguished truth from falsity, a combined index representing the overall pattern of physiological activity was far more reliable than any single measure.

But beyond the theoretical lessons of lie detection, there are serious ethical questions concerning its use even by the most expert. For example, J. Barthel's book, *A Death in Canaan*, describes the controversial case of Peter Reilly, who was jailed in 1973 when he confessed during an intensive polygraph examination to murdering his mother, despite the fact that he reneged the next day. The *New York Times* reviewer described this book as a "chilling. . .exposure of the Connecticut State Police's dependence upon and mindless faith in these damned machines" (C. D. B. Bryan, *New York Times Book Review*, December 12, 1976).

Biofeedback

While lie detection grew up as an industry, biofeedback got its start in a rather esoteric academic controversy. Psychologists have argued for some time about just how many kinds of learning there are. Some, as discussed below, were not willing to accept the traditional distinction between classical conditioning (Pavlov's dogs) and operant conditioning (Skinner's rats). These theorists wanted to prove that the involuntary processes of the ANS could be manipulated by operant conditioning. And so Neal Miller and his associates began their famous experiments in which paralyzed rats were taught to raise their HR, BP, renal blood flow, and so on. At about the same time, Joe Kamiya was beginning a series of studies at the University of Chicago to see whether people could tell when they were producing occipital alpha. They could, and he continued this work at San Francisco's Langley Porter Neuropsychiatric Institute to demonstrate that people could learn to control how much occipital alpha they produced.

This history of biofeedback is a good example of the way in which basic research, whose concerns often seem far removed from the "real world," sometimes provides new techniques and new ways of looking at things that yield unexpected applications.

The basic principle of biofeedback is quite simple: Feedback makes learning possible. Imagine trying to learn to play the piano while you were wearing very effective earplugs. Without the feedback of hearing your cacophonous errors, you would never stop driving the neighbors crazy. It is only through the feedback of hearing your mistakes that your playing ever improves. Or imagine trying to learn to throw darts when you were blindfolded. You'd never know when you hit the bull's-eye.

Our bodies are not designed to provide subtle feedback about internal physiological states. Without taking my pulse, I cannot tell whether my HR is now 60 or 70. I don't have any idea at all what my BP is or how many SSCRs I am producing. We do not ordinarily consciously control these processes; they go on outside our awareness. I can probably distinguish the relatively high HR in a game of tennis from the low HR as I sit here and plan the next sentence. But this type of feedback is quite crude.

This leads us directly to the operant principle of shaping: Feedback for very small changes is generally more helpful than feedback for gross changes. One way to keep track of your weight is to notice when you're too fat for all of your clothes. However, if the only reinforcement you get on a diet is fitting into your favorite dungarees after six months of starving yourself, chances are that you won't last. If, instead, you stand on the scale and note, for example, that your weight has plummeted overnight from 413 to 411, you might be better inclined to face at least today's black coffee and unbuttered toast.

Biofeedback, then, involves making one aware of very subtle changes in physiological state in the hope of bringing those processes under conscious control. If a meter tells you from moment to moment whether your HR is 75 or 80, you can gradually learn to keep it closer to either of these figures. What precisely do you do to control your HR? It's hard to say. David Shapiro (1973) reports the following interchange with one successful HR manipulator: "When I asked 'How do you do it?', he replied, 'How do you move your arm?' " However people do it, a wide variety of physiological changes have been brought under conscious control, including various EEG rhythms, HR, BP, peripheral circulation, and EMG.

As noted above, biofeedback developed at least partially as a result of a controversy in the field of learning. Traditionally, psychologists have considered learning to be of two distinct types: Pavlov's classical conditioning and Skinner's operant or instrumental conditioning. It was widely believed (Kimble, 1961) that CNS-controlled behaviors were instrumentally conditioned, while ANS response was amenable only to classical conditioning (Skinner, 1953). Neal Miller (1969) challenged this view with a series of demonstrations of operant conditioning of autonomic function in the paralyzed rat. He argued vehemently against the "invidious dichotomy" of CNS and ANS functions, which he traced all the way back to Plato's *Dialogues*. The suggestion that there is only one kind of learning is hardly a new one (Smith, 1954), but it was Neal Miller and his students who gave impetus to the argument that biofeedback procedures were true instances of instrumental conditioning of the ANS.

The controversy revolved around the "mediation" issue. If I want to raise my HR, I can easily do it by running around the block, hyperventilating, or even just tensing my muscles. All would agree that, using these "mediators," I could "voluntarily" control an involuntary process. The question, then, is not whether HR (for example) can be controlled but, rather, whether it can be controlled directly. If, when HR increases are reinforced, HR automatically goes up, then the laws of operant conditioning apply to the autonomic nervous system. Thus Miller and his students set out to demonstrate that ANS changes could be induced directly.

Their efforts to rule out the possibility of skeletal system "mediation" were truly heroic: In most of their experiments, their subjects were rats paralyzed with curare, a drug that selectively blocks the motor end plates of muscles. These unfortunate animals were kept alive by artificial respirators while they were under the influence of the drug. Since it is rather difficult to do anything nice for a paralyzed rat, reinforcement was given by means of electrical stimulation of the "pleasure centers" of the brain. Care was taken to show that all biofeedback effects produced under these restricted conditions were also bidirectional; this precaution made it almost impossible to argue that the results were simply elaborate instances of classical conditioning.

In 1968, a number of studies on the paralyzed rats appeared. Miller and Banuazizi showed that their rate of intestinal contractions could be increased or decreased without affecting HR. Conversely, HR could be raised or lowered without affecting the rate of intestinal contractions. Miller and DiCara presented data to prove that the rate of urine formation in the kidney (accomplished by altering renal blood flow) could be increased or decreased without affecting HR, blood pressure, or peripheral vasomotor activity. DiCara and Miller (1968a) taught rats to blush in either the right or the left ear by rewarding vasodilation in the pinnae on the appropriate side. Again, HR, BP, and peripheral vasomotor activity showed no effects. Using tail shock as a reinforcer in an avoidance paradigm, DiCara and Miller (1968b) taught rats to raise and lower their systolic BPs and observed no corresponding HR changes.

However, when Miller and his associates carefully attempted to replicate their own work several years later, they found to their surprise that they could not (Miller and Dworkin, 1974). A set of elaborate manipulations has failed thus far to discover just what has gone wrong.

Before the replication difficulties, the Miller work was widely accepted as a legitimate example of the instrumental conditioning of autonomic responses. A controversy arose when human biofeedback researchers extrapolated from these results to claim that operant conditioning also accounted for the results in studies of humans. In historical terms, the Miller results encouraged such claims. Authenticated cases of voluntary HR control in humans, for example, predated the invention of the polygraph by many years (King, 1920). Similarly, in 1938 Skinner conceded that it was possible for man to gain control over autonomic responses, as does the child who learns to cry at will. But, he argued, this response is mediated by other processes.

Katkin and Murray (1968) considered the issue of the theoretical status of human biofeedback in detail. Although they were willing to accept the performance of the curarized rats as legitimate examples of operant conditioning, they were unwilling to make the theoretical leap that similar processes were involved in human ANS control. In short, they argued that, if a given physiological response is mediated either cognitively or physiologically, then one cannot contend that the response being measured is truly conditioned. This drives them to the extreme position that a demonstration of human instrumental conditioning of the ANS "would require unconscious subjects to eliminate cognitive mediation and complete curarization to eliminate somatic mediation."

In fairness to them, they admit that the theoretical issue is hardly worth the trouble of resolving. However, this kind of argument was taken so seriously that one researcher actually permitted himself to be partially curarized in a biofeedback study of skin potential responses (Birk et al., 1966). (He successfully produced more skin potential responses but, since he was conscious and only partially paralyzed, the results were "not conclusive.")

A number of rejoinders followed. Crider, Schwartz, and Schnidman (1969) criticized the argument on a number of grounds, most notably the failure of Katkin and Murray to identify the mediators that they so frequently invoked. However, it soon became clear, even to Katkin and Murray (1969), that his was becoming "a controversy more based in epistemology than in data."

The issue of total specificity, and with it the question of the true status of biofeedback as conditioning, gradually seemed less important as people realized, as Engel (1972) put it: "Specificity to the point of physiological disintegration would be disastrous." Given this fact, Lynch and Paskewitz (1971) have this to say about the conditioning argument: "Is it ever possible for a physiological system to be conditioned without some sort of mediation? Can we, for instance, increase HR without affecting changes in blood flow, blood pressure, or peripheral vasomotor tone? This would seem to be a hydraulic impossibility and, therefore, following the strictest interpretation of Katkin and Murray's proposals, heart rate cannot be operantly conditioned in any direct sense."

"With the luxury of hindsight," as Schwartz (1974) put it, this controversy does not seem to be a very useful one. Indeed, the reader who has been successfully indoctrinated into accepting the emphasis of this text on the centrality of brain processes in all psychophysiological response may wonder how the controversy arose in the first place. We should note that, historically, the increased acceptance of the fundamentally biological view presented here arose partially from the ashes of the mediation issue. At this point, it is fair to discuss biofeedback as an aspect of "applied psychophysiology," since the theoretical issues now seem considerably less important.

The most important applications of biofeedback were in the clinical sphere. Its potential was obvious: Why not teach people with high blood pressure, for example, to maintain BP at healthy levels?

Many clinicians began experimenting with biofeedback devices. The first reports provided the mass media with an onslaught of biofeedback cures (for example, Pines, 1970; Karlins and Andrews, 1972). The problem of evaluating such claims is an old one in medical history. Clinicians are interested in curing their patients by whatever means are available, and rightly so. However, their enthusiasm for a new method of treatment may have as much to do with its success as the treatment itself. Indeed, there is an ancient medical maxim that states: "Treat many patients with the new remedies while they still have the power to heal" (in Shapiro, 1971).

The confusion is partly due to a phenomenon that cancer research and writer Lewis Thomas calls "the great secret of doctors," still hidden from the public: "[M]ost things get better by themselves. . . . Most things, in fact, are better by the morning" (Thomas, 1974).

In his delightful and scholarly writings on the placebo effect, Arthur Shapiro (1960, 1971) carefully traces the history of the power of suggestion in psychiatry and medicine. He notes, "Despite Galen's and Hippocrates' acumen, none of the drugs they used were of any use" (Shapiro, 1971). Consider, for example, a well-documented eighteenth century British cure for toothaches: "Fill your mouth with milk and shake it until it becomes butter" (Shapiro, 1960). And yet patients did get better in vast numbers by using the ancient cures. Present medical practice continues to rely on the placebo effect. In one study of 17,000 prescriptions written by British physicians (Dunlap, Henderson, and Inch, 1952), about one-third of the drugs prescribed had no known medical value. The placebo effect is so well documented that today no drug is considered to have established pharmacologic value until its effects have been demonstrated in a "double blind" study, that is, one in which some patients are given the active drugs while others are given placebos and neither doctor nor patient knows which people are which.

In our technological age, biofeedback may represent "the ultimate placebo" (Stroebel and Glueck, 1973), for it combines the notion of patient self-help with all the trappings of electronic gadgetry.

Miller (1974) pointed out that the decreases in BP seen in biofeedback studies have been comparable in size to the reductions one sees with placebos. The patient may not really care why his condition improves, as long as it does. But the clinician would like to tease out placebo effects from true clinical advantages, so that he can best choose the treatment for other patients. Blanchard and Young (1974) provide an excellent summary of the kinds of experimental designs required to demonstrate clinical effectiveness and review clinical biofeedback studies in the light of this scheme. In general terms, they conclude that biofeedback is promising but not yet proven. As we review this and more recent evidence, we shall urge an extreme caution in evaluating biofeedback, in keeping with the Blanchard and Young discussion. At least part of this caution is probably a response to the over-enthusiasm of the late 1960s.

Some of the best-documented clinical applications of biofeedback involve EMG training. It is not surprising that a person can learn to control his muscles. That, after all, is what we do whenever we scratch our noses. What is surprising is the degree of control that we can attain with the aid of biofeedback technology.

If I tense my forehead in puzzlement, I receive some feedback; I can feel that the muscles of my forehead are tightened. However, unless I look in a mirror, I find it hard to distinguish any but the crudest categories of tension. Suppose now that electrodes were attached to my frontalis muscle (see Figure 8.4) and an electronic circuit were built so that even the most miniscule changes in muscle tension altered the brightness of the room lighting. This would be a kind of biofeedback. After practice, I could learn to control far more subtle changes in the tonus of my frontalis muscle than are presently possible.

EMG biofeedback can be used clinically, then, to provide an unusually sensitive degree of muscle control in certain patients. Andrews (1964), for example, studied twenty patients suffering from hemiplegia for whom traditional forms of neuromuscular rehabilitation had failed. He found that after a simple biofeedback training procedure, these patients could produce muscle tension in the paralyzed arm at will. Johnson and Garton (1973) found a similar technique helpful in retraining normal limb function in ten hemiplegic patients who were forced to wear a leg brace. Each of these patients had shown little or no progress after a year of traditional physical therapy. After two to sixteen weeks of biofeedback training, five of the ten patients improved enough to eliminate the brace, while the remainder showed less dramatic, but still significant, improvements.

More commonly, biofeedback procedures have been used to teach patients how to relax. Levee, Cohen, and Rickles (1976), for example, reported the case of a woodwind musician with a long history of tics and excessive tension in throat and facial muscles. With the aid of EMG feedback for these specific muscle groups, the patient learned to relax these symptoms away.

Tension headaches often appear to result from tension in the frontalis muscle. Budzynski, Stoyva, and their associates have conducted a series of studies showing that biofeedback training of frontalis relaxation can help to reduce the frequency of headache attacks. In one well-controlled study (Budzynski et al., 1973), six subjects received extended biofeedback training for frontalis relaxation. Four of the six were totally cured. This was compared with two control groups: in the first, six subjects were given "pseudofeedback," that is, they were told that they were receiving EMG relaxation training when in fact the tone emitted by their practice devices bore no relation to true muscle tension levels. Only one of these patients improved. Another control group had weekly contact with the experimenter but no feedback treatment. None of these six patients improved.

Less systematic evidence has been presented that biofeedback may be useful in the treatment of certain cardiovascular disorders. Weiss and Engel (1971) found biofeedback useful in the reduction of preventricular contractions, a certain type of cardiac arrhythmia. Benson et al. (1971) found that five of seven hypertensives were able to reduce systolic BP by at least 16 mm Hg with the help of biofeedback training; Schwartz and Shapiro (1973) found the technique less useful in reducing diastolic BP. Elder et al. (1973) found just the opposite: Biofeedback could be used to decrease diastolic BP but not systolic BP.

Peripheral circulatory changes have also been manipulated by biofeedback. Schwartz (1972a) presented suggestive data on the treatment of two patients with Raynaud's disease, a disorder in which excessive vasoconstriction yields pathologically cold hands and feet. Migraine headaches have also been treated by teaching people to warm their hands; presumably, digital arteries dilate and cerebral arteries constrict during this process. In the most systematic study to date, Sargent, Green, and Walters (1972) confirmed clinical improvement in only 29% to 39% of the migraine patients, a proportion that might easily be explained by placebo effects.

Perhaps the most widely publicized biofeedback "cure" has been the EEG treatment of epilepsy that actually provided the plot for one episode of "Marcus Welby, M.D.," the now-defunct TV show. The treatment involves increasing the frequency and amplitude of the sensorimotor rhythm (SMR—a 12–16 Hz rhythm recorded from sensorimotor cortex, typically C_z-T_3 and/or C_z-T_4, a procedure pioneered by Barry Sterman (1973). Although there have been some negative reports (Kaplan, 1974), most researchers have reported that SMR biofeedback training has been useful in the reduction of seizure frequency (Sterman, MacDonald, and Stone, 1974; Finley, Smith, and Etherton, 1975; Lubar and Bahler, 1976).

Very few studies have even hinted that alpha biofeedback may have some clinical significance. Despite this fact, the "alpha state" has received a tremendous amount of popular attention. Some quasi-religious groups describe alpha as an almost mystical level of consciousness that may open the door to ESP and psychic healing. Others who are only slightly more cautious see alpha biofeedback as a key to achieving their full potential, whatever that means. Counterculture entrepreneurs fanned these flames. Forming companies with names like Whole Earth Electronics, they mass-marketed inexpensive alpha biofeedback devices, often of rather dubious technical quality. Some came complete with instruction books showing how alpha biofeedback could be used to develop ESP, cure baldness, and end the heartbreak of psoriasis.

Those with even a nodding familiarity with the EEG viewed such claims with a certain skepticism. Of course, there is no such thing as the "alpha state"; the brain is not a single undifferentiated mass of tissue that remains in one state or another. Most frequently, alpha biofeedback involves increasing the amplitude of 8–13 Hz activity recorded from occipital cortex at the back of the skull. The simplest way to achieve this effect is by closing the eyes.

Much of the excitement about alpha biofeedback was generated by the reports of subjects in the earliest experiments that they enjoyed the experience. In two of the most frequently cited examples (Nowlis and Kamiya, 1970; Brown, 1971), about half of the subjects reported that alpha production led to or was accompanied by feelings of pleasant relaxation. This was the half that everybody talked about. The other half didn't notice much of anything. More recent studies (Travis, Kondo, and Knott, 1975) have come up with the same proportion; about half describe alpha generation as "pleasant." However, in one of the earliest studies (Brown, 1970) two of ten subjects reported feeling relaxed while producing alpha, while another three "actively attempted to relax." This raises some question as to whether these subjects came to the experiment with some well-defined ideas about what alpha was supposed to feel like, a point to which we shall return later.

If that doesn't sound like enough to go out and found a religion on, there was one more source of inspiration for the alpha fans. Systematic EEG changes, including increased amplitude of occipital alpha, were observed during meditation in Zen monks (Kasamatsu and Hirai, 1969), Indian yogis (Anand, Chhina, and Singh, 1961), and in practitioners of Transcendental Meditation (Wallace, 1970). Alpha biofeedback, then, became seen as a kind of TV-dinner approach to meditation, cutting down on the preparation time for harried Westerners.

Of course, increased occipital alpha is also seen as a person falls asleep. And indeed, one group of researchers at the University of Washington (Pagano et al., 1976) argued that, at least for Transcendental Meditation, meditative periods are quite similar physiologically to afternoon naps. Others have made far more dramatic claims. Some of the earliest research characterized meditation as a "wakeful hypometabolic state" (Wallace, Benson, and Wilson, 1971). Transcendental Meditation was seen as a "fourth kind" of consciousness, different from waking, sleeping, and dreaming. Herbert Benson, one of the original TM researchers, went on to develop his own more secular version, which he described in his best seller, *The Relaxation Response* (Benson, 1975). Woolfolk reviewed the meditation literature in 1975 and provides a good summary of general psychophysiological findings to that date.

The meditation literature includes several examples of more interesting findings than simple relaxation. For example, Zen monks, whose meditation involves focusing attention on the external environment, failed to show habituation of alpha blocking to a sound stimulus (Kasamatsu and Hirai, 1969). That is, while the EEG response to a tone gradually decreased for a control group, Zen monks continued to respond to the stimulus. Thus, the EEG evidence supported their contention that they were "more aware" of the world around them. Indian yogis, on the other hand, practice a very different kind of meditation, which involves attending to inner states and shutting out the external environment. These meditators did not show alpha blocking to several rather dramatic stimuli (for example, placing a hot test tube against the arm), although these same stimuli caused alpha blocking when they were not in the meditative state (Anand, Chhina, and Singh, 1961). Thus, the EEG evidence suggested just the opposite of the pattern in the Zen monks; the yogis had successfully cut themselves off from the external world.

Such niceties, however, are forgotten by those who argue that alpha biofeedback can help produce a state resembling a meditative trance. Also forgotten is the critical importance of oculomotor adjustments in the generation of occipital alpha. As discussed in Chapter 9, some researchers have gone so far as to argue that occipital alpha is nothing but a reflection of eye movements. While this is a bit extreme, there is no question that relaxing and unfocusing the eyes will ordinarily increase the amplitude of occipital alpha. Indeed, in an overwhelming display of pedantic virtuosity, Dewan (1967) taught people to send Morse code with their brain waves simply by focusing and defocusing the eyes. Oculomotor defocusing produced high-amplitude alpha, which in turn produced an audible tone as a dot or dash, depending on how long the alpha was maintained. Mulholland (1968, 1972), Peper (1970, 1971), Peper and Mulholland (1970), and Plotkin (1976) have further stressed the importance of oculomotor adjustments in alpha suppression. Plotkin and Cohen (1976) manipulated five dimensions of subjective experience and found that oculomotor processing and, to a less extent, sensory awareness were involved in alpha control, while body awareness, deliberateness of thought, and pleasantness of emotional state were not.

Some of the researchers who stress the importance of oculomotor adjustments doubt that people ever learn to generate alpha at all. What is learned, they suggest, is an ability to turn alpha off, not on. Lynch and Paskewitz (1971) wrote the classic paper in this area. Hardt and Kamiya (1976) provide a more recent view.

Mulholland (1971) has argued that the "pleasantness" of alpha may have as much to do with a person's expectations and feelings of success in the experiment as with its inherent effects. He has reported several cases of subjects who claimed dramatic experiences while they were producing alpha with feedback. However, when the feedback was discontinued, they seemed unable to tell when they were producing alpha.

More recently, one of Mulholland's students, David Walsh (1974), examined the importance of expectancy effects more systematically. Subjects were given either true alpha feedback or pseudofeedback, in combination with instructions that emphasized that alpha was a "calm, contemplative, dreamlike, or 'high' state" or more neutral instructions. Only those subjects who received the value-laden instructions *and* were actually trained to maintain alpha (recorded from O_1-P_3 or O_2-P_4, whichever was larger) reported that alpha was indeed a pleasant state to be in. That is, neither the instructions alone nor the physiological state by itself was enough to produce the "alpha state"; this was observed only when the two worked together. This finding reemphasizes the importance of cognitive factors in determining what a person feels. It also emphasizes, once again, the need for physiological and psychological sophistication. There is not likely to be any simple correspondence between a physiological variable as crude as occipital alpha and subjective experience. To some extent, early biofeedback researchers had been tantalized by the hope that scientifically minded researchers would be able to reopen a door that behaviorism had long ago shut—the door to inner experience.

Stoyva and Kamiya (1968) describe this possibility in terms of the principle of converging operations. Simply stated, they argue that by looking at the "public accompaniments of an inferred state" (in this case, physiological alternative measures), it may be possible to eliminate hypotheses about the validity of these states. They give the example of rapid eye movement, an accompaniment of most dreams. The fact that the length of a REM period is highly correlated with the reported length of a dream experience (Dement and Kleitman, 1957) helps to rule out the possibility that the subject's reports of dreams are merely fabricated.

Biofeedback procedures, they hoped, would offer a similar solution for the waking subject. From our review here, it is clear that there is no easy correspondence. If there is any hope at all in that direction, it probably comes from the more sophisticated approaches of pattern biofeedback.

The notion of pattern biofeedback was pioneered by Schwartz (1971) with his proposal of the Integration-Differentiation (ID) Model. The ID Model was developed to help explain a troubling result for biofeedback researchers: Although HR is known to be one determinant of BP (see Chapter 5), Shapiro, Tursky, and Schwartz (1970a) found that subjects taught to raise or lower their systolic BPs showed no HR effects and, conversely, subjects who raised or lowered their HRs showed no changes in systolic BP (1970b). Schwartz explains the ID

Model resolution of this paradox: "These results are understandable and predictable from an operant conditioning point of view *only* if the assumption is made that BP and HR are in fact *unrelated* (uncorrelated in time) to the extent that when one is contingently reinforced, the other is *simultaneously* receiving some form of *random* reinforcement."

Given this model, it is possible to predict the effects of HR biofeedback on BP, for example, from the pattern of their "normal" relationship to one another. Conversely, given the effects of HR feedback on BP, one can predict their normal degree of covariation. In this case, the correlation between the two (defined in terms of the probability of HR and BP both being in the same state relative to their respective medians) should be close to zero. In fact, Schwartz found, this is the case.

Schwartz (1971) then suggested that feedback for *patterns* of HR and BP might reveal relationships between physiological systems that would not be observed with more traditional biofeedback procedures. He coined the terms *integration* and *differentiation* to describe two possible types of patterns. As stated by Schwartz (1972a): "The term *integration* is reserved for the response pattern in which two functions simultaneously change in the same direction (both increasing and decreasing together in a sympathetic-like pattern), and the term *differentiation* refers to the response pattern in which two functions simultaneously change in opposite directions."

Schwartz (1971) did indeed find that the pattern procedure was sensitive to the constraints each measure imposed on the other, where the single system approach was not. A later application of the model to diastolic BP and HR (Schwartz, Shapiro, and Tursky, 1972) again showed the sensitivity of the pattern approach.

Thus, the ID model can be seen as a first step in more sophisticated biofeedback approaches to physiology. As Schwartz (1971) demonstrated, the pattern approach gives us information that cannot be uncovered with more simple-minded techniques. If a person cannot learn to raise his systolic BP while lowering his HR (as Schwartz's subjects could not), this gives valuable information about the relationship between the two systems. If the HR-down/BP-down pattern produces larger HR decreases than HR-down/BP-up (again the case in this study), this tells us of a kind of natural integration within the cardiovascular system which was not uncovered by the training of either system alone or by an analysis of typical phasic relations between the two.

Hassett (1974) extended the pattern approach to the study of ANS/CNS interrelationships. Subjects were first trained to manipulate HR and occipital alpha separately and then were asked to combine the two in all possible combinations. Under pattern conditions, a unidirectional influence of occipital alpha manipulation on HR was observed which could not be seen when single systems were manipulated. (See also Hassett and Schwartz, 1975.) Also in this study, evidence was found that some biofeedback subjects are "better learners" than others; people who produced large-magnitude HR effects tended to have the best control over occipital alpha.

Pattern biofeedback, then, may have important implications for understanding the relationships between common physiological measures (Hassett, 1974) as well as potential clinical applications (Schwartz, 1974). This and other recent technical advances will surely lead to more sophisticated applications of biofeedback in the future.

The fact that biofeedback training encourages the patient to take an active role in his own treatment may ultimately have a major impact on modern medicine, regardless of the final verdict on its value in the treatment of any specific disorder.

11

Psychophysiology in Perspective

As we leave the study of psychophysiology, let us attempt to gain some perspective on the key issues we have discussed. The conclusion begins with a summary of the arousal approach vs. the patterning approach and then proceeds to look briefly at issues raised by the fact that different people frequently respond to identical events in different ways. Finally, we shall look at the place of psychophysiology in the social sciences.

Arousal and Patterning Revisited

And so we return, one last time, to the question of patterning of physiological responses. Virtually all of the early research on autonomic function is based on the arousal perspective. A person is more alert at some times than at others, and many physiological measures index that fact. EDA was seen to increase in an air raid. HR goes up when we sit in a dentist's chair. Even a mild handshake elicits pupil dilation. The notion of arousal is indeed a reasonable first approximation that ties together these disparate observations. But we must not mistake this promising beginning for the whole story.

Psychophysiology would have a dismal future indeed if every one of its variables were telling the same simple tale. We have seen Kilpatrick's (1972) promising work on SSCRs and emotionality and SCL and cognitive factors. We have seen Ax's (1953) differentiation of fear and anger as distinct physiological states. We have seen what Schwartz et al. (1976) learned from investigating patterns of facial muscular activity in different emotions. We have seen in studies of the cortical evoked potential how different brain sites yield different responses to the same stimuli.

And yet, somehow, all of these studies leave us unsatisfied. Important as they are in calling attention to the simultaneous measurement of many physiological systems, and even in analyzing a single system in many ways, they never quite come to grips with the problem of defining a *pattern* as such. It is always a question of Variable A does *x* and Variable B does *y* rather than A and B together form the pattern *xy*. This latter demands a very high level of mathematical sophistication. Let us examine a few attempts to define patterns.

In 1939, Dr. Marion Wenger began a long series of studies of "autonomic balance" in children and adults. Starting with Cannon's ideas about sympathetic and parasympathetic innervation underlying autonomic function, Wenger hoped to develop a single index of relative activation in these two antagonistic systems by combining information from many different measures.

The actual physiological measures finally used in this index included salivary output, several measures of EDA, heart rate, systolic and diastolic blood pressure, finger temperature, sublingual temperature, respiration period, and pupillary diameter. Information from all these measures was combined in a single weighted average representing a person's overall level of apparent sympathetic or parasympathetic activation (autonomic balance). Such measures were found to be reasonably characteristic of an individual. That is, the measures were reliable; the same individual showed similar scores on two different occasions. In some cases, these autonomic balance scores were consistent with psychosomatic complaints. Anxious subjects, for example, gave evidence of "sympathetic dominance," a fact which is quite consistent with Cannon's "fight or flight" formulation. Wenger and Cullen (1972) present an excellent summary of both the history and current status of this approach.

More recently, Stephen Porges (in press, 1977) has called attention to the link between ANS balance and CNS neurotransmitter biochemistry. He reviews the work of several theorists, suggesting that the inhibitory activity of the CNS neurotransmitter, acetylcholine, may be reflected in the parasympathetic nervous system, while the excitatory CNS effects of the catecholamines may be reflected in the sympathetic nervous system. Porges then argues that autonomic balance may have an important role in understanding behavioral pathologies such as hyperactivity, psychopathy, and infantile autism.

He goes on to propose a new method for assessing autonomic balance that is physiologically quite simple but mathematically quite complex. One begins simply by measuring phasic HR and respiration. Respiratory influences on HR are mediated by the parasympathetic nervous system; thus, quantifying the respiratory influence on HR gives a measure of relative parasympathetic/sympathetic activation. This quantification involves an elaborate statistical technique called cross-spectral analysis, in which two separate rhythms (here, HR and respiration) are analyzed into Fourier series (the same technique as described in Chapter 9 for providing power spectra of EEG) and then the influence of one rhythm on the other is assessed.

Several studies (see Porges, 1976) support the value of this basic formulation, particularly for understanding hyperactivity and its treatment with drugs. The ultimate fate of the model, of course, will depend on the proverbial further research. It should serve in this context to remind us of the increasingly prominent role of computers in psychophysiology. The computer allows analyses that would once have been unthinkable, if only by virtue of their sheer tediousness.

Both the Wenger and Porges approaches to autonomic balance reflect greater sophistication than measurement of a single psychophysiological system, but they fall short of a true pattern approach. For the attempt to form a single index from this wealth of information represents a "smoothing over" of the pattern information, rather than an attempt to pinpoint the areas in which measures vary together in some more complicated fashion. From our point of view, some of their apparent failures are more interesting than their successes. In one report of 534 adult males (Wenger, 1966), for example, more than half of their subjects showed anomalous patterns of activity that could be characterized as neither sympathetic nor parasympathetic activation.

This arousal-oriented approach can be contrasted with several recent studies of patterning within the cardiovascular system conducted at the National Institute of Mental Health (Williams et al., 1975; Bittker et al., 1975). These experiments began with Lacey's distinction between "sensory intake" and "sensory rejection." As discussed in Chapter 5, Lacey has argued that attentive observance of the environment (sensory intake) is accompanied by cardiovascular relaxation, while focusing the attention inward, as in mental arithmetic (sensory rejection), is signaled by increases in cardiovascular function. The Williams group went beyond the simple recording of HR to include measures of systolic and diastolic BP, forearm blood flow, and digital pulse volume in order to investigate a more complete pattern of cardiovascular changes in these situations. Three experimental tasks were included: reading slides of words that were blurred, backwards, or upside down (sensory intake); subtracting the number 12 from 1179 and then from the difference between the two, and so on (sensory rejection); and finally a clinical type of interview, in which the subject described his life (a combination of intake and rejection).

Williams et al. (1975) reported that each of these three conditions was characterized by a unique pattern of cardiovascular adjustments, as seen in Figure 11.1. A further statistical analysis of these findings indicated that there were two major factors underlying the results. The first corresponded to the

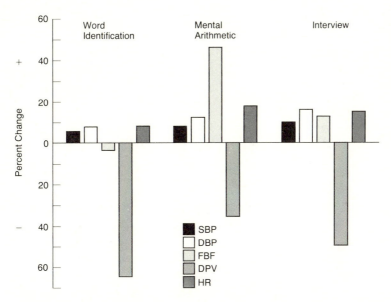

Figure 11.1 *Cardiovascular Patterning for Different Tasks.* SBP = systolic blood pressure; DBP = diastolic blood pressure; FBF = forearm blood flow; DPV = digital pulse volume; HR = heart rate. (After Williams et al., 1975.)

traditional arousal view: increases in HR, BF, and BP along with decreases in PV. But beyond this covariation, a second competing pattern was found in which diastolic BP decreases were coupled with increases in HR and forearm BF (FBF), and vice versa. That is to say, the arousal pattern was only *part* of the story. The additional information gained by this more sophisticated analysis led to several fascinating hypotheses about the mechanisms of cardiovascular change.

In a separate analysis of the interview data from this same experiment (Bittker et al., 1975), these researchers related the physiological changes to behavioral ratings of the subject's behavior during the interview. Throughout the discussion of life history, each subject was observed by two raters who estimated his "attentiveness" to the situation. On the basis of these ratings, the subjects were divided into equal groups of "attenders," who were actively involved in the discussion, and "non-attenders," whose interest seemed to wander. As might be expected, the "attenders" showed decreased FBF during the interview—the same physiological response that characterized the entire group when they were forced to focus on the slides of words. Correspondingly, the "non-attenders" had increased FBF during the interview, the response previously seen during mental arithmetic. Although physiological differences between the two groups appeared in all three tasks, it was only in the relatively ambiguous interview that these differences became statistically significant. This brings us to the topic of using physiological patterns of response to study the differences between people.

Individual Differences

Throughout our discussion of psychophysiology, we have often proceeded as if the personalities of all the experimental subjects we discussed were the same. That is, if you are interested in studying normal human physiological function, it doesn't particularly matter who the normal human is. This assumption is characteristic of all attempts to formulate general laws of behavior. It is also very often false.

This brings us face-to-face with one of the most fundamental controversies in a science of man. Mischel (1973) has argued persuasively that, in behavioral studies, the situation in which a person finds himself is far more important than the specific person in that situation. To use an extreme example, a man offered $5,000 to cross the street will cross the street no matter who he is. Bowers (1973) has countered that, for many less extreme cases, the personality of the individual interacts with the situation. One man may respond to his wife's threat to leave him by bashing her over the head, while another goes to the local bar to drown his troubles, and a third tries to talk it over.

The Bittker et al. (1975) data discussed above contain the germ of the solution. They found that in the extreme situation of sensory intake or rejection, individual differences were relatively minor. However, in a more ambiguous situation where the subjects clearly had an opportunity to pay attention to the interviewer or not as they chose, the characteristic individual differences appeared. Thus, once again, both positions are right. General laws of behavior or general laws of physiological response will be quite appropriate for some situations and inappropriate for others. The catch, then, is in discovering which situations are particularly constraining and which are not.

Let us put this conclusion another way. Suppose a researcher is interested in the importance of individual differences to studies of weight lifting. Imagine two possible experiments. In the first, all subjects are asked to lift a paper clip and then lift an elephant. Virtually everyone will be able to pick up the paper clip; virtually no one will be able to lift the elephant. Ergo, there are no individual differences. In the second experiment, the same people are asked to lift weights of 20 lbs., 40 lbs., 60 lbs., and so on. Here, important individual differences *are* found—same people, different conclusion. Thus, one cannot ask the question: Are individual differences important in weight lifting (or in physiology)? There is no abstract general answer. If you want to choose people for Olympic weight-lifting competitions, individual differences are critical. If you want to hire people to load a truck with paper clips or elephants, they couldn't be less important. It all depends on the question you ask.

In the search for general physiological laws, the researcher may be easily misled by a facile application of the physical sciences model. Newton taught us that any action produces an equal and opposite reaction. To the physical scientist, the way in which this force is applied is irrelevant. The type of rocket propulsion system does not matter; if a rocket is to take off, all that matters is that sufficient driving force be available.

Standardization of stimuli is a mammoth task for the psychologist. Consider any study of EDA responses to a series of words. The word *parachute* is tape-recorded and presented along with many other emotionally neutral or stimulating words. One subject in the laboratory stifles a yawn and waits for the experiment to end when he hears the word *parachute*. No EDR is observed. Then another person hears the same tape recording. The word *parachute* reminds him that he has agreed to try skydiving with his new girl friend the following weekend. The thought of jumping 3000 feet for love scares him silly, and a massive SRR is observed. This is the eternal problem of studying people: Ultimately, their complicated internal lives must be brought into the equations.

Many psychophysiologists attempt to circumvent this problem as much as possible. Elaborate pains are taken to present the same stimulus to all individuals. Instead of a series of words, an interminable series of 86-decibel, 1000-Hz tones is presented to each volunteer. Each tone is precisely equated for its physical characteristics. But human complications once more muddy the picture. One person has the utmost confidence that the experimenter is on the verge of revolutionizing human knowledge and concentrates intently on the situation. Another, who woke up too late to eat breakfast and had to hurry over to the lab to take part, is cooperating only so that he can collect his $3.00 fee and go out for a large stack of pancakes with a side order of sausage. No matter how carefully the experimenter standardizes the stimulus presentations, he is left with the fact that he is studying the most complicated topic ever approached by science—you and me.

Like all behavioral scientists, most psychophysiologists have concentrated on the search for general laws that apply equally to all human beings. The topic of a distinctive physiological pattern that characterizes a given state is sometimes referred to as "response stereotypy." Thus Ax's (1953) physiological distinction between anger and fear and Lacey's (1959) distinction between sensory intake and sensory rejection are examples of response stereotypy.

A few researchers have focused instead on how one individual's responses differ from another's. Wenger's (1966) attempt to discover stable scores of autonomic balance is one example of this search for "individual stereotypy." Malmo and Shagass (1949) were involved in a series of classic experiments on this topic of individual differences. Briefly, they studied the stress responses of two groups of psychiatric patients, some with cardiovascular symptoms and others with a history of head and neck pains. As expected, the cardiovascular patients showed large HR and BP changes to stress, while the second group gave more evidence of muscle tension in the same situations. Lacey, Bateman, and Van Lehn (1953) extended these findings to normal individuals; some people seem to respond more in one physiological system than another regardless of the type of stress.

In a series of papers whose mathematical sophistication is rarely approached even today, Engel (1960) showed how response stereotypy and individual stereotypy can coexist. The total pattern of physiological response to a given situation is a function *both* of the situation and of the individual.

The point to be made here is that, as psychology matures, it will increasingly recognize the importance of the individual tested as well as the conditions of testing. Given the intimate tie of physiological responses to mental life, the psychophysiologist must be particularly sensitive to this interaction.

Psychophysiology and the Social Sciences

Throughout this book we have emphasized the importance of a biological perspective on human behavior. In concluding, it is only fair to look at the other side of the coin. For this book is not meant as an imperialistic attempt to subsume the social sciences into biology. Rather it is a plea that psychologists should be open to the importance of biological factors, and human biologists should be closely attuned to psychological variables.

In a classic paper entitled "A Biologist Examines the Mind and Behavior," Seymour Kety (1960) makes the point that, as his subtitle put it, "Many disciplines contribute to understanding human behavior, each with peculiar virtues and limitations."

It all depends on the kind of question one asks. Suppose we want to know who will win the next Presidential election. As psychobiologists, we might assume that the decision for one candidate over another is based on a specific molecular configuration in the brain. Perhaps the psychophysiology of the future will able to detect that configuration, so that one way to find out who will be elected would be to place each citizen in this expensive machine. Another way would be to ask people. When we are looking across large populations, asking people is likely to remain the most practical approach.

Behaviorists love to bring up the proverb about how you can lead a horse to water, but you can't make him drink. "Horsefeathers," they say. "All you have to do is make the animal thirsty enough." Now it is also true that one could accomplish that today by opening the horse's skull and electrically stimulating thirst centers in the hypothalamus. Which is easier?

Thus psychophysiology does not pretend to have the best answer to every question in the social sciences, though all of the social sciences are its subject matter.

Psychophysiology is the study of human biology as a means for understanding human behavior and experience. Its strength is its weakness: the attempt to study human behavior in all its complexity. It is an infant science, just beginning to develop appropriate techniques. Its future is intimately tied up with technological and methodological advances, like facial thermography (Chapter 5) and magnetoencephalography (Chapter 9). If a new technique is developed tomorrow to measure levels of synaptic transmitters in specific brain sites in the normal human, the psychophysiology of tomorrow may bear little resemblance to what we've sketched here—except in its commitment to study the psychobiology of human function with the least possible interference.

Appendices

Appendix A: Technical Notes for Chapter 3

Recording Human Physiological Response

An Introduction to Electricity

All matter is composed of atoms, nature's basic building blocks. Atoms were once thought to be indivisible, but we now know that they are composed of protons, electrons, and neutrons, in turn. Electrical charge is a fundamental property of protons (positively charged particles) and electrons (negatively charged particles). Electrons can be detached from an atom by a number of forces; friction, pressure, light, heat, chemicals and magnetism all operate to move these "free electrons" from one place to another.

We are all familiar with many examples of these principles. Walking across a carpet (friction) builds up a charge of electricity, which your body discharges to a door knob or some other good conductor; pressure on certain crystal materials produces an electrical charge that is used in one kind of microphone; batteries (chemical) make use of the fact that some materials readily give up electrons and others readily accept them.

An electric current is simply the flow of electrons through some material. Some materials allow far more of this flow than others; basically, it depends on their structure and how tightly bound the electrons are to their atoms. If electrons can be detached easily and thus flow through a material, it is said to be a good conductor. Most metals are good conductors of electricity. Electrical wire is typically made of copper because it is relatively cheap and allows electrons to flow freely. Insulators are materials that do not allow a free electron flow. Rubber, for example, is a complex substance with very tightly bound electrons. Most electrical wire is insulated with rubber, so that if you touch it the electrons will not flow through you and interfere with the body's own electrochemical circuits.

It may be useful to think of a simple electrical circuit as analogous to the flow of water through a pipe. We must have a pump, or power source, to keep water flowing in such a plumbing system. Depending on how powerful this pump is, it will exert a certain pressure on the water that passes through it. If we wanted to, we could also measure the water current, or how fast the water is flowing. Let us arbitrarily say that we are concerned with the amount of water that flows through a certain section of the pipe every second.

Obviously, the water current or rate of flow will depend at least partially upon the pressure that the pump exerts. It will also depend on how wide our pipe is. Assuming that the pipe is entirely filled with water, whenever the pressure of the pump is increased, the amount of water that flows past a certain point will also be increased.

Another thing that will influence the rate of water flow will be any resistance that the water encounters. Suppose, for example, that we want to purify the water flowing through the pipe. The first thing we might do is put in a screen somewhere along the pipe to keep out small pebbles or other impurities. The water is now encountering some *resistance*—its current or rate of flow will be decreased because the water is being slowed down by the screen.

So, in this more complicated example, the current depends both on the pressure of the pump and the size of any resistance that it encounters along the way.

Now, let's get back to electricity. Remember that an electric current is merely a flow of electrons. If we replace the pump with a battery and the pipe with a piece of wire, we will have a complete electrical circuit. Instead of a piece of wire mesh, we can substitute a length of material that is a relatively poor conductor of electricity—typically, a kind of carbon compound. We now have a complete electrical circuit. The pressure that a battery exerts is called its *voltage*. Electrons flow from the negative pole of a battery to the positive pole. The *current*, or rate of flow of electrons, again will be determined by the *voltage* or pressure and *resistance* to the flow. The relationship between these quantities is summarized in Ohm's law, which can be simply stated as:

$$\text{Voltage} = \text{Current} \times \text{Resistance}$$

or

$$\text{Resistance} = \frac{\text{Voltage}}{\text{Current}}$$

or

$$\text{Current} = \frac{\text{Voltage}}{\text{Resistance}}$$

The units of these quantities are arbitrarily defined so that:

$$1 \text{ Volt} = 1 \text{ Ampere} \times 1 \text{ Ohm}$$

Thus, using Ohm's law, if we know the current and voltage in a circuit, we can easily calculate the resistance. Or, if we know the voltage and resistance in ohms we can calculate the current in amperes. Thus, electrical resistance is arbitrarily defined in units called ohms.

Alternatively, one may talk about a material's conductance. A material that resists the flow of electrons is a relatively poor conductor. By definition, conductance is the reciprocal of resistance. That is:

$$mhos \quad = \quad \frac{1}{ohms}$$

$$ohms \quad = \quad \frac{1}{mhos}$$

Thus, a resistance of 10 ohms = .1 mho. A resistance of 200 ohms = .005 mho. Again, as resistance increases, conductance decreases. As resistance decreases, conductance increases. Every resistance can be expressed as a conductance.

Technically, an ampere is defined as the passage of 6.24×10^{18} electrons past a given point in one second. Current is rarely measured directly in the psychophysiology laboratory. What is measured directly is voltage, the potential difference between two sides of an energy source. (Remember, electrons must always flow from one place to another.) The typical order of magnitude for psychophysiological variables is in millivolts (mV—thousandths of a volt) and microvolts (μV—millionths of a volt).

Note that all that we have said here can be simply summarized as follows: Electricity is the flow of electrons; for electrons to flow there must be a power source of potential difference in a complete circuit; the basic electrical variables are related according to Ohm's Law: Voltage = Current × Resistance.

Electronic Filtering

The basic principle in electronic filtering has to do with altering the frequency characteristics of an electrical signal. Electrical power is supplied in two different forms: DC (direct current), in which electrons flow in a single direction, and AC (alternating current), in which electron flow is periodically reversed. If we were to graphically represent what happens to electricity when you turn on a flashlight (DC), it might look something like this:

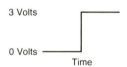

When the flashlight is turned on, 3 volts of potential difference appears in the electric circuit. But ordinary house current (AC), when it is turned on, looks something like this:

−110 Volts

0 Volts

+ 110 Volts

The direction of electron flow is periodically reversed. In the United States, AC house current ordinarily has a frequency of 60 Hz; that is, the direction of electron flow is reversed twice a second. (Thus the voltage goes from +110 to −110 to +110 60 times.) Elsewhere, 50 Hz is often the rule.

Similar principles of direct and alternating current are involved in recording certain physiological signals; this may be a source of confusion for those unfamiliar with polygraph conventions. In the EEG, for example, we are usually more interested in the frequency with which current flow reverses than we are in the actual magnitude of the potential difference itself. On some polygraphs, the distinction is made by labeling some preamplifiers DC, because they allow us to measure the actual potential difference between two points on the body, while other preamplifiers are called AC (although not in the same sense as is AC house current) because they are built to ignore the true potential difference while they concentrate on the rate of change. These "AC" preamplifiers further allow us to filter out, or ignore, certain frequencies.

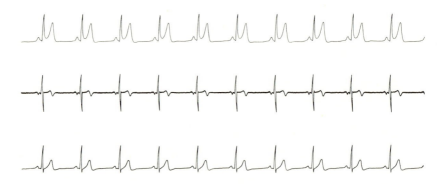

Figure A.1 *EKG Filtered Through Three Different Circuits.* The same electrical signal is filtered simultaneously through three different amplifiers on a Grass Model 7 polygraph. Top channel: ½ amp, low frequency, 1 Hz; ½ amp, high frequency, 15 Hz. Middle channel: ½ amp, low frequency, 10 Hz; ½ amp, high frequency, 75 Hz. Bottom channel: ½ amp, low frequency, 1 Hz; ½ amp, high frequency, 75 Hz. Normal EKG usually displayed as on the bottom channel.

The effect of this filtering is difficult to explain in the abstract but can easily be seen in Figure A.1. This represents an actual polygraph record of the EKG, indicating contraction of the heart muscles. The exact same electrical signal is passed through three different preamplifiers at the same time to illustrate the effects of filtering. Often the psychophysiologist is concerned only with the rate at which the heart beats (indicated by the "spikes" in the record). In the first record of this same EKG, other aspects of the wave-form are emphasized by the filtering apparatus. This may be of special interest to the psychophysiologist who is concerned with more than just the major pumping action of the heart (see Chapter 5).

Thus, through electronic filters, the researcher is able to focus on specific aspects of a complex electronic signal, much as one might choose to focus his attention on a familiar person in a group photograph. The actual effects of a specific kind of filtering on a complex physiological wave-form are difficult to predict and often established by trial and error.

Paper Speeds

The same electronic signal may look very different if it is recorded at two different paper speeds. A faster paper speed provides more detail about the characteristics of a given wave, but runs the risk of providing so much detail that the overall picture is lost. Figure A.2 shows similar EKG signals recorded at four different paper speeds. The actual paper speed chosen depends on the goals of the experimenter; the top tracing recorded at 5

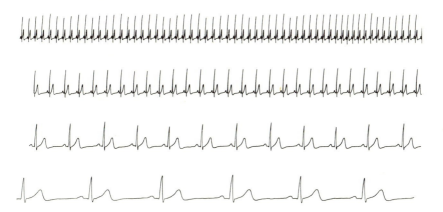

Figure A.2 *EKG at Four Paper Speeds.* Four EKG records from the same subject. Paper speed for the top channel is 5 mm/sec; for the second channel, 10 mm/sec; for the third channel, 25 mm/sec; for the bottom channel, 50 mm/sec. Note that faster paper speeds give additional information about wave-form.

mm/sec is an example of the kind of record usually seen in psychophysiological research. An experimenter who was interested in subtle changes in EKG might use a much faster paper speed; one who was only interested in slower sweat gland changes might use a slower speed.

Safety

Modern commercial polygraphs are designed to eliminate the risk of shock hazard to an experimental subject. However, psychophysiological investigators must always remain keenly aware of potential shock hazards. This is particularly true when one is using "makeshift" or additional experimental equipment.

Table A.1 summarizes the effects on the human body of various current intensities delivered to the skin surface. According to Ohm's law, the actual current delivered by a given voltage will depend on the impedance (resistance to an alternating current) of the subject. This in turn is determined by factors like the dampness of the skin. Note that if shock were delivered to electrodes that pierce the skin, the hazards would be increased considerably.

Although sensation thresholds vary from person to person, somewhere around one milliampere the first "tingling" sensations will be felt. Near 5 mA, the feeling becomes so painful that the subject is likely to jump away. Also starting around this level, motor nerves are stimulated, causing muscular contraction. Somewhere between 10 and 20 mA, these muscle spasms become so strong that a person cannot release the current source. Up to 100 mA, the shock becomes increasingly painful; the uncontrolled contraction of skeletal muscles may lead to physical injury.

Table A.1   Effects of 60 Hz Electric Shock Through the Body on an Average Human

Current Intensity (1-second contact)	
1 milliampere	Sensation threshold.
5 milliamperes	Maximum harmless current intensity.
	Person can just manage to release grip on conductors. Above this level, sustained muscular contractions result.
50 milliamperes	Pain. Possible fainting, exhaustion, mechanical injury. Heart and respiratory functions continue.
100–300 milliamperes	Ventricular fibrillation starts. Respiratory centers remain intact.
6 amperes	Sustained myocardial contraction followed by normal heart rhythm. Temporary respiratory paralysis. Burns if current density is high.

Source: Based on Bruner, 1967.

Around 100 mA, life-threatening forces come into play, most notably ventricular fibrillation. The blood-pumping action of the heart depends on the coordinated electrical firing of the myocardial tissue. With sufficiently high external currents, some of the heart's muscle cells are stimulated to fire randomly, upsetting the pumping action. This ventricular fibrillation, as the random firing is called, is fatal unless corrected within minutes.

Sustained electrical currents at 6 amperes force the heart into sustained contraction, much as currents over 20 mA affect the skeletal musculature. But if the current is only a few thousandths of a second in duration, the normal coordinated pumping pattern may reappear. This principle is used in "defibrillation," when a massive shock is provided to the chest of a patient with a fibrillating heart to restore the normal rhythm.

Appendix B: Technical Notes for Chapter 4

The Sweat Gland

Resistance vs. Conductance

Although conductances can be computed directly from resistances by the following transformation:

$$\text{conductance (mhos)} \quad = \quad \frac{1}{\text{resistance (ohms)}}$$

this transformation is nonlinear. Therefore, use of the two measures may lead to very different conclusions. Suppose, for example, that we wish to compare two responses made by the same subject, starting from different EDA baselines. Consider the following hypothetical data:*

	SR (in ohms)	SC (in micromhos)
	Preresponse Values	
Response 1	100,000	10
Response 2	20,000	50
	Postresponse Values	
Response 1	99,000	10.1
Response 2	19,000	52.6
	Actual Response	
Response 1	1,000	0.1
Response 2	1,000	2.6

* See Woodworth and Schlosberg, 1954, p. 141, for a more elaborate example.

Thus, in this example, the two SRRs appear equal, but SCRs based on the same data vary by a factor of 26:1. Clearly, then, the choice of which units to analyze is a critical one, particularly when linear statistics like the correlation coefficient are considered.

As noted in the text, both biological and statistical considerations suggest that conductance is to be preferred as a dependent measure. However, apparatus for the direct recording of SC is only now becoming widely available. Some experimenters record SR and then convert each relevant data point to SC before data analysis. Given the non-linearity of the transformation, direct measurement of conductances would yield responses with a different wave-form.

Typical Values

All electrodermal measures vary according to such factors as electrolytes, recording site on the body, and room temperature, as well as individual differences. The following ranges are for "standard conditions":

SCL	2–100 μmhos/cm^2
SRL	10–500 kilohms/cm^2
SPL	+10 to −70 mv (skin with reference to neutral site on body)

SCL and SRL vary with electrode size (SPL does not), and so values are given per square centimeter of electrode surface.

Responses vary with level. A very powerful stimulus (like an electric shock) might result in a 50% decrease in SRL, while the normally moderate experimental stimuli could be expected to yield about 5% decreases. Typically, response latency is 1–2 *seconds, with* 50% recovery time about the same. These values are approximate.

Defining Spontaneous Activity

Defining the minimum amplitude of a response that is to be considered a "spontaneous electrodermal response" is presently not standardized. Experimenters frequently choose a fairly arbitrary cutoff point (typically between 100 and 1000 ohms). Edelberg (1972) suggests that, when resistance is measured, 0.1% of baseline resistance be considered the minimum amplitude for an SSRR. (This value is based on the original resting SRL and then held constant until SRL changes by 10%. A new minimum amplitude based on this SRL is then computed.) If conductance is being measured directly, a cutoff of 0.1% μmhos is suggested by the same author.

These two procedures are not directly comparable, nor are they in widespread use. One of the present difficulties in talking about psychological correlates of spontaneous activity is the lack of standardization; two experimenters who find different results may have defined the term very differently. Although standardization is extremely important in attempts to replicate findings, the present diversity of systems may be useful in helping us to determine the implications of choosing a given cutoff point. Given the attitude of the present work toward specificity in the electrodermal system, we might even find that different cutoff points were appropriate for different experimental questions.

Recording Procedure

The electrodes used to record EDA may be as simple as two silver quarters strapped to the wrist with rubber bands. However, primitive electrodes of this sort are likely to become electrically unstable, particularly if SR is recorded for a long period of time. Polarization, or the build-up of a counterelectromotive force at the interface of electrode and electrolyte, is the most common problem in recording EDA. (The polarization of a pair of electrodes may be directly tested by recording the potential difference or resistance between two electrodes whose surfaces are brought into contact with the electrolyte.) This problem may largely be avoided by the use of high-quality commercial electrodes, silver/silver chloride (silver covered with a thin film of the alloy silver chloride) being the most common type.

As noted in the introductory section, an electrolyte is ordinarily placed between the electrode and the skin surface. Many commercial creams are available with the approximate chemical composition of sweat, and these are to be preferred for EDA measurement. Some electrode pastes contain a mild abrasive (for example, Sanborn's Redux) which strips away the outer horny layer of skin. Such pastes should not be used for EDA measurement, because they alter the electrical properties of the skin.

The actual electrode placements for SC and SP should be quite different. For SC or SR, two "emotionally reactive" sites (for example, palms, fingertips, soles of the feet) are preferred because this choice maximizes the observed activity by summing across two sites. Since the major pathway for current flow is at the highly conductive dermal layer, the actual distance between the electrodes on the epidermal layer is, for all practical purposes, irrelevant. However, since an electrical current is being introduced into the body, two sites on the same side of the heart are probably preferable for safety reasons. (The actual magnitude of the current introduced for EDA is extremely small; the suggestion serves only as a sort of fail-safe device.) Edelberg (1972) suggests recording SC from the medial phalanx of the second and third fingers of one hand, since small surface cuts may bias recordings by providing a direct current pathway to the dermal layer and these sites appear to be least likely to have these minor abrasions. Another common choice for SR recording is from the thenar and hypothenar eminences of the palm.

Obviously, to record resistance, a very small electrical current must be introduced into the body. In all probability, the magnitude of this current will be predetermined by the manufacturer of the specific device you are using. Ideally, it should be on the order of 8 microamps/cm^2 or smaller (Edelberg, 1972).

SP recordings reflect a potential difference between the sweat glands and internal body tissues. Thus, for the ideal recording, one electrode is placed on an "emotionally active"

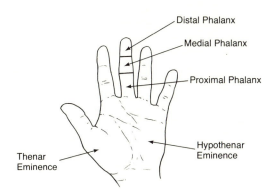

site and a small hole is drilled in the skin under the second electrode. For ordinary recordings, a second electrode placed on an inactive site (usually the forearm, four-fifths of the way to the elbow) is quite satisfactory. Note that, if two active sites are used to record potential difference, sweat glands that show similar activity in phase will tend to cancel each other out, and the total potential difference observed may be quite small.

Filtering EDA

One frequent annoyance for the EDA researcher is the fact that, for some subjects, level changes may be of relatively large magnitude compared to responses. Thus, for example, a person sitting quietly may show an increasing SR of 5000 ohms per minute, when one is interested in measuring SSRRs of 100 ohms. Thus, the desired detectable change is only 1/50 of unwanted level shifts for each minute. Given a limited range of measurable values, this implies that the SR scale will have to be changed at regular intervals (usually manually).

One way to solve this problem is to filter out the slower frequency level changes (for example, a high pass filter of 3 Hz). Many of the simpler EDA meters on the market make use of a filter of this sort. This is a quite satisfactory solution for many applications. However, several words of warning should be kept in mind if one is considering such a system. Obviously, level information and data on response topography are lost when this method is used. Less obvious is the fact that true response amplitude information is also unavailable; the filtering circuits may change the characteristics of the rising limb of the EDR. Thus, with a system of this sort, one can only speak with assurance of the *relative* ordering of responses.

Range Correction

For the sake of argument, let us extrapolate from the Kilpatrick (1972) results and state that SCL, being linked with cognitive problem-solving activity, is a measure of "alertness." Suppose now that we want to deduce the alertness of the following two people:

| Subject 1 | SCL | = | 10 μmhos |
| Subject 2 | SCL | = | 25 μmhos |

On the basis of just this data, we would have to argue that Subject 2 is "more alert." This is immediately suspect, however, because we know that individual differences in SCL depend on the thickness of the skin, precise recording site, and so on.

Suppose we also know that over the course of an hour and a half in this experiment, the variation of each subject was as follows:

	Minimum	*Maximum*
Subject 1	3 μmhos	11 μmhos
Subject 2	23 μmhos	40 μhos

On the basis of this additional information, we can see that, for our original measurements, Subject 1 was almost as "alert" as he gets (maximum 11 μmhos; actual value 10 μmhos). Subject 2, on the other hand was at the relaxation end of his continuum (minimum 23 μmhos; actual value 25 μmhos).

This is the principle of range correction, a statistical correction procedure proposed by Lykken et al. (1966). Although actual baseline values may be telling us in the above example that Subject 2 was always more alert than Subject 1 ever got, more likely they were telling us about the relative number of sweat glands or the quality of the electrode contact in each. And so, we would be well advised to talk about how "alert" a person is in reference to his normal range of variation.

Range-corrected scores are computed as follows:

$$\text{Range-corrected SCL} \quad = \quad \frac{\text{SCL} - \text{SCL}_{min}}{\text{SCL}_{max} - \text{SCL}_{min}}$$

Note that these values will always fall between 0 and 1, the 0 implying that a subject is at his physiological minimum and the 1 that he is at his maximum.

For the above examples, then, range-corrected scores would be as follows:

$$\text{Subject 1} \quad = \quad (10 - 3) / (11 - 3) \quad = \quad 0.88$$

$$\text{Subject 2} \quad = \quad (25 - 23) / (40 - 23) \quad = \quad 0.18$$

In the original report, Lykken et al. (1966) found that use of this procedure increased the correlation they found between SCL and the two-flash threshold—a psychophysical task in which one attempts to discriminate two brief flashes of light from each other. Thus, this approach has more than just the powerful intuitive appeal to recommend it.

Note that this procedure presupposes estimates of physiological maxima and minima. For SCL, Lykken suggests sitting quietly with the eyes closed (for minimum) and blowing up a balloon until it bursts (for the maximum).

Appendix C: Technical Notes for Chapter 5

The Cardiovascular System

Recording the Electrocardiogram

Electrode quality and the precision of electrode placement are less important for the EKG than for any other popular physiological measure. Given the large magnitude of the signal (on the order of 1 mv), its easily recognized form, and the fact that most researchers are simply interested in the number of R-spikes (that is, heart rate) rather than more subtle characteristics of the wave, it is quite easy to record. Electrodes are frequently large silver discs that are strapped to the arms and legs. All skin sites are first cleaned with alcohol or acetone and then rubbed with a mild abrasive.

Electrode placement for psychophysiological research (as opposed to diagnostic cardiology) is usually limited to one of three possible pairings summarized by Einthoven's triangle (see diagram). Lead I involved recording from the right and left arms, Lead II

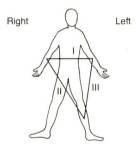

Right   Left

from the right arm and left leg, and Lead III from the left arm and left leg. The actual form of the EKG varies for these three "leads." Lead II is generally preferred since, for the normal subject, it yields the strongest signal with the most accentuated R-spikes (from which HR is computed). Lead I results in a relatively larger T-wave, while Lead III gives a much smaller signal.

Amplification and filtering circuits are also fairly flexible. Some filtering of slow frequency changes must be done to avoid "drift" (see Figure 3.10). Other filter settings are done empirically to maximize the relative height of the R-spikes.

Measuring Blood Pressure

Blood pressure is one of the most difficult systems to measure accurately within the limits of present technology. Many researchers have settled for the simple system described in the text: cutting off the circulation with an inflatable cuff, decreasing the cuff pressure until the first K-sound (Korotkoff sound) is heard, indicating that blood is now coming through (systole), and then continuing to decrease cuff pressure until the K-sounds disappear, indicating that blood flow is no longer interfered with (diastole).

But this system is not entirely satisfactory, for several reasons. The psychophysiologist is frequently interested in phasic (or moment-to-moment) responses to environmental stimuli. The clinical method allows only about one determination every minute. This ignores the fundamental problem of beat-to-beat variability. Like HR, BP varies from one beat to the next. The method described above bases its estimate on the presence or absence of the K-sound at a single beat. This can be seen as analogous to measuring HR by precisely timing the interval between any two beats, and then extrapolating this rate to a longer time period. Thus, the HR or BP will be dependent on the two specific beats chosen and will not be a good estimate of longer time trends.

Several systems have been developed for the continuous measurement of BP. The oldest system (still used in lie detection) simply inflates a cuff to a point midway between systolic and diastolic pressures. With each beat of the heart, the volume of the arm increases and decreases as blood is pumped through it, and changes in the pressure mechanically exerted on the cuff are noted. It should be clear from our discussion in the text that this is not really a measure of blood pressure at all but rather of blood volume. The intrusive effects of keeping a cuff inflated around the arm are also not entirely understood. Thus, it is impossible at this time to specify the lawful relationship of this measure to true BP.

Recently, biofeedback researchers have developed a number of more sophisticated systems for continuous BP measurement. We shall discuss the procedure recommended by Tursky, Shapiro, and Schwartz (1972). Further details on this and alternate procedures can be found in Tursky (1974). In these systems, a microphone is strapped near the elbow to electrically detect K-sounds. The EKG is simultaneously recorded. A cuff is then inflated to a point near the estimated systolic pressure. With each beat of the heart (as seen on the EKG channel), electronic equipment notes whether or not a K-sound occurred. If it did, then the systolic pressure for that beat was greater than the cuff pressure, since the K-sound represents blood being forced past the cuff barrier. If no K-sound was detected, then the artery was occluded and systolic BP for that beat must be below the cuff pressure. Note that this system tells us whether systolic BP was above or below cuff pressure for each beat; it does not tell us how far above or below.

In biofeedback studies for training patients to lower systolic BP, the cuff is first inflated to a point at which half the beats are followed by K-sounds and half are not. By definition, this could be referred to as the median systolic pressure. A subject can then be reinforced for those beats which are not followed by a K-sound (that is, lower than median systolic BP). Once the patient masters this task, the cuff is deflated by 2 mmHg at a time until the new lower median systolic pressure is located, and the process is repeated. A similar system can be used with diastolic BP. For both procedures, the cuff can remain inflated for only a relatively short period of time before the patient experiences discomfort. In these experiments, a "trial" lasted 50 beats, and then the cuff was deflated for a short rest period.

Photoplethysmography

In plethysmography, one measures the volume of a body part. This increases as the member fills with blood with each beat of the heart, and decreases as the blood is drained. In Chapter 3, we referred to the technique of volume plethysmography, in which the body part was placed in a sealed container (for example, a jar filled with water) and changes in pressure were noted. Needless to say, this is not a particularly convenient procedure.

It is far easier to use the technique of photoplethysmography, which takes advantage of the optical properties of the blood. In "transmitted" photoplethysmography, a small light source is taped, for example, to the tip of a finger. A light-sensitive electronic device is placed opposite the light on the bottom of the finger. The light transmitted through the finger to the photocell varies systematically with the amount of blood in the digit. This system is possible only with relatively thin body parts like a finger or the earlobe. An alternative system depends on "reflected" light. Here the light source and photodetector are placed side by side, both "aimed" at the same section of tissue.

Commercial photoplethysmographs of many types are now widely available. Since BV varies with each beat of the heart (as tissues are alternately filled with and emptied of blood), HR can be assessed by using a plethysmograph rather than the EKG. This is sometimes preferred for reasons of safety and convenience.

Two Views of the Cardiac Function

The two major contemporary theories of the functional significance of cardiovascular response have been formulated by John Lacey and Paul Obrist. They were discussed in general terms in the main text under the heading "What Does the Heart Respond To?" Here let us consider some of their implications in more detail.

Lacey's work harks back to a classic experiment performed by Chester Darrow in 1929. Darrow believed that the general term *emotion* referred to a number of physiologically distinct subcategories. Specifically, he showed that physiological reactions distinguished "sensory" from "ideational" stimuli. He used groups of "disturbing" and "indifferent" ideational stimuli in his experiment. Examples of indifferent stimuli were the words *apple, table* and *paper*. For disturbing stimuli, his examples included the words *toilet* and *masturbation* as well as pictures of men's and women's underwear. His sensory stimuli included ringing a bell, pulling a subject's hair, and slapping him in the face.

Dr. Darrow notes that he had some trouble getting subjects to complete the entire experiment, but his results do indeed show that the "immediate reflex response to sensory excitation" is physiologically distinct from responses "mediated by associative or ideational processes." More specifically, BP and HR increases were seen more frequently in response to the disturbing ideational than to sensory stimuli. Indeed, sensory stimuli were sometimes accompanied by decreases in both systems. EDRs also distinguished the two groups, being far more common for the disturbing ideational stimuli. On the average, the indifferent ideational stimuli fell between the other two.

This research remained just one more fact that didn't quite fit in with activation theory until it was revised and extended by the work of Professors John and Beatrice Lacey. The Laceys called attention to phenomena of "directional fractionation" of responses—that is, cases in which physiological systems did not covary in an arousal-like fashion. Their major example of this contrasted "environmental intake" (attention directed outwards; Darrow's sensory stimuli) in which HR decreased to "environmental rejection" (attention directed inward; Darrow's ideational stimuli) which typically led to an increase of HR. They further suggested an underlying biological mechanism for this phenomenon: increases in HR or BP lead to feedback that inhibits cortical activity.

The aortic arch and the carotid sinus are richly endowed with baroreceptors. When blood pressure rises, these receptors fire more frequently and produce a variety of homeostatic changes to keep the blood pressure at an acceptable level. A number of animal studies have suggested that an increase in baroreceptor firing can also lead to cortical deactivation.

One series of studies has tested this hypothesis behaviorally. This group depends on the fact that with each beat of the heart, BP rises to a peak (systole) and then gradually drops off to a minimum (diastole) until the heart beats again. Resulting changes in aortic pressure, and thus baroreceptor activity, can be approximately related to wave-forms in the electrocardiogram. During the S-T and T phases of the cardiac cycle, aortic pressure should be at its peak; baroreceptor activity is minimal, and, therefore, the cortex should be relatively inhibited. Similarly, during the T-P and P phases, pressure should be low, baroreceptor firing reduced, and thus cortical activation highest. If one further assumes that behavioral measures such as reaction times and sensory thresholds reflect "cortical activation," one would expect to find short reaction times and low sensory thresholds to stimuli presented near the T-P and P waves of the electrocardiogram if Lacey's theory is correct. Longer reaction times and higher sensory thresholds would be found to stimuli presented in the S-T and T waves of the cycle.

Two early studies of reaction time and the cardiac cycle (Birren et al., 1963; Callaway and Layne, 1964) found precisely these results. However, a series of attempted replications by Thompson and Botwinick (1970) failed to find any effects of the cardiac cycle on reaction time. Along the same lines, an early report on cardiac cycle effects on the auditory thresholds of four subjects (Saxon, 1970) suggested support of Lacey's hypothesis, while later more careful studies (Delfini and Campos, 1972) failed to verify this result.

There have been a few more directly physiological tests of the Lacey baroreceptor hypothesis. Boyle, Dykman, and Ackerman (1965) used five separate methods of EEG analysis (including frequency counts) to look for cortical accompaniments of spontaneously high HRs (defined as 6 beat-per-minute (BPM) accelerations in a 5-second period). None of their EEG measures showed any correlation to HR changes in their group of thirty 10-year-olds. They concluded, however, that more EEG leads or more subtle analyses of the EEG might support Lacey's contention. Even if they didn't, they persisted, it could just mean that the EEG is too crude a measure of cortical activation.

On the other hand, an unpublished study by Lacey and Coquery (reported in Lacey, 1967) supported the baroreceptor mechanism. They used a primitive type of biofeedback in which high-voltage alpha turns a light on. The light goes off when alpha blocks in response to it. Subjects were not aware of the reinforcement contingency, nor were they asked to try to keep the light on or off—they were merely to watch it. In 20 of these 24 subjects, the HR for alpha on was greater than the HR for alpha off. Says Lacey (1967): "The HR differences are small but very consistent." For the group as a whole, the results were significant at the .001 level of confidence.

However, it is well known that attending to a light results in a transient HR deceleration (Lacey, 1967) as well as alpha blockade (Lynch and Paskewitz, 1971). The convenient pairing of these events could account for the small group trend observed. If the experiment could be replicated with the light going off when alpha appears, the results would inspire considerably more confidence.

In general, then, the baroreceptor hypothesis has proven difficult to substantiate. One set of problems revolves around the use of phasic HR to test a hypothesis about phasic BP. Schwartz (1971) demonstrated that the two were not highly correlated. More subtle tests of the hypothesis (Lacey and Lacey, 1974) continue to provide some support for this formulation. Using quite sophisticated analyses, the Laceys (1976) now argue that phase relations between the cardiac cycle and baroreceptor activity may systematically vary with HR.

Obrist et al. (1970a) stress the importance of metabolic demand in the determination of HR—that is, an increase in a person's HR generally indicates that his body is more active. HR is thus a peripheral measure of total somatic activity rather than a cause of CNS change.

In a direct test of the alternative view, Obrist et al. (1970b) used atropine (which blocks cardiac response) in preparing subjects for a reaction-time task. According to the Lacey argument, this HR decrease prepares the organism to respond via baroreceptor activation of the cortex. The Obrist group argued that, if this transient HR deceleration is a *cause* of improved performance, then blocking it pharmacologically should lead to longer reaction times. If deceleration was just a by-product of general somatic adjustments to the situation, then atropine should have no effect on reaction time. The findings clearly favored Obrist's view that HR is less a cause than an effect.

This kind of argument immediately brings us back to the question of CNS mechanisms of cardiac control. There is no simple "HR center" in the brain. Among areas of the brain that will produce HR accelerations upon electrical stimulation, Gunn et al. (1972) list the following: sensorimotor cortex; some areas of the cingulate gyrus, septum, and amygdala; the lateral and posterior hypothalamus; the mesencephalic reticular formation; and the medullary reticulum.

In a review of these CNS mechanisms of cardiac control, Rushmer and Smith (1959) provide an overview that strongly supports Obrist:

> Virtually all portions of the CNS which consistently yield cardiovascular responses when stimulated also induce behavioral changes which would normally be associated with cardiovascular adjustments. . . . In general, those portions of the brain which do not elicit cardiovascular responses to electrical stimulation also fail to induce behavioral changes which would be expected to involve circulatory alterations.

They go on to point out, "The fact that profound cardiovascular changes can be induced in anesthetized preparations demonstrates that these changes are under direct neural control and not the result of muscular responses."

The primacy of CNS commands in HR control was elegantly demonstrated in an experiment by Goodwin, McCloskey, and Mitchell (1972). Subjects first learned to maintain a constant level of tension in the biceps or triceps muscle with the aid of visual biofeedback. The experimenters then applied a vibratory stimulus to the muscle or its antagonist while the tension was maintained. This stimulus produced afferent feedback, which would ordinarily result in a reflex increase of tension when the muscle was stimulated or a decrease when its antagonist was. Thus, for subjects to maintain the required constant tension levels, CNS commands had to decrease with muscle stimulation and increase with antagonist stimulation. They found that, under these conditions of constant energy expenditure, cardiovascular and respiratory variables increased and decreased with the CNS commands. This is similar to the Schwartz and Higgins (1971) finding that the thought of pushing a telegraph key yields cardiovascular responses similar to those in the actual act of pushing it.

Still more support for this view comes from the fact that subjects who attempted to tense muscles paralyzed by drugs (Freyschuss, 1970) showed increased HRs despite the obvious lack of actual somatic changes. Thus, there is strong anatomical support for the notion of cardiac-somatic coupling. As Obrist et al. (1974) summarize their view, "It would appear that we have available in the action of one muscle, the heart, an index of the activity of striate musculature." Of course, this is difficult to test absolutely, because any measurement of EMG is tied to a specific muscle group; HR is in fact the only measure we have of total somatic activity. However, a number of experiments including measurements of chin EMG and general bodily twitching (assessed by a pressure-sensitive transducer placed under the seat of the subject's chair) indicate that this is a good first approximation.

However, as Elliott (1974) points out, to the extent that it is true that HR is *nothing but* an indicator of bodily activity, HR is of relatively less interest to psychophysiology as a whole. It is too crude a measure of overall activity to be of much use.

The most interesting question for psychophysiology is, then, when does the heart function independently of other muscles? Even the Laceys (1974) accept the view that HR is primarily an indicator of metabolic demand. The question is: What else does it tell us? Thus once more we return to the problem of response patterning.

Obrist et al. (1974) showed that it is indeed possible to uncouple HR from somatic measures under stressful conditions of "active coping." Subjects were given a reaction-time task in which fast reactions were rewarded with a monetary bonus and slow reactions punished with a strong shock. The threat of this unknown shock did increase HR, while somatic activity showed no corresponding increase. This effect can be attributed to accelerating influences of the sympathetic nervous system. Evidence from many sources indicates that under conditions of "passive coping" HR is controlled by the PNS via the vagus nerve. Under "active coping" conditions of stress, SNS activation is also seen. This has been demonstrated by the fact that when subjects in this experiment were given a drug that blocked SNS activity, the HR increases were no longer seen. It is also possible to monitor this SNS activity directly under nonstressful conditions. While the PNS normally controls HR, SNS influences are seen on contractility, or the force with which the heart beats (Lawler and Obrist, 1974). Thus, our awareness of the heart pounding in fear in the chest reflects this increased SNS contractility as well as an increase in HR.

Psychophysiological measurements of contractility are technically difficult compared to other cardiovascular recordings. According to Lawler and Obrist (1974) the best procedure involves analysis of the pulse wave recorded from a microphone strapped over the carotid artery (in the neck). This procedure is rather difficult all around and as a result will probably not be used in casual experimentation. Nevertheless, this information has proven invaluable in resolving the mechanisms of HR control and understanding their implications.

Thus, the Obrist et al. (1970) view of "cardiac-somatic coupling" is widely accepted —the primary information offered by HR reflects the total level of bodily energy mobilization. However, the most interesting advances in sophisticated use of cardiovascular measures are likely to come from analysis of situations in which HR is telling us something more. The most obvious example at the present time is SNS-mediated HR increases in response to stress.

Appendix D: Technical Notes for Chapter 7

The Eyes

Photographic Recording

The simplest way to record eye movements and/or pupil size is to take a movie of the eye. Needless to say, this sounds simpler than it is. For one thing, scoring data with a tedious frame-by-frame review has been responsible for the headaches of many research assistants. But more than that, great attention must be paid to keeping head position constant and the lighting correct. For the first, a "bite board"—a fixed piece of wood which the subject bites into and then holds in his mouth throughout the experiment—is the most common solution. Various sophisticated technical systems have been developed to solve the lighting problem. For example, a beam of light directed at the cornea is reflected as an identifiable bright spot that can be easily tracked in a series of photographs. This spot can be made even more identifiable with the aid of a special reflective contact lens fitted over the eye (Tursky, 1974).

Technological advances in photography and television opened up whole new avenues of research for the corneal reflection techniques. Mackworth and Mackworth (1958), for example, directed one TV camera at a scene being viewed by the subject while a second recorded eye movements. The two images were then superimposed so that the eye movements could actually be matched to features of the scene as it was watched.

A problem with this technique, as with many other eye movement recording systems, is that the "bite board" used to keep the head stationary was rather inconvenient. Further refinements, then, involved mounting a camera on the subject's head so that it "sees" the same scene as the eyes. Such a system allows recording of eye movements under more natural conditions.

Other refinements in the photographic method have also increased their scope. Photoelectric recording involves a direct conversion of video information into electrical potentials, which can then be adapted to the polygraph. Haith (1969) developed special procedures for recording infant eye movements. Being less inhibited and cooperative than adult subjects, infants tend to blink too often under the harsh glare required for normal corneal reflection photography. Haith developed a quite sophisticated system based on the reflection of infrared light, which is not visible to the human eye.

Recording EOG

The EOG is a relatively easy measure to record. As discussed in the text, it consists of a simple standing electrical potential. DC recordings will give true information about eye position; AC recordings reflect only transitory movements. When calibrating a DC recording, one usually asks the subject to "look straight ahead," "look left," "look up," and so on, and sets the electrical limits accordingly.

Very small electrodes are used for the EOG. Skin surfaces should first be cleaned with alcohol and then rubbed briskly with a mild abrasive to decrease electrical resistance. Probably the most difficult aspect of recording EOG is the care required to do this work, since the electrodes are placed so close to the eyeball. Two basic electrode placements are common:

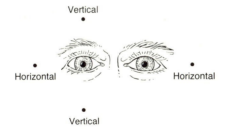

An alternative to the EOG also permits eye-movement recording with the eyes closed. Baldridge, Whitman and Kramer (1963) simply taped a sensitive strain gauge to their subject's eyelids. If you close one eye and place your hand over the lid, you will notice that you can feel the eye moving back and forth under the lid since it is not completely spherical. The strain gauge converts these bulges under the lid into a changing electrical resistance.

Appendix E: Technical Notes for Chapter 8

The Muscles

Recording EMG

Skin sites are prepared for EMG recording much as they are for EOG: The skin is first cleaned with alcohol or acetone and then rubbed briskly with a mild abrasive. To reduce skin resistance to a minimum, the skin should be rubbed until it turns light pink. Miniature silver/silver-chloride electrodes are then attached to the skin. Precise placement depends, of course, on the muscles of interest (see Figures 8.3 and 8.4).

EMG is one of the more difficult measures to record with standard polygraph equipment because components of very high frequency are common. The typical ink writing device has a physical limitation in that it simply cannot move faster than 75 times each second; thus, 75 Hz is the highest frequency that it can record. There is some controversy in the psychophysiological literature as to the seriousness of this limitation. In laboratories devoted exclusively to electromyography, cathode ray oscilloscopes are used to allow the high-frequency components to emerge (Basmajian, 1967). Some researchers claim that a frequency band as wide as 2–10,000 Hz may be required for undistorted EMG recording (Buchthal, Pinelli, and Rosenfalck, 1954). Less conservative experimenters have argued that the range of 10–70 Hz may be quite representative of the larger frequency spectrum (Friedman, 1951). This is probably sufficient for the relatively crude recordings of the psychophysiology laboratory, where one is simply interested in the relative action of various muscle groups. For clinical consideration of possible muscular damage, the oscilloscope method of displaying high-frequency components is probably required.

Appendix F: Technical Notes for Chapter 9

The Brain

The 10–20 System

The 10–20 system is a standardized guide to locating EEG electrodes on the scalp. It corrects for individual differences in skull size by beginning with two measurements: the distance from the front to the back of the head, and the distance from side to side. To begin, locate the nasion by moving your finger up the top surface of the nose until you come to a depression right under the eyebrows. Locate the inion with your finger up the back of the neck. You should feel a bone on either side if your finger is properly centered. Continue up the back of the skull until you feel a large bone protruding over the middle. This is the inion. Now measure the distance from nasion to inion. Then move your fingers up the side of the skull, just in front of the ear on each side. The slight depression you feel on either side just above the earlobe is called the preauricular depression. Again, use a tape measure to find the precise distance across the top of the head from the left preauricular depression to the right.

Now consult Figure 9.3 to determine the precise placement of electrodes based on these distances. Note that the placement of each of the electrodes along the major lines of the skull is based on taking either 10% or 20% of these two distances. See Jasper (1958) for further details.

Stretchable electrode caps that fit over the subject's head are commercially available. These have holes for each of the standard placements and considerably speed the process of electrode application.

Recording EEG

There are many different types of electrodes that can be used to record EEG, and the actual methods of affixing them to the scalp also vary widely. For normal EEG recording, the electrode stability is not especially critical, because slow electrical changes are filtered out. What is critical is the use of a relatively small electrode that is firmly attached to the scalp. The electrodes should be checked before recording to be certain that the resistance between them is less than 10,000 ohms. (Many researchers use 5000 ohms as the highest acceptable resistance.) If the resistance is greater, the electrodes should be reattached to the scalp. Rubbing the spot on the scalp with a mild abrasive, as in EMG recording, will frequently help to lower the resistance. In a clinical setting, the more immediate concern with precise localization of unusual rhythms has led to the use of needle electrodes that pierce the scalp.

Recordings may be monopolar or bipolar, depending on the experimenter's intent. Earclip electrodes attached to one or both earlobes frequently serve as a ground for bipolar recording or a reference point for monopolar.

Given the very small electrical magnitude of the EEG (peak-to-peak voltage is on the order of 100 μV), a high degree of amplification is required. This may lead to artifact problems. This is particularly critical with frontal recordings, which are often contaminated by the corneoretinal potential. See Shagass (1972) for a detailed discussion of EEG artifacts.

Filtering the EEG

Most casual users of EEG are interested only in response within a discrete frequency band, usually 8–13 Hz (that is, alpha). General-purpose polygraphs, however, do not have special filtering circuits for these frequencies. Therefore, the EEG is frequently recorded across a more normal range of about 1–60 Hz. Filters are set on an AC preamplifier to cut off very slow and very high frequency shifts. This "raw" EEG (which has already been through substantial filtering) is then put through a band-pass filter, set for the appropriate frequencies, and displayed on a second polygraph channel.

More sophisticated electroencephalographers are likely to experiment with many different filter settings to determine which is most appropriate to the problem at hand. It was just this type of experimentation that led to Gray-Walter's discovery of the CNV.

Recording Averaged Evoked Potentials

AEPs involve a higher level of technological sophistication than any of the psycho-physiological measures we have discussed thus far. In addition to high-quality EEG recording, this technique requires a computerized averaging system. The average may be computed on-line (as the experiment progresses) or off-line (analyzed by a computer after the experiment is over, from magnetic-tape records of the EEG and stimulus presentations).

Typically, the stimulus is repeated 20–100 times. The EEG record must be marked for the precise instant of the onset of each stimulus. (A one-second period after stimulus onset is then averaged across all trials.)

Recording the Contingent Negative Variation

Since the CNV represents a very small and slowly shifting electrical potential, it is critical that stable electrodes be used; any slight electrode polarization might be confused with potentials originating over the cortex. For this reason, the standard practice of measuring resistance between electrodes with an ohmmeter is inappropriate for CNV recording. Because an ohmmeter introduces a transient electrical potential across the electrodes, it can easily have the undesired side effect of creating a potential difference between them. Therefore, an impedance meter must be used to verify good electrical contact. Obviously, the amplifier used must either be direct-coupled or have a very long time constant (at least several seconds).

Under uncontrolled conditions, most people will tend to look down (even with the eyes closed) when they press a button. The relatively large changes in corneoretinal potential that this movement produces can be detected at the vertex. Thus, eye-movement artifact can easily contaminate the true cortical potentials of the CNV. There are a number of different electronic systems for simultaneous EOG recording and automatic subtraction of the corneoretinal potentials. However, it is much easier and probably more accurate to have the subject fix his eyes on a given point and discard those trials on which major eye movements appear.

Clearly, CNV recording also implies some electronic means of averaging. About twelve stimuli are usually adequate, and AEP apparatus can frequently be adapted. Hillyard (1974) provides a good overview of these and other technical problems.

References

Adler, F. H. *Physiology of the eye* (4th ed.). St. Louis: C. V. Mosby, 1965.

Anand, B. K., Chhina, G. S., and Singh, B. Some aspects of electroencephalographic studies in yogis. *Electroencephalography and Clinical Neurophysiology*, 1961, *13*, 452–456.

Andersen, P., and Andersson, S. A. *Physiological basis of the alpha rhythm*. New York: Appleton-Century-Crofts, 1968.

Andrews, J. M. Neuromuscular re-education of the hemiplegic with the aid of the electromyograph. *Archives of Physical Medicine and Rehabilitation*, 1964, *45*, 530–532.

Aserinsky, E., and Kleitman, N. Regularly occurring periods of eye motility and concomitant phenomena, during sleep. *Science*, 1953, *118*, 273–274.

Astrand, P. O., and Rodahl, K. *Textbook of work physiology*. New York: McGraw-Hill, 1970.

Atwood, R. W., and Howell, R. J. Pupillometric and personality test score differences of female aggressing pedophiliacs and normals. *Psychonomic Science*, 1971, *22*, 115–116.

Ax, A. F. The physiological differentiation between anger and fear in humans. *Psychosomatic Medicine*, 1953, *15*, 433–442.

Bakan, P. The eyes have it. *Psychology Today*, 1971, *4*, 64–69.

Baldridge, B. J., Whitman, R., and Kramer, M. A. A simplified method for detecting eye movement during dreaming. *Psychosomatic Medicine*, 1963, *25*, 78–82.

Balshan, I. D. Muscle tension and personality in women. *Archives of General Psychiatry*, 1962, 7, 436–448.

Bard, P. B. Some further analyses of the function of the cerebrum. In P. B. Bard (Ed.), *Medical physiology* (11th ed.). St. Louis: C. V. Mosby, 1961.

Barland, G. H., and Raskin, D. C. Detection of deception. In W. F. Prokasy and D. C. Raskin (Eds.), *Electrodermal activity in psychological research*. New York: Academic Press, 1973.

Barland, G. H., and Raskin, D. C. Psychopathy and detection of deception in criminal suspects. *Psychophysiology*, 1975, 12, 224.

Bartlett, F., and John, E. R. Equipotentiality quantified: The anatomical distribution of the engram. *Science*, 1973, 181, 764–767.

Bartlett, R. G., Jr. Physiologic responses during coitus. *Journal of Applied Physiology*, 1956, 9, 469–472.

Basmajian, J. V. Control and training of individual motor units. *Science*, 1963, 141, 440–441.

Basmajian, J. V. Control and training of individual motor units. *Science*, 1963, 141, Williams & Wilkins, 1967.

Bayley, N. A study of fear by means of the psychogalvanic technique. *Psychological Monographs*, 1928, 38 (1–38, Whole No. 176).

Beaumont, W. *Experiments and observations on the gastric juice and the physiology of digestion*. Plattsburgh, N.Y.: F. P. Allen, 1833.

Benson, H. *The relaxation response*. New York: Avon, 1975.

Benson, H., Shapiro, D., Tursky, B., and Schwartz, G. E. Decreased systolic blood pressure through operant conditioning techniques in patients with essential hypertension. *Science*, 1971, 173, 740–742.

Benussi, V. Die Atmungssymptome der Lüge. *Archiv für die gesamte Psychologie*, 1914, 31, 244–273.

Berger, H. Über das elektrenkephalogramm des menschen. *Archiv für Psychiatrie und Nervenkrankheiten*, 1929, 87, 527–570.

Bernstein, A. S., Taylor, K. W., and Weinstein, E. The phasic electrodermal response as a differentiated complex reflecting stimulus significance. *Psychophysiology*, 1975, 12, 158–169.

Birk, L., Crider, A. B., Shapiro, D., and Tursky, B. Operant conditioning under partial curarization. *Journal of Comparative and Physiological Psychology*, 1966, 62, 165–166.

Birren, J. E., Cardon, P. V., and Phillips, S. L. Reaction time as a function of the cardiac cycle in young adults. *Science*, 1963, 146, 195–196.

Bittker, T. E., Buchsbaum, M. S., Williams, R. B., and Wynne, L. C. Cardiovascular and neurophysiologic correlates of sensory intake and rejection. II. Interview Behavior. *Psychophysiology*, 1975, 12, 434–438.

Blatz, W. E. The cardiac, respiratory and electrical phenomena involved in the emotion of fear. *Journal of Experimental Psychology*, 1925, 8, 109–132.

Blanchard, E. B., and Young, L. D. Clinical applications of biofeedback training: A review of evidence. *Archives of General Psychiatry*, 1974, 30, 573–589.

Boissonneault, D. R., Dorosh, M. E., and Tong, J. E. The effect of induced heart rate change and neuroticism on the resolution of temporally paired flashes. *Psychophysiology*, 1970, 7, 465–474.

Boring, E. G. A *history of experimental psychology*. New York: Appleton-Century-Crofts, 1950.

Bowers, K. S. Situationism in psychology: An analysis and a critique. *Psychological Review*, 1973, 80, 307–336.

Boyle, R. H., Dykman, R. A., and Ackerman, P. T. Relationships of resting autonomic activity, motor impulsivity, and EEG tracings in children. *Archives of General Psychiatry*, 1965, 12, 314–323.

Brown, B. Recognition of aspects of consciousness through association with EEG alpha activity represented by a light signal. *Psychophysiology*, 1970, 6, 442–452.

Brown, B. Awareness of EEG-subjective activity relationships detected within a closed-feedback system. *Psychophysiology*, 1971, 7, 451–464.

Brown, C. H., and Van Gelder, D. Emotional reactions before examinations. I. Physiological changes. *Journal of Psychology*, 1938, 5, 1–9.

Bruner, J. M. R. Hazards of electrical apparatus. *Anesthesiology*, March 1967.

Buchthal, F., Pinelli, P., and Rosenfalck, P. Action potential parameters in normal human muscle and their physiological determinants. *Acta Physiologica Scandinavica*, 1954, 32, 219–229.

Budzynski, T. H., Stoyva, J. M., Adler, C. S., and Mullaney, D. J. EMG biofeedback and tension headache: A controlled-outcome study. *Psychosomatic Medicine*, 1973, 35, 484–496.

Bull, R. H. C., and Gale, M. A. Electrodermal activity recorded concomitantly from the subject's two hands. *Psychophysiology*, 1975, 12, 94–97.

Bumke, O. *Die Pupillenstorungen, Bie Geistes—und Nervenkrankheiten*. Jena: Fischer, 1911.

Burtt, H. E. The inspiration-expiration ratios during truth and falsehood. *Journal of Experimental Psychology*, 1921, 4, 1–23.

Callaway, E., and Layne, R. S. Interaction between the visual evoked response and two spontaneous rhythms: The EEG alpha cycle and the cardiac arousal cycle. *Annals of the New York Academy of Sciences*, 1964, 112, 421–431.

Cannon, W. B. The James-Lange theory of emotions: A critical examination and an alternative. *American Journal of Psychology*, 1927, 39, 106–124.

Champion, R. H. (Ed.). *An introduction to the biology of the skin*. Philadelphia: Davis, 1970.

Clarke, E., and Dewhurst, K. *An illustrated history of brain function*. Berkeley and Los Angeles: University of California Press, 1972.

Cohen, D. Magnetoencephalography: Detection of the brain's electrical activity with a superconducting magnetometer. *Science*, 1972, 175, 664–666.

Cohen, D. H., and MacDonald, R. L. A selective review of central neural pathways involved in cardiovascular control. In P. A. Obrist, A. H. Black, J. Brener, and L. V. DiCara (Eds.). *Cardiovascular psychophysiology*. Chicago: Aldine, 1974.

Cohen, J. Very slow brain potentials relating to expectancy: The CNV. In E. Donchin and D. B. Lindsley (Eds.), *Average Evoked Potentials*. Washington, D.C.: NASA SP–191, 1969.

Cohen, J. Cerebral psychophysiology: The contingent negative variation. In R. F. Thompson and M. M. Patterson (Eds.), *Bioelectric recording techniques. Part B. Electroencephalography and human brain potentials*. New York: Academic Press, 1974.

Cook, M. R. Psychophysiology of peripheral vascular changes. In P. A. Obrist, A. H. Black, J. Brener, and L. V. DiCara (Eds.), *Cardiovascular Psychophysiology*. Chicago: Aldine, 1974.

Crider, A. B., Schwartz, G. E., and Schnidman, S. On the criteria for instrumental conditioning: A reply to Katkin and Murray. *Psychological Bulletin*, 1969, 71, 455–461.

Cutrow, R. J., Parks, A., Lucas, N., and Thomas, K. The objective use of multiple physiological indices in the detection of deception. *Psychophysiology*, 1972, 9, 578–588.

Dalessio, D. J. *Wolff's headache and other head pain* (3rd ed.). New York: Oxford University Press, 1972.

Darrow, C. W. Electrical and circulatory responses to brief sensory and ideational stimuli. *Journal of Experimental Psychology*, 1929, 12, 267–300.

Darrow, C. W. The relation of the galvanic skin reflex recovery curve to reactivity, resistance level, and perspiration. *Journal of General Psychology*, 1932, 7, 261–271.

Darrow, C. W. The galvanic skin reflex (sweating) and blood pressure as preparatory and facilitative functions. *Psychological Bulletin*, 1936, 33, 73–94.

Darrow, C. W. Psychophysiology, yesterday, today, and tomorrow. *Psychophysiology*, 1964a, 1, 4–7.

Darrow, C. W. The rationale for treating the change in galvanic skin response as a change in conductance. *Psychophysiology*, 1964b, 1, 31–38.

Darwin, C. *The expression of emotion in man and animals*. London: Murray, 1872.

Davis, F. C. The functional significance of imagery differences. *Journal of Experimental Psychology*, 1932, 15, 630–661.

Dawson, G. D. Cerebral responses to electrical stimulation of peripheral nerve in man. *Journal of Neurology, Neurosurgery and Psychiatry*, 1947, 10, 137–140.

Delebarre, E. B. A method of recording eye movements. *American Journal of Psychology*, 1898, 9, 572–574.

Delfini, L. F., and Campos, J. J. Signal detection and the "cardiac arousal cycle." *Psychophysiology*, 1972, 9, 484–491.

Dement, W. C. The effect of dream deprivation. *Science*, 1960, 131, 1705–1707.

Dement, W., and Kleitman, N. The relationship of eye movements during sleep to dream activity: An objective method for the study of dreaming. *Journal of Experimental Psychology*, 1957, 53, 339–346.

Dewan, E. D. Occipital alpha rhythm, eye position and lens accommodation. *Nature*, 1967, *214*, 975–977.

DiCara, L. V., and Miller, N. E. Instrumental learning of systolic blood pressure by curarized rats: Dissociation of cardiac and vascular changes. *Psychosomatic Medicine*, 1968a, *30*, 489–494.

DiCara, L. V., and Miller, N. E. Instrumental learning of vasomotor responses by rats: Learning to respond differentially in the two ears. *Science*, 1968b, *159*, 1485.

Dichtburn, R. W. *Eye movements and visual perception*. Oxford: Clarendon Press, 1973.

Dichtburn, R. W., and Ginsborg, B. L. Vision with a stabilized retinal image. *Nature*, 1952, *170*, 36.

Doyle, J. C., Ornstein, R., and Galin, D. Lateral specialization of cognitive mode: II. EEG frequency analysis. *Psychophysiology*, 1974, *11*, 567–578.

Duffy, E. Emotion: An example of the need for reorientation in psychology. *Psychological Review*, 1934, *41*, 184–198.

Duffy, E. Activation. In N. S. Greenfield and R. A. Sternbach (Eds.), *Handbook of psychophysiology*. New York: Holt, Rinehart and Winston, 1972.

Dumas, R., and Morgan, A. EEG asymmetry as a function of occupation, task, and task difficulty. *Neuropsychologia*, 1975, *13*, 219–228.

Dunlap, D. M., Henderson, T. L., and Inch, R. S. A survey of 17,301 prescriptions on form E10. *British Medical Journal*, 1952, *I*, 292.

Eccles, J. C. *The neurophysiological basis of mind*. London: Clarendon Press, 1953.

Eckstrand, G., and Gilliland, A. R. The psychogalvanometric method for measuring the effectiveness of advertising. *Journal of Applied Psychology*, 1948, *32*, 415–425.

Edelberg, R. The information content of the recovery limb of the electrodermal response. *Psychophysiology*, 1970, *6*, 527–539.

Edelberg, R. Electrical activity of the skin: Its measurement and uses in psychophysiology. In N. S. Greenfield and R. A. Sternbach (Eds.), *Handbook of psychophysiology*. New York: Holt, Rinehart and Winston, 1972.

Edelberg, R. *The dual character of electrodermal activity*. Address presented to the American Psychological Association, 1973.

Ekman, P. Universals and cultural differences in facial expressions of emotion. In J. K. Cole (Ed.), *Nebraska Symposium on Motivation*. Lincoln: University of Nebraska Press, 1971.

Elder, S. T., Ruiz, Z. R., Deabler, H. L., and Dillenkoffer, R. L. Instrumental conditioning of diastolic blood pressure in essential hypertensive patients. *Journal of Applied Behavioral Analysis*, 1973, *6*, 377–382.

Elliott, R. The motivational significance of heart rate. In P. A. Obrist, A. H. Black, J. Brener, and L. V. DiCara (Eds.), *Cardiovascular psychophysiology*. Chicago: Aldine, 1974.

Engel, B. T. Stimulus response and individual-response specificity. *Archives of General Psychiatry*, 1960, *2*, 305–313.

Engel, B. T. Operant conditioning of cardiac function: A status report. *Psychophysiology*, 1972, 9, 161–177.

Feleky, A. The expression of the emotions. *Psychological Review*, 1914, 21, 33–41.

Feleky, A. The influence of emotions on respiration. *Journal of Experimental Psychology*, 1916, 1, 218–241.

Féré, C. Note sur les modifications de la résistance électrique sous l'influence des excitations sensorielles et des émotions. *Comptes Rendus des Séances de la Société de Biologie*, 1888, 5, 217–219.

Finley, W. W., Smith, H. A., and Etherton, M. D. Reduction of seizures and normalization of the EEG in a severe epileptic following sensorimotor biofeedback training: Preliminary study. *Biological Psychology*, 1975, 2, 189–203.

Fisher, C., Gross, J., and Zuch, J. Cycle of penile erection synchronous with dreaming (REM) sleep. *Archives of General Psychiatry*, 1965, 12, 29–45.

Freyschuss, V. Cardiovascular adjustments to somatomotor activation: The elimination of increments in heart rate, aortic pressure and venomotor tone with the initiation of muscle contraction. *Acta Physiologica Scandinavica*, 1970, Suppl. 342, 1–63.

Freund, K. A laboratory method for diagnosing predominance of homo- and heteroerotic interest in the male. *Behavior Research and Therapy*, 1963, 1, 85–93.

Friedman, N. E. Instrumentation requirements for continuous magnetic tape recording of muscle potentials. Unpublished doctoral dissertation, University of California, Los Angeles, 1951.

Galin, D., and Ornstein, R. Lateral specialization of cognitive mode: An EEG study. *Psychophysiology*, 1972, 9, 412–418.

Galin, D., and Ornstein, R. Individual differences in cognitive style. I. Reflective Eye Movements. *Neuropsychologia*, 1974, 12, 367–376.

Gardner, H. *The shattered mind*. New York: Vintage Books, 1974.

Gastaut, H. Étude électrocorticographique de la réactivité des rhythmes rolandiques. *Revue Neurologique*, 1952, 87, 176–182.

Gibbs, F. A., Davis, H., and Lennox, W. G. The electroencephalogram in epilepsy and in conditions of impaired consciousness. *Archives of Neurology and Psychiatry*, 1935, 3, 1133–1148.

Goff, W. R. Human average evoked potentials: procedures for stimulating and recording. In R. F. Thompson and M. M. Patterson (Eds.), *Bioelectric recording techniques*, part B. New York: Academic Press, 1974.

Goldstein, I. B. Electromyography: A measure of skeletal muscle response. In N. S. Greenfield and R. A. Sternbach (Eds.), *Handbook of psychophysiology*. New York: Holt, Rinehart and Winston, 1972.

Goldwater, B. C. Psychological significance of pupillary movements. *Psychological Bulletin*, 1972, 77, 340–355.

Goleman, D., and Schwartz, G. E. Meditation as an intervention in stress reactivity. *Journal of Consulting and Clinical Psychology*, 1976, 44, 456–463.

Goodwin, G. M., McCloskey, D. I., and Mitchell, J. H. Cardiovascular and respiratory responses to changes in central command during isometric exercise at constant muscle tension. *Journal of Physiology*, 1972, 226, 173–190.

Green, E. E., Green, A. M., and Walters, E. D. Biofeedback for mind-body self-regulation: Healing and creativity. Talk given at the symposium called *The Varieties of Healing Experience* at DeAnza College, Cupertino, California, 1971.

Gregory, R. L. *Eye and brain: The psychology of seeing.* New York: McGraw-Hill, 1966.

Greenfield, N. S., and Sternbach, R. A. (Eds.). *Handbook of psychophysiology.* New York: Holt, Rinehart and Winston, 1972.

Grinspoon, L. *Marihuana reconsidered.* Cambridge, Mass.: Harvard University Press, 1971.

Grossman, S. P. *A textbook of physiological psychology.* New York: Wiley, 1967.

Groves, P. M., and Thompson, R. Habituation: A dual process theory. *Psychological Review,* 1970, 77, 419–450.

Gunn, C. G., Wolf, S., Block, R. T., and Person, R. J. Psychophysiology of the cardiovascular system. In N. S. Greenfield and R. A. Sternbach (Eds.), *Handbook of psychophysiology.* New York: Holt, Rinehart and Winston, 1972.

Gur, R. E., Gur, R. C., and Harris, L. J. Cerebral activation, as measured by subjects' lateral eye movements, is influenced by experimenter location. *Neuropsychologia,* 1975, 13, 35–44.

Gustafson, L. A., and Orne, M. T. Effects of heightened motivation on the detection of deception. *Journal of Applied Psychology,* 1963, 47, 408–411.

Haith, M. M. Infrared television recording and measurement of ocular behavior in the human infant. *American Psychologist,* 1969, 24, 279–283.

Hall, R. J., and Cusack, B. L. *The measurement of eye behavior: Critical and selected reviews of voluntary movement and blinking* (Technical Memorandum 18–72). Aberdeen Proving Ground, Md.: Human Engineering Laboratory, 1972 (AMCMS Code 501B.11.84100).

Hardt, J. V., and Kamiya, J. Conflicting results in EEG alpha feedback studies: Why amplitude integration should replace percent time. *Biofeedback and Self-Regulation,* 1976, 1, 63–76.

Hare, R. D. Orienting and defensive responses to visual stimuli. *Psychophysiology,* 1973, 10, 453–464.

Hassett, J. *Relationships between heart rate and occipital alpha: A biofeedback approach.* Unpublished doctoral dissertation, Harvard University, 1974.

Hassett, J., and Schwartz, G. E. Relationships between heart rate and occipital alpha: A biofeedback approach. *Psychophysiology,* 1975, 12, 228.

Hassett, J., and Zelner, B. Correlations between measures of cerebral asymmetry. *Psychophysiology,* 1977, 14, 79.

Hess, E. H. Pupillometrics. In N. S. Greenfield and R. A. Sternbach (Eds.), *Handbook of Psychophysiology.* New York: Holt, Rinehart and Winston, 1972.

Hess, E. *The tell-tale eye.* New York: Van Nostrand Reinhold, 1975.

Hess, E. H., Seltzer, A. L., and Shlien, J. M. Pupil responses of hetero- and homosexual males to pictures of men and women: A pilot study. *Journal of Abnormal Psychology,* 1965, 70, 165–168.

Hillyard, S. A. Methodological issues in CNV research. In R. F. Thompson and M. M. Patterson (Eds.), *Bioelectric recording techniques. Part B. Electroencephalography and Human Brain Potentials.* New York: Academic Press, 1974.

Hillyard, S. A., Hink, R. F., Schwent, V. L., and Picton, T. W. Electrical signs of selective attention in the human brain. *Science,* 1973, *182,* 177–180.

Hoon, P. W., Wincze, J. P., and Hoon, E. F. Physiological assessment of sexual arousal in women. *Psychophysiology,* 1976, *13,* 196–204.

Jacobs, L., Feldman, M., and Bender, M. B. Are the eye movements of dreaming sleep related to the visual images of the dreams? *Psychophysiology,* 1972, 9, 393–401.

Jacobson, E. *Progressive relaxation.* Chicago: University of Chicago Press, 1938.

Jacobson, E. Muscular tension and the estimation of effort. *American Journal of Psychology,* 1951, *64,* 112–117.

Janisse, M. P. Pupil size and effect: A critical review of the literature since 1960. *The Canadian Psychologist,* 1973, *14,* 311–329.

Janisse, M. P., and Peavler, W. S. Pupillary research today: Emotion in the eye. *Psychology Today,* February 1974, 7, 60–63.

Jasper, H. H. Electrical signs of cortical activity. *Psychological Bulletin,* 1937, *34,* 411–481.

Jasper, H. H. Report of committee on methods of clinical examination in EEG: Appendix: The ten–twenty electrode system of the International Federation. *Electroencephalography and Clinical Neurophysiology,* 1958, *10,* 371–375.

John, E. R. Switchboard vs. statistical theories of learning and memory. *Science,* 1972, *177,* 850–864.

Johnson, H. E., and Garton, W. H. Muscle re-education in hemiplegia by use of electromyographic device. *Archives of Physical Medicine and Rehabilitation,* 1973, *54,* 320–325.

Johnston, V. S., and Chesney, G. L. Electrophysiological correlates of meaning. *Science,* 1974, *186,* 944–946.

Kaplan, B. J. Biofeedback in epileptics: Equivocal relationship of reinforced EEG frequency to seizure reduction. *Epilepsia,* 1975, *16,* 477–485.

Karlins, M., and Andrews, L. M. *Biofeedback: Turning on the power of your mind.* New York: Lippincott, 1972.

Kasamatsu, A., and Hirai, T. An electroencephalographic study on the Zen meditation (Zazen). *Psychologia,* 1969, *12,* 205–225.

Katchadourian, H. A., and Lunde, D. T. *Fundamentals of human sexuality.* New York: Holt, Rinehart and Winston, 1975.

Katkin, E. S., and Murray, E. N. Instrumental conditioning of autonomically mediated behavior: Theoretical and methodological issues. *Psychological Bulletin,* 1968, *70,* 52–68.

Katkin, E. S., Murray, E. N., and Lachman, R. Concerning instrumental autonomic conditioning: A rejoinder. *Psychological Bulletin,* 1969, *71,* 462–466.

Kelly, D., Brown, C. C., and Shaffer, J. W. A comparison of physiological and psychological measurements on anxious patients and normal controls. *Psychophysiology*, 1970, *6*, 429–441.

Kennard, D. S., and Glasser, G. H. An analysis of eyelid movements. *Journal of Nervous and Mental Diseases*, 1963, *139*, 31–48.

Kennedy, J. L. A possible artifact in electroencephalography. *Psychological Review*, 1959, *66*, 347–352.

Kety, S. A biologist examines the mind and behavior. *Science*, 1960, *132*, 1861–1870.

Kilpatrick, D. G. Differential responsiveness of two electrodermal indices to psychological stress and performance of a complex cognitive task. *Psychophysiology*, 1972, *9*, 218–226.

Kimble, G. A. *Hilgard and Marquis' conditioning and learning revised* (2nd ed.). New York: Appleton-Century-Crofts, 1961.

King, J. T. An instance of voluntary acceleration of the pulse. *Johns Hopkins Hospital Bulletin*, 1920, 303–305.

Kinsbourne, M. Eye and head turning indicates cerebral lateralization. *Science*, 1972, *176*, 539–541.

Kleitman, N. Patterns of dreaming. *Scientific American*, November 1960.

Kornhuber, H. H., and Deecke, L. Hirnpotentialandererungen bei Willkurbewegungen und passiven Bewegungen des Menschen: Bereitschaftspotential und reafferente Potentiale. *Pflüger's Archiv für die gesamte Physiologie des Menschen und der Tiere*, 1965, *284*, 1–17.

Kornmüller, A. E. Die bioelektrischen erscheinungen architektonischer felder der grosshirnrinde. *Biol. Reus.*, 1935, *10*, 383–426.

Krogh, A. G. *The Comparative Physiology of Respiratory Mechanisms*. New York: Dover, 1941.

Kuno, Y. *Human perspiration*. Springfield, Ill.: Thomas, 1956.

Lacey, B. C., and Lacey, J. I. Studies of heart rate and other bodily processes in sensorimotor behavior. In P. A. Obrist, A. H. Black, J. Brener, and L. V. DiCara (Eds.), *Cardiovascular psychophysiology*. Chicago: Aldine, 1974.

Lacey, J. I. Psychophysiological approaches to the evaluation of psychotherapeutic process and outcome. In E. A. Rubinstein and M. B. Parloff (Eds.), *Research in Psychotherapy*. Washington, D.C.: American Psychological Association, 1959.

Lacey, J. I. Somatic response patterning and stress: Some revisions of activation theory. In M. H. Apley and R. Trumbull (Eds.), *Psychological Stress*. New York: Appleton-Century-Crofts, 1967.

Lacey, J. I., Bateman, D. E., and Van Lehn, R. Autonomic response specificity: An experimental study. *Psychosomatic Medicine*, 1953, *15*, 8–21.

Lacey, J. I., Kagan, J., Lacey, B. C., and Moss, H. A. The visceral level: Situational determinants and behavioral correlates of autonomic response patterns. In P. H. Knapp (Ed.), *Expression of the emotions in man*. New York: International Universities Press, 1963.

Lacey, J., and Lacey, B. Baroreceptors, brain and behavior (and bits of boloney). Invited lecture at Society for Psychophysiological Research Convention, San Diego, 1976.

Lader, M. H., and Montagu, J. D. The psycho-galvanic reflex: A pharmacologic study of the peripheral mechanism. *Journal of Neurology, Neurosurgery, and Psychiatry*, 1962, 25, 126–133.

Lambert, R. H., Monty, R. A., and Hall, R. J. High-speed data processing and unobtrusive monitoring of eye movements. *Behavior Research Methods and Instrumentation*, 1974, 6, 525–530.

Landis, C. Studies of emotional reactions. V. Severe emotional upset. *Journal of Comparative Psychology*, 1926, 6, 221–242.

Landis, C., and Wiley, L. E. Changes in blood pressure during deception. *Journal of Comparative Psychology*, 1926, 6, 1–19.

Larson, J. A. *Lying and its detection: A study of deception and deception tests.* Chicago: University of Chicago Press, 1932.

Lawler, J. E., and Obrist, P. A. Indirect indices of contractile force. In P. A. Obrist, A. H. Black, J. Brener, and L. V. DiCara (Eds.), *Cardiovascular psychophysiology.* Chicago: Aldine, 1974.

Levee, J. R., Cohen, M. J., and Rickles, W. H. Electromyographic biofeedback for relief of tension in the facial and throat muscles of a woodwind musician. *Biofeedback and Self-Regulation*, 1976, 1, 113–120.

Liberson, W. T. Problem of sleep and mental disease. *Digest of Neurology and Psychiatry*, The Institute of Living, Hartford, Conn., 13, 1945.

Linde, E. Zur frage vom psychischen korrelate des psychogalvanischen reflexphänomens. *Proceedings of Eighth International Congress of Psychology*, 1928, 8, 351–352.

Lindsley, D. B. Emotion. In S. S. Stevens (Ed.), *Handbook of experimental psychology.* New York: Wiley, 1951.

Lindsley, D. B. Basic perceptual processes and the EEG. *Psychiatric Research Reports*, 1956, 6, 161–170.

Lindsley, D. B., and Wicke, J. D. The electroencephalogram: Autonomous electrical activity in man and animals. In R. F. Thompson and M. M. Patterson (Eds.), *Bioelectric recording techniques. Part B. Electroencephalography and human brain potentials.* New York: Academic Press, 1974.

Lippold, D. C. J., and Novotny, G. E. K. Is alpha rhythm an artifact? *Lancet*, 1970, I, 976–979.

Livanov, M. N., Gavrilova, N. A., and Aslanov, A. S. Cross correlation between different areas of the human brain during mental work. *Zhurnal Vysshei Nervoi. Deiate l'nosti*, 1964, 14.

Livingston, W. K. *Pain mechanisms.* New York: Macmillan, 1943.

Lowenstein, O., and Loewenfeld, I. E. The pupil. In H. Davson (Ed.), *The eye* (Vol. 3). New York: Academic Press, 1962.

Lubar, J. L., and Bahler, W. W. Behavioral management of epileptic seizures following EEG biofeedback training of the sensorimotor rhythm. *Biofeedback and Self-Regulation*, 1976, *1*, 77–104.

Luce, G. G., and Segal, J. *Sleep*. New York: Lancer, 1966.

Luria, A. R. *The working brain*. New York: Basic Books, 1973.

Lykken, D. T. The GSR in the detection of guilt. *Journal of Applied Psychology*, 1959, *43*, 385–388.

Lykken, D. T. The validity of the guilty knowledge technique: The effects of faking. *Journal of Applied Psychology*, 1960, *44*, 258–262.

Lykken, D. T. Psychology and the lie detector industry. *American Psychologist*, 1974, *29*, 725–739.

Lykken, D. T., Rose, R. J., Luther, B., and Maley, M. Correcting psychophysiological measures for individual differences in range. *Psychological Bulletin*, 1966, *66*, 481–484.

Lykken, D. T., Tellegen, A., and Thorkelson, K. Genetic determination of EEG frequency spectra. *Biological Psychology*, 1974, *1*, 245–259.

Lykken, D. T., and Venables, P. H. Direct measurement of skin conductance: A proposal for standardization. *Psychophysiology*, 1971, *8*, 656–672.

Lynch, J. J., and Paskewitz, D. A. On the mechanisms of the feedback control of human brain wave activity. *Journal of Nervous and Mental Disease*, 1971, *153*, 205–217.

Lynn, R. *Attention, arousal and the orienting reflex*. New York: Pergamon, 1966.

McAdam, D. W. The contingent negative variations. In R. F. Thompson and M. M. Patterson (Eds.), *Bioelectric recording techniques. Part B. Electroencephalography and human brain potentials*. New York: Academic Press, 1974.

McAdam, D. W., and Whitaker, H. A. Language production: Electroencephalographic localization in the normal human brain. *Science*, 1971, *172*, 499–502.

McClintock, M. K. Menstrual synchrony and suppression. *Nature*, 1971, *229*, 244–245.

McCurdy, H. D. Consciousness and the galvanometer. *Psychological Review*, 1950, *57*, 322–327.

McFie, J. Recent advances in phrenology. *Lancet*, 1961, *2*, 360–363.

McKonkie, G. W. The use of eye movement data in determining the perceptual span in reading. In R. A. Monty and J. W. Senders (Eds.), *Eye movements and psychological processes*. Hillsdale, N.J.: Erlbaum Associates, 1976.

Mackworth, J. F., and Mackworth, N. H. Eye fixations recorded on changing visual scenes by the television eye marker. *Journal of the Optical Society of America*, 1958, *48*, 439–445.

Maher, B. A. *Principles of psychopathology*. New York: McGraw-Hill, 1966.

Malmo, R. B., and Shagass, C. Physiologic study of symptom mechanisms in psychiatric patients under stress. *Psychosomatic Medicine*, 1949, *11*, 25–29.

Mangelsdorff, A. D., and Zuckerman, M. Habituation to scenes of violence. *Psychophysiology*, 1975, *12*, 124–129.

Margerison, J. H., St. John-Loe, P., and Binnie, C. D. Electroencephalography. In P. H. Venables and I. Martin (Eds.), *A manual of psychophysiological methods.* New York: Wiley, 1967.

Masters, W. H., and Johnson, V. E. *Human sexual response.* Boston: Little, Brown, 1966.

Max, L. W. An experimental study of the motor theory of consciousness. III. Action current responses in deaf-mutes during sleep. *Journal of Comparative Psychology,* 1935, *19,* 469–486.

Max, L. W. An experimental study of the motor theory of consciousness. IV. Action current responses of the deaf during awakening, kinesthetic imagery and abstract thinking. *Journal of Comparative Psychology,* 1937, *24,* 301–344.

Melzack, R. *The puzzle of pain.* New York: Basic Books, 1973.

Mesulam, M. M., and Perry, J. The diagnosis of love-sickness: Experimental psycho-physiology without the polygraph. *Psychophysiology,* 1972, *9,* 546–551.

Miller, N. E. Learning of visceral and glandular responses. *Science,* 1969, *163,* 434–445.

Miller, N. E. Biofeedback: Evaluation of a new technic. *New England Journal of Medicine,* 1974, *290,* 684–685.

Miller, N. E., and Banuazizi, A. Instrumental learning by curarized rats of a specific visceral response, intestinal or cardiac. *Journal of Comparative and Physiological Psychology,* 1968, *65,* 1–7.

Miller, N. E., and DiCara, L. V. Instrumental learning of urine formation by rats: Changes in renal blood flow. *American Journal of Physiology,* 1968, *215,* 677–683.

Miller, N. E., and Dworkin, B. R. Visceral learning: Recent difficulties with curarized rats and significant problems for human research. In P. A. Obrist, A. H. Black, J. Brener, and L. V. DiCara (Eds.), *Cardiovascular psychophysiology.* Chicago: Aldine, 1974.

Mischel, W. Toward a cognitive social learning reconceptualization of personality. *Psychological Review,* 1973, *80,* 252–283.

Mittleman, B., and Wolff, H. G. Affective states and skin temperature: Experimental study of subjects with "cold hands" and Raynaud's syndrome. *Psychosomatic Medicine,* 1939, *1,* 271–292.

Morgan, A. H., MacDonald, H., and Hilgard, E. R. EEG alpha: Lateral asymmetry related to task, and hypnotizability. *Psychophysiology,* 1974, *11,* 275–282.

Morgan, J. J. B. The overcoming of distraction and other resistances. *Archives of Psychology,* 1916, *35.*

Mowrer, D. H., Ruch, R. L., and Miller, N. E. The corneo-retinal potential difference as the basis of the galvanometric method of recording eye movements. *American Journal of Physiology,* 1936, *114,* 423–428.

Mulholland, T. Feedback electroencephalography. *Activas Nervosa Superior,* 1968, *10,* 410–438.

Mulholland, T. *Can you really turn on with alpha?* Paper presented at the meeting of the Massachusetts Psychological Association, 1971.

Mulholland, T. Occipital alpha revisited. *Psychological Bulletin,* 1972, 78, 176–182.

Myslobodsky, M. S., and Rattok, J. Asymmetry of electrodermal activity in man. *Bulletin of Psychonomic Society,* 1975, 6, 501–502.

Nidever, J. E. A factor analytic study of general muscular tension. Unpublished doctoral dissertation, University of California, Los Angeles, 1959.

Nissen, A. E. Influence of emotions upon systolic blood pressure. Unpublished Master's thesis, Columbia University, 1928.

Noback, C. R., and Demarest, R. J. *The nervous system: Introduction and review.* New York: McGraw-Hill, 1972.

Nowlis, D. P., and Kamiya, J. The control of electroencephalographic alpha rhythms through auditory feedback and the associated mental activity, *Psychophysiology,* 1970, 6, 476–484.

Obrist, P. A. The cardiovascular-behavioral interaction—as it appears today. *Psychophysiology,* 1976, 13, 95–107.

Obrist, P. A., Howard, J. L., Lawler, J. E., Galosy, R. A., Meyers, K. A., and Gaebelein, C. J. The cardiac somatic interaction. In P. A. Obrist, A. H. Black, J. Brener, and L. V. DiCara (Eds.), *Cardiovascular psychophysiology.* Chicago: Aldine, 1974.

Obrist, P. A., Webb, R. A., Sutterer, J. R., and Howard, J. L. The cardiac-somatic relationship: Some reformulations. *Psychophysiology,* 1970a, 6, 569–587.

Obrist, P. A., Webb, R. A., Sutterer, J. R., and Howard, J. L. Cardiac deceleration and reaction time: An evaluation of two hypotheses. *Psychophysiology,* 1970b, 6, 695–706.

Orlansky, J. An assessment of lie detection capability. In *Use of polygraphs and "lie detectors" by the Federal Government* (House Report No. 198, 89th Congress, 1st Session). Washington, D.C.: U.S. Government Printing Office, 1965.

Orme-Johnson, D. W. Autonomic stability and transcendental meditation. *Psychosomatic Medicine,* 1973, 35, 341–349.

Orne, M. T., Thackray, R. I., and Paskewitz, D. A. On the detection of deception. In N. S. Greenfield and R. A. Sternbach (Eds.), *Handbook of psychophysiology.* New York: Holt, Rinehart and Winston, 1972.

Ornstein, R. E. *The psychology of consciousness.* San Francisco: W. H. Freeman, 1972.

Pagano, R. R., Rose, R. M., Stivers, R. M., and Warrenburg, S. Sleep during Transcendental Meditation. *Science,* 1976, 191, 308–310.

Patterson, T. Skin conductance recovery and pupillometrics in chronic schizophrenia. *Psychophysiology,* 1976, 13, 189–195.

Peper, E. Feedback regulation of the alpha electroencephalogram activity through control of the internal and external parameters. *Kybernetik,* 1970, 7, 107–112.

Peper, E. Reduction of efferent motor commands during alpha feedback as a facilitator of EEG alpha and a precondition for changes in consciousness. *Kybernetik,* 1971, 9, 226–231.

Peper, E., and Mulholland, T. Methodological and theoretical problems in the voluntary control of electroencephalographic occipital alpha by the subject. *Kybernetik*, 1970, 7, 10–13.

Peterson, F., and Jung, C. Psychophysical investigations with the galvanometer and plethysmograph in normal and insane individuals. *Brain*, 1907, 30, 153–218.

Picton, T. W., and Hillyard, S. A. Human auditory evoked potentials. II. Effects of attention. *Electroencephalography and Clinical Neurophysiology*, 1974, 36, 191–199.

Picton, T. W., Hillyard, S. A., Krausz, H. I., and Galambos, R. Human auditory evoked potentials. I. Evaluation of components. *Electroencephalography and Clinical Neurophysiology*, 1974, 36, 179–190.

Pines, M. Train yourself to stay well. *McCall's*, 1970, 48, 137–138.

Plotkin, W. B. On the self-regulation of the occipital alpha rhythm: Control strategies, states of consciousness, and the role of physiological feedback. *Journal of Experimental Psychology: General*, 1976, 105, 66–99.

Plotkin, W. B., and Cohen, R. Occipital alpha and attributes of the "alpha experience." *Psychophysiology*, 1976, 13, 16–21.

Plutchik, R. The psychophysiology of skin temperature: A critical review. *Journal of General Psychology*, 1956, 55, 249–268.

Ponder, E., and Kennedy, W. P. On the act of blinking. *Quarterly Journal of Experimental Physiology*, 1927, 18, 89–110.

Porges, S. W. Peripheral and neurochemical parallels of psychopathology: A psychophysiological model relating autonomic imbalance to hyperactivity, psychopathy, and autism. In H. W. Reese (Ed.), *Advances in child development and behavior* (Vol. II), 1977, in press.

Rehwoldt, F. Über respiratorische affektsymptome Mit Atlas von 25 Taflen. *Ps. St.*, 1911, 7, 141–195.

Rice, B. Rattlesnakes, French fries, and pupillometric oversell. *Psychology Today*, February 1974, 7, 55–59.

Rickles, W. H. Central nervous system substrates of some psychophysiological variables. In N. S. Greenfield and R. A. Sternbach (Eds.), *Handbook of psychophysiology*. New York: Holt, Rinehart and Winston, 1972.

Rickles, W. H., Jr., and Day, J. L. Electrodermal activity in non-palmar skin sites. *Psychophysiology*, 1968, 4, 421–435.

Riddle, E. M. Aggressive behavior in a small social group. *Archives of Psychology*, 1925, 78.

Risberg, J., and Ingvar, D. H. Patterns of activation in the gray matter of the dominant hemisphere during mental arithmetic and memorizing: A study of regional blood flow changes during psychological testing in a group of neurologically normal patients. *Brain*, 1973, 96, 737–756.

Roffwarg, H. P., Muzio, J. N., and Dement, W. C. Ontogenetic development of the human sleep-dream cycle. *Science*, 1966, 152, 604–619.

Romig, C. H. A. The status of polygraph legislation in the fifty states. *Police*, 1971.

Rose, S. *The conscious brain*. New York: Vintage Books, 1976.

Rothman, S. (Ed.). *Physiology and biochemistry of the skin.* Chicago: University of Chicago Press, 1954.

Rushmer, R. F., and Smith, D. A. Cardiac control. *Psychological Reviews*, 1959, 39, 41–68.

Russell, R. W., and Stern, R. M. Gastric motility: The electrogastrogram. In P. H. Venables and I. Martin (Eds.), *A manual of psychophysiological methods.* New York: Wiley, 1967.

Rust, J. Genetic effects in the cortical auditory evoked potential: A twin study. *Electroencephalography and Clinical Neurophysiology*, 1975, 39, 321–327.

Sargent, J. D., Green, E. E., and Walters, E. D. The use of autogenic feedback training in a pilot study of migraine and tension headaches. *Headache*, 1972, 12, 120–125.

Sargent, J. D., Green, E. E., and Walters, E. D. Preliminary report on the use of autogenic feedback training in the treatment of migraine and tension headaches. *Psychosomatic Medicine*, 1973, 35, 129–134.

Saxon, S. A. Detection of near threshold signals during four phases of the cardiac cycle. *The Alabama Journal of Medical Sciences*, 1970, 7, 427–430.

Schachter, S. *Emotion, obesity, and crime.* New York: Academic Press, 1971.

Schwartz, G. E. *Operant conditioning of human cardiovascular integration and differentiation through feedback and reward.* Unpublished doctoral dissertation, Harvard University, 1971.

Schwartz, G. E. Clinical applications of biofeedback: Some theoretical issues. In D. Upper and D. S. Goodenough (Eds.), *Behavior modification with the individual patient: Proceedings of third annual Brockton Symposium on behavior therapy.* Nutley, N.J.: Roche, 1972a.

Schwartz, G. E. Voluntary control of human cardiovascular integration and differentiation through feedback and reward. *Science*, 1972b, 175, 90–93.

Schwartz, G. E. Toward a theory of voluntary control of response patterns in the cardiovascular system. In P. A. Obrist, A. H. Black, J. Brener, and L. V. DiCara (Eds.), *Cardiovascular psychophysiology.* Chicago: Aldine, 1974.

Schwartz, G. E., Davidson, R., and Maer, F. Right hemisphere lateralization for emotion in the human brain: Interactions with cognition. *Science*, 1975, 190, 286–288.

Schwartz, G. E., Davidson, R. J., Maer, F., and Bromfield, E. Patterns of hemispheric dominance in musical, emotional, verbal, and spatial tasks. *Psychophysiology*, 1974, 11, 227.

Schwartz, G. E., Fair, P. L., Salt, P., Mandel, M. R., and Klerman, G. L. Facial muscle patterning to affective imagery in depressed and nondepressed subjects. *Science*, 1976, 192, 489–491.

Schwartz, G. E., and Higgins, J. D. Cardiac activity preparatory to overt and covert behavior. *Science*, 1971, 173, 1144–1146.

Schwartz, G. E., and Logue, A. Facial thermography in the assessment of emotion. In preparation, 1977.

Schwartz, G. E., and Shapiro, D. Biofeedback and essential hypertension: Current findings and theoretical concerns. In L. Birk (Ed.), *Biofeedback: Behavioral medicine.* New York: Grune & Stratton, 1973.

Schwartz, G. E., Shapiro, D., and Tursky, B. Self-control of patterns of human diastolic blood pressure and heart rate through feedback and reward. *Psychophysiology,* 1972, 9, 270.

Schwartz, H. G. Reflex activity within the sympathetic nervous system. *American Journal of Physiology,* 1934, 109, 593–604.

Shackel, B. Eye movement recording by electro-oculography. In P. H. Venables and I. Martin, *A manual of psychophysiological methods.* New York and Amsterdam: American Elsevier, 1967.

Shagass, C. Electrical activity of the brain. In N. S. Greenfield and R. A. Sternbach (Eds.), *Handbook of psychophysiology.* New York: Holt, Rinehart and Winston, 1972.

Shapiro, A., Cohen, H. D., DiBianco, P., and Rosen, G. Vaginal blood flow changes during sleep and sexual arousal. *Psychophysiology,* 1968, 4, 394 (abstract).

Shapiro, A. K. Contribution to a history of the placebo effect. *Behavior Science,* 1960, 5, 109–135.

Shapiro, A. K. Placebo effects in medicine, psychotherapy, and psychoanalysis. In A. E. Bergin and S. L. Garfield (Eds.), *Handbook of Psychotherapy and behavior change: Empirical analysis.* New York: Wiley, 1971.

Shapiro, D. Preface. In D. Shapiro, T. X. Barber, L. V. DiCara, J. Kamiya, N. E. Miller, and J. Stoyva (Eds.), *Biofeedback and self-control 1972.* Chicago: Aldine, 1973.

Shapiro, D., Tursky, B., and Schwartz, G. E. Control of blood pressure in man by operant conditioning. *Circulation Research,* 1970a, 1, 27–32 (supplement 1).

Shapiro, D., Tursky, B., and Schwartz, G. E. Differentiation of heart rate and blood pressure in man by operant conditioning. *Psychosomatic Medicine,* 1970b, 32, 417–423.

Shaw, J. C., Foley, J., and Blowers, G. H. Alpha rhythm: An artifact? *Lancet,* 1970, I, 1173.

Shaw, W. A. The relation of muscular action potentials to imaginal weight lifting. *Archives of Psychology,* 1940, 247.

Shepard, J. F. Organic changes and feeling. *American Journal of Psychology,* 1906, 17, 522–584.

Sintchak, G., and Geer, J. H. A vaginal plethysmograph system. *Psychophysiology,* 1975, 12, 113–115.

Skinner, B. F. *The behavior of organisms.* New York: Appleton-Century-Crofts, 1938.

Skinner, B. F. *Science and human behavior.* New York: Macmillan, 1953.

Smith, K. Conditioning as an artifact. *Psychological Review,* 1954, 61, 217–225.

Snyder, F., and Scott, J. The psychophysiology of sleep. In N. S. Greenfield and R. A. Sternbach (Eds.), *Handbook of psychophysiology.* New York: Holt, Rinehart and Winston, 1972.

Sterman, M. B. Neurophysiological and clinical studies of sensorimotor EEG biofeedback training: Some effects on epilepsy. In L. Birk (Ed.), *Biofeedback: Behavioral medicine.* New York: Grune & Stratton, 1973.

Sterman, M. B., MacDonald, L. R., and Stone, R. K. Biofeedback training of the sensorimotor electroencephalogram rhythm in man: Effects on epilepsy. *Epilepsia,* 1974, *15,* 395–416.

Stern, J. A. Toward a definition of psychophysiology. *Psychophysiology,* 1964, *1,* 90–91.

Sternbach, R. A. *Principles of psychophysiology.* New York: Academic Press, 1966.

Sternbach, R. A., Gustafson, L. A., and Colier, R. L. Don't trust the lie detector. *Harvard Business Law,* 1962, *40,* 127–134.

Stoerring, G. Experimentelle beitraege zur Lehre vom gefuehl. *Archiv ges Psychologischen,* 1906, *6,* 316–356.

Stoyva, J. M. Finger electromyographic activity during sleep: Its relation to dreaming in deaf and normal subjects. *Journal of Abnormal Psychology,* 1965, *70,* 343–349.

Stoyva, J., and Kamiya, J. Electrophysiological studies of dreaming as the prototype of a new strategy in the study of consciousness. *Psychological Review,* 1968, *75,* 192–205.

Strahan, R. F., and Ho, C. Palmar sweat response to surgery. *Psychophysiology,* 1976, *13,* 168.

Strahan, R. F., Todd, J. B., and Inglis, G. B. A palmar sweat method particularly suited for naturalistic research. *Psychophysiology,* 1974, *11,* 715–720.

Stroebel, C. F., and Glueck, B. C. Biofeedback treatment in medicine and psychiatry: An ultimate placebo? *Seminars in Psychiatry,* 1973, *5,* 379–393.

Stunkard, A. J. Obesity and the denial of hunger. *Psychosomatic Medicine,* 1959, *21,* 281–289.

Svebak, S. Respiratory patterns as predictors of laughter. *Psychophysiology,* 1975, *12,* 62–65.

Syz, H. Observations on unreliability of subjective reports of emotional reactions. *British Journal of Psychology,* 1926–1927, *17,* 119–126.

Tarchanoff, J. Über die galvanischen erscheinungen an der haut des menschen bei reizung der sinnesorgane und bei verschiedenen formen der psychischen tatigkeit. *Pflüger's Archiv Psycholischen,* 1890, *46,* 46–55.

Thomas, L. *The lives of a cell.* New York: Bantam, 1974.

Thompson, L. W., and Botwinick, J. Stimulation in different phases of the cardiac cycle and reaction time. *Psychophysiology,* 1970, *7,* 57–65.

Tinker, M. A. Recent studies of eye movements in reading. *Psychological Bulletin,* 1958, *55,* 215–231.

Travis, T. A., Kondo, C. Y., and Knott, J. R. Subjective aspects of alpha enhancement. *British Journal of Psychiatry,* 1975, *127,* 122–126.

Treager, R. T. *Physical functions of skin.* New York: Academic Press, 1966.

Tryon, W. W. Pupillometry: A survey of sources of variation. *Psychophysiology,* 1975, *12,* 90–93.

Tursky, B. The indirect recording of human blood pressure. In P. A. Obrist, A. H. Black, J. Brener, and L. V. DiCara (Eds.), *Cardiovascular psychophysiology*. Chicago: Aldine, 1974a.

Tursky, B. Recording of human eye movements. In R. F. Thompson and M. M. Patterson (Eds.), *Bioelectric recording techniques*, part C. New York: Academic Press, 1974b.

Tursky, B., Shapiro, D., and Schwartz, G. E. Automated constant cuff pressure system to measure average systolic and diastolic pressure in man. *Transactions on Bio-Medical Engineering*, 1972, *19*, 271–275.

U.S. Congress. Use of polygraphs and "lie detectors" by the Federal Government (House Report No. 198, 89th Congress, 1st Session). Washington, D.C.: Government Printing Office, 1965.

Vaitl, D. Heart rate control under false feedback conditions. Paper presented at the meeting of the Biofeedback Research Society, 1972.

Varni, J. G. Learned asymmetry of localized electrodermal responses. *Psychophysiology*, 1975, *12*, 41–45.

Venables, P. H., and Warwick-Evans, L. A. Cortical arousal and the two-flash threshold. *Psychonomic Science*, 1967, *8*, 231–232.

Vierling, J. S., and Rock, J. Variations in olfactory sensitivity to exaltolide during the menstrual cycle. *Journal of Applied Physiology*, 1967, *22*, 311–315.

Voas, R. B. *Generalization and consistency of muscle tension level*. Unpublished doctoral dissertation, University of California, Los Angeles, 1952.

Wallace, R. K. Physiological effects of transcendental meditation. *Science*, 1970, *167*, 1751–1754.

Wallace, R. K., Benson, H., and Wilson, A. F. A wakeful hypometabolic physiological state. *American Journal of Physiology*, 1971, *221*, 795–799.

Waller, A. D. Galvanometric observation of the emotivity of a normal subject during the German air-raid of Whit-Sunday, May 19, 1918. *Lancet*, 1918, *194*, 916.

Walsh, D. H. Interactive effects of alpha feedback and instructional set on subjective state. *Psychophysiology*, 1974, *11*, 428–435.

Walter, W. G. The location of cerebral tumors by electroencephalography. *Lancet*, 1936, 2, 305–308.

Walter, W. G. Discussion of Mulholland chapter. In C. R. Evans and T. B. Mulholland (Eds.), *Attention in neurophysiology*. New York: Appleton-Century-Crofts, 1969.

Walter, W. G., Cooper, R., Aldridge, V. J., McCallum, W. C., and Winter, A. L. Contingent negative variation: An electric sign of sensorimotor association and expectancy in the human brain. *Nature*, 1964, *203*, 380–384.

Watson, J. B. *Psychology from the standpoint of a behaviorist*. Philadelphia: Lippincott, 1919.

Weerts, T. C., and Roberts, R. The physiological effects of imagining anger-provoking and fear-provoking scenes. *Psychophysiology*, 1976, *13*, 174.

Weiss, T., and Engel, B. T. Operant conditioning of heart rate in patients with premature ventricular contractions. *Psychosomatic Medicine*, 1971, *33*, 301–321.

Wendt, G. R. An analytic study of the conditioned knee-jerk. *Archives of Psychology*, 1930, *123*.

Wenger, M. A., Bagchi, B. K., and Anand, B. K. Experiments in India on "voluntary" control of the heart and pulse. *Circulation*, 1961, *CCIV*.

Wenger, M. A. Studies of autonomic balance: A summary. *Psychophysiology*, 1966, 2, 173–186.

Wenger, M. A., and Cullen, T. D. Studies of autonomic balance in children and adults. In N. S. Greenfield and R. A. Sternbach (Eds.), *Handbook of psychophysiology*. New York: Holt, Rinehart and Winston, 1972.

Williams, R. B., Bittker, T. E., Buchsbaum, M. S., and Wynne, L. C. Cardiovascular and neurophysiologic correlates of sensory intake and rejection. I. Effect of cognitive tasks. *Psychophysiology*, 1975, *12*, 427–433.

Wilman, C. W. *Seeing and perceiving*. Oxford: Pergamon Press, 1966.

Wolf, S., and Welsh, J. D. The gastrointestinal tract as a responsive system. In N. S. Greenfield and R. A. Sternbach (Eds.), *Handbook of psychophysiology*. New York: Holt, Rinehart and Winston, 1972.

Wolf, S., and Wolff, H. G. *Human gastric function: An experimental study of a man and his stomach*. New York: Oxford University Press, 1947.

Woodworth, R. S., and Schlosberg, H. *Experimental psychology*. New York: Holt, Rinehart and Winston, 1954.

Woolfolk, R. L. Psychophysiological correlates of meditation. *Archives of General Psychiatry*, 1975, *32*, 1326–1333.

Yarbus, A. L. *Eye movements and vision*. New York: Plenum, 1967.

Zahn, T. P., Rosenthal, D., and Lawlor, W. G. Electrodermal and heart rate orienting reactions in chronic schizophrenia. *Journal of Psychiatric Research*, 1968, *6*, 117–134.

Zimny, G. H., and Miller, F. L. Orienting and adaptive cardiovascular responses to heat and cold. *Psychophysiology*, 1966, *3*, 81–92.

Zuckerman, M. Physiological measures of sexual arousal in the human. In N. S. Greenfield and R. A. Sternbach (Eds.), *Handbook of psychophysiology*. New York: Holt, Rinehart and Winston, 1972.

Index of Names

Index of Subjects